Last Chapters
A Sociology of Aging and Dying

Brooks/Cole Series in Social Gerontology

Vern Bengtson, *University of Southern California*
Series Editor

HEALTH AND AGING
Tom Hickey, *University of Michigan*

ENVIRONMENT AND AGING
M. Powell Lawton, *Philadelphia Geriatric Center*

LAST CHAPTERS: A SOCIOLOGY OF AGING AND DYING
Victor W. Marshall, *University of Toronto and McMaster University*

AGING AND RETIREMENT
Anne Foner, *Rutgers University*
Karen Schwab, *Social Security Administration, Washington, D.C.*

ROLE TRANSITIONS IN LATER LIFE
Linda K. George, *Duke University Medical Center*

STRATIFICATION AMONG THE AGED
James J. Dowd, *University of Georgia*

Last Chapters
A Sociology of Aging and Dying

Victor W. Marshall

University of Toronto
and
McMaster University

Brooks/Cole Publishing Company
Monterey, California
A Division of Wadsworth, Inc.

I dedicate this book to my father, Victor G. Marshall, and to the memory of my mother, Esther Marshall, in loving thanks.

Printed in the United States of America

10 9 8 7 6 5 4 3 2 1

Library of Congress Cataloging in Publication Data

Marshall, Victor W
    Last chapters, a sociology of aging and dying.

    (Brooks/Cole series in social gerontology)
    Bibliography: p. 197
    Includes index.
    1. Death—Social aspects. 2. Gerontology.
3. Aged—Psychology. I. Title. II. Series.
HQ1073.M37   305.2'6   79-26915
ISBN 0-8185-0399-8

Acquisition Editor: *Todd Lueders*
Manuscript Editor: *Susan Meadows*
Production Editor: *Fiorella Ljunggren*
Series Design: *John Edeen*
Illustrations: *AYXA Art*
Typesetting: *Graphic Typesetting Service, Los Angeles, California*

Foreword

Until quite recently death and dying were not considered proper topics for serious professional and scholarly discussion. Then, with a suddenness that surprised many of us, things changed. The social and psychological aspects of death became the object of attention, discussion, analysis, and even popularization. Books and courses, symposia and journals appeared in astonishing numbers, reflecting the growing professional and intellectual respectability of the study of death.

But awareness does not necessarily mean understanding, any more than description can be equated with analysis. Too often death and dying have been treated as abstractions hardly connected to other aspects of social life, without systematic attention to the existing theoretical frameworks of related issues such as social organization and aging.

This volume represents an exception. Students, professionals, and lay persons will find it a significant advance in our understanding of the last chapters of life. Not only does it bring together an impressive array of recent research, but it codifies and amplifies the findings by examining the issues and data within explicit theoretical approaches, both traditional and emergent. In passing, it exposes many myths, misconceptions, and stereotypes held by both professionals and lay persons.

Most importantly, Dr. Victor Marshall has formulated a sociology of aging and dying that, by going far beyond the minute event of individual death, offers a valuable context for understanding the conflicts accompanying the end of life. The book's central theme is that the problems connected with aging and dying are essentially rooted in our need to construct meaning in a continually changing social world. From birth to death, Marshall notes, human beings continuously negotiate with one another to work out some sense and substance of order with regard to who they are, who they were, and who they will be. Inevitably, this effort involves attempts to give meaning to death itself, as well as to the process of aging and dying. Such a process can be correctly viewed as a career in its own right and as a status passage over which the individual attempts to maintain some control.

Dr. Marshall observes that two levels of analysis are necessary to understand aging and dying in any culture. The first concerns the individual as a social being attempting to create and negotiate meaning throughout the course of life; the second involves society as constituted and reconstituted through the actions of a continually changing cast of individuals. The author emphasizes the dialectics between the individual and the social system and between the individual as producer of the social world and that world as a social product.

Dramatic changes have occurred in the last few human generations to alter the content, but not the process, of that dialectics as it concerns death. Profound demographic changes have caused death to be increasingly associated with old age. Death and dying have become progressively bureaucratized and separated from the day-to-day events of community living. Individuals have lost control of their dying, and the search for meaning is often rendered very difficult by a cultural context heavily influenced by the past.

But perhaps Dr. Marshall's key contribution is his concern for *theory* —a concern expressed by his analysis of observations and data in the context of contemporary scholarly attempts to reach a deeper understanding of aging and dying. Current theories of aging are weighed in the balance and found wanting as explanations. Role theory, disengagement theory, Kübler-Ross' clinical thanatology, developmental theories—all have made important contributions, but all have their limits. Marshall's critiques of these and other theories in Chapters Four and Six should be required reading for every student of gerontology.

This is an important book. It is a model of clear thinking and writing that will influence the literature about death and dying for the next decade.

Vern Bengtson
Series Editor

Preface

This book is a sociological analysis of the relationship between aging and dying at both the individual and the social level. At the individual level, my interest is in how the inevitability of death influences older people's lives. At the social level, my main concern is with the ways in which the fact of human mortality affects social organization. The two concerns are interrelated because, recognizing their own mortality and its impact on social organization, people collaboratively devise ways to deal with death and dying. These ways of dealing with mortality become institutionalized and form the setting in which any individual will age and die.

Although my analysis is basically sociological and social psychological, I have attempted to integrate anthropological and psychological research where it is relevant. I have not attempted, however, to write a comprehensive psychology or anthropology of aging and dying. Some may question my delimitation of the topic. The research literature on aging and dying is extensive, and I have focused on that which brings aging and dying together, to the exclusion of material from either area that is relatively independent of the other—for example, dying children and their care. Others may wonder why I have not maintained an explicitly comparative perspective throughout the book. If I had done so, I would have exceeded my competence and greatly extended the length and scope of the book. I would, of course, be delighted to see these issues dealt with in a more comprehensive manner than was possible here.

In writing this book, I have attempted to cover a wide sweep of the literature. I have not hesitated, however, to ignore material I judge to be methodologically unsound, and my selection of sources has been strongly guided by my own theoretical objective. The book attempts to be more than a review and summary of the literature. It presents an argument in terms of the literature, and I have worked back and forth between the research literature and my developing theoretical argument to weave them together into an integrated whole.

The book provides a systematic assessment of several important strands of theory in human development and social gerontology, including developmental theory, activity and disengagement theory, role theory, and symbolic interactionist approaches. This feature enhances the book's relevance for general courses in social gerontology and social theory. My own perspective is that of interpretive sociology and is based on phenomenological and symbolic interactionist foundations. However, I do not strive for theoretical purity within any one sociological perspective, because I do not think that such a purity is an important goal in its own right. The book is not simply eclectic. Rather than just report diverse theoretical approaches, it uses them analytically and offers a view that integrates the individual and social levels.

In writing this book, I drew on my major research interests and activities of the past 11 years. Over that period, I have accumulated many debts of gratitude, only some of which I can acknowledge in this space. In the beginning, Steve Klineberg and Bob Scott encouraged my investigation of this topic, and Dick Kalish, Bob Kastenbaum, and Leonard Pearson helped me discover what can now be considered the early literature in this area. These people, with Walter Beattie, Jr., Leonard Cain, and Bernice Neugarten, have continued to offer their intellectual and moral support to my work in the sociology of aging and dying. At various stages, the work that eventually found its way into *Last Chapters* benefited from all the above. I have also learned much of value to this book from Neena Chappell, Cathy Calkins Charmaz, Lynn Lofland, Joep Munnichs, Carolyn Rosenthal, Don Spence, Teri Spinola, and Joe Tindale. I remain especially indebted to Tony Harris.

John Knodel helped me reinterpret some questions concerning demographic history in Chapter Two and generally improved the flow of that chapter a great deal. I was aided by Jane Synge in finding some relevant historical material on the family, which also appears in that chapter. Lew Hendrix, whose work is discussed in Chapter Three, provided valuable comments. Mary Vachon thoroughly reviewed a draft of Chapter Six and broadened the scope of the research literature I used to cover bereavement.

Dick Kalish and Sarah H. Matthews read the manuscript in its entirety and provided invaluable critical comments and attention to detail beyond the call of duty. Together with the fine-grained, knowledgeable, and practical critique of the draft given by Series Editor Vern Bengtson, these comments provided the major bases on which I could prepare the final manuscript. Of course, none of these people are responsible for any weaknesses that remain in the book. I stubbornly refused at times to take advice, but it was nice to have it. The remarkable generosity of these scholars and friends reaffirmed my conviction that knowledge and its production are inherently social.

I have also had a great deal of institutional support. During the long history of my involvement with this area of research, I have had doctoral fellowships from The Canada Council and from Princeton University and research support from The Canada Council, The Midwest Council for Social Research on Aging, The Ontario Ministry of Health, and Health and Welfare Canada—all of which have directly or indirectly aided the writing of this book. I have had office and secretarial support from the Department of Sociology, McMaster University; from the Département d'Administration de la Santé, Université de Montréal; and from the Department of Behavioural Science, University of Toronto. I am especially grateful to the latter institute and to Wendy Peace for seeing this manuscript through. During the crucial final year of preparing this book, I have been supported as a National Health Scientist by Health and Welfare Canada. I am grateful to all these institutions and to the individuals in them who have facilitated my work and made it enjoyable.

My special thanks to Vern Bengtson for his trust in asking me to write this book for his series and for his good humor and encouragement in helping me finish it. The support I received from Todd Lueders and Fiorella Ljunggren at Brooks/Cole was very valuable, and so was the sympathetically aggressive editing of Susan Meadows.

I wish to express my appreciation to my wife, Joanne Gard Marshall, for her intellectual support. As a health-sciences librarian working in a clinical capacity in a hospital setting, she was able to provide not only invaluable bibliographical and reference assistance but also practical critical reactions based on her clinical experience. I also thank Joanne and my daughter, Emily, for their loving support, their patience, and the time they let me take from them.

Victor W. Marshall

Contents

Introduction

> We are, from birth on, beings that will die. We are this, of course, in different ways. The manner in which we conceive this nature of ours and its final effect, and in which we react to this conception, varies greatly. So does the way in which this element of our existence is interwoven with its other elements.
>
> Georg Simmel (1908)

Some 4000 years ago the ancient peoples of the Tigro-Euphrates Valley placed their thoughts on the inevitability of death on the tablets of the Gilgamesh Epic (Heidel, 1963), and at least since then we humans have been recording our preoccupation with finitude. The epic tells the story of Gilgamesh, who was one-third god and two-thirds man. Being partly human, Gilgamesh lamented at the death of his friend Enkidu: "When I die, shall I not be like unto Enkidu?" he asked. Obsessed with the fear of death, Gilgamesh went through a series of adventures seeking to prevent his own death. He was willing to endure the greatest hardships and perils in his quest for a "fountain of youth," and he almost succeeded, by finding a plant that, if eaten, would rejuvenate his life. But a serpent stole the plant and ate it. At last Gilgamesh realized that he could not transcend his mortality, took consolation in the fact that he had done good and wondrous things in his life, and accepted the inevitability that he, like all of us, would die.

Death is an inevitable part of the human condition. Most of us "face death" as, seeing our families and friends die, we reflect on our own mortal state. Each of us is, to some extent, conscious of the "inevitable scarcity" (Moore, 1963) that plagues our existence—our time will run out too.

It is not only that we die that is important. More fundamentally important is our knowledge that we shall die. This book explores the implications of that knowledge: How is it that people die in different ways? How do people conceive of their nature and its "final effect"? How do people react to their conceptions of death? In what ways are individual conceptions of mortality interwoven with other aspects of life? The focus will be on the aging, for whom these questions have the greatest importance.

Death and mortality are important not only to individuals but also to a society, since it is the case that, if everyone died, there would be no society left. Some societies have ceased to exist, and many others, particularly small ones with little technological control over their environment, live under the threat of total annihilation through famine, flood, war, or pestilence. The massive expenditures of highly modernized societies to control disease and natural disasters testify to the continuing concerns that people in society have for the control of death. In perhaps more subtle ways, the societal character of death—the frequency and distribution of death among a population—influences social processes and institutions. For example, because some people die, others must be recruited and socialized to fill the vacancies. Social institutions, such as education, and practices, such as those governing retirement policies and rules of inheritance, are affected by the social character of death (Blauner, 1966).

There are then two faces of death that I wish to explore in this book: the individual and the social. As the perspective is sociological, even my concern with the mortal individual will be social. I will take a dialectical approach that sees the individual as a social being and the society as constituted, and always reconstituted, through the actions of individuals (Berger & Luckmann, 1967).

Theoretical Perspective

In this book I adopt the analytical distinction between what people do together and the meaning they share about what they do—between what has been called *social system* and what has been called *culture* (see especially Geertz, 1957, pp. 32–54), although both these terms have been defined in many different ways (see Inkeles, 1963; Kroeber & Kluckhohn, 1952; Parsons et al., 1961; Spiro, 1961). On the cultural level is found "the framework of beliefs, expressive symbols, and values in terms of which individuals define their world, express their feelings, and make their judgments (Geertz, 1957, p. 549). These beliefs are utilized by individuals to render meaningful their behavior. We humans are fundamentally symbolic creatures. Our world is more than a world of concrete objects; it is a world in which the past and the future exist, in which we can orient our activities in relation to distant events or abstract ideas.

Many of our ideas about the world are shared with others, and they come to us from the past. It is therefore useful, for analytical purposes, to think of shared meanings as the culture of a people and of individuals growing into a culture and learning these meanings. The family is a major mediator between the culture of the society and the meanings held by an individual (Spiro, 1951). Over time, however, the culture changes. In being passed on to successive generations, meanings are altered or lost, and new interpretations are invented and shared. I might add that, since meanings serve as guides to action, patterns of action and interaction both attain some stability and undergo innovation in the same way. It would be folly to attribute massive inertia or stability to contemporary society but equally fallacious to make an assumption about the massive impermanence of premodern and nonindustrialized societies.

The key assumption underlying the perspective of this book is that individuals are at least partially free to create their own world, even if at times that world of their own creation poses a constraint on their own freedom. If this is so, it follows that an understanding of the individual in a social context is best gained when attention is paid to the individual's own definition of the situation.

Briefly stated, this position approximates what has been called the secondary, or less predominant, of the "two sociologies" described in a recent article by Dawe (1970; see also Silverman, 1970, pp. 126–146). Rooted in the *verstehen* sociology of Max Weber (1964, pp. 87–123) and the symbolic interactionist social psychology of George H. Mead (1934a) and others, this perspective takes as a basic postulate the human capacity for constructing and sharing meaning:

> The key notion . . . is that of autonomous man, able to realize his full potential and to create a truly human social order only when freed from external constraint. Society is thus the creation of its members; the product of their construction of meaning, and of the action and relationships through which they attempt to impose that meaning on their historical situations [Dawe, 1970, p. 216].

In an important theoretical statement within this perspective, Berger and Luckmann (1967) emphasize the dialectical relationship between humans as producers of their world and that world as social product. Thus, while humans socially construct the reality of their world through what Berger and Luckmann call *externalization,* that social reality comes to be experienced as having a reality of its own, "a reality that confronts the individual as an external and coercive fact" (Berger & Luckmann, 1967, p. 58). This is the process of *objectivation*. The third moment in this dialectic between the individual and the social world is *internalization*—the process by which the "objectivated social world is retrojected into consciousness in the course of socialization" (Berger & Luckmann, 1967, p. 61).*

As Berger and Luckmann note, and has been emphasized most strongly by Schutz (1953), the intersubjective or social world is experienced as unquestioned in its typicality. Through internalization the individual acquires the typification schemes that are shared by other members of the collectivity and partakes of the "social stock of knowledge." As Schutz (1967) puts it:

> This world existed before our birth, experienced and interpreted by others, our predecessors, as an organized world. Now it is given to our experience and interpretation. All interpretation of this world is based on a stock of previous experiences of it, our own or those handed down to us by parents or teachers; these experiences in the form of "knowledge at hand" function as a scheme of reference. . . .
>
> [This stock of knowledge is] just taken for granted until further notice as the unquestioned, *though at any time questionable* stock of knowledge at hand [1967, p. 7; italics mine].

The process by which new objects or events come to be taken for granted is the process of *legitimation*. That which has been taken for granted *may* come to be questioned. Conversely, legitimation processes *may* incorporate that which had been questioned into the unquestioned stock of knowledge. In both cases, I emphasize the word *may* because these are empirical questions.

I assume, with Schutz and Berger and Luckmann, that social reality, and hence legitimation, is maintained primarily through the objectivation of language. As Berger and Luckmann (1967) state, "Language provides the fundamental superimposition of logic on the objectivated social world. The edifice of legitimations is built upon language and uses language as its principal instrumentality. We can only 'know' reality through the medium of language" (p. 64). Winch (1958) states "Our idea of what belongs to the realm of reality is given for us in the language that we use. The concepts we have settle for us the form of the experience we have of the world. . . . The world is for us what is presented through these concepts" (p. 15). If we know our world through language, then "the most important vehicle of reality-maintenance is conversation" (Berger & Luckmann, 1967, p. 152), and

> the plausibility and stability of the world, as socially defined, is dependent upon the strength and continuity of significant relationships in which conver-

---

*From *The Social Construction of Reality* (2nd Ed.), by P. L. Berger and T. Luckmann. Copyright © 1966, 1967 by P. L. Berger and T. Luckmann. These and all other quotations from this source are reprinted by permission of Doubleday & Co., Inc.

sation about this world can be continually carried on. Or, to put it a little differently: the reality of the world is sustained through conversation with significant others [Berger & Kellner, 1964, pp. 4–5].

This general perspective is useful at both the microlevel, when considering the individual interacting with others, and at the macrolevel, when considering the relationship between societal features and broadly shared meanings. It is necessary to bear in mind that, when addressing macroissues, many of the fine details are of necessity lost in the higher level of abstraction employed.

The final crucial theoretical point is that we humans not only endow our world with meaning; we have no choice but to do so. Not being genetically preprogrammed, we have to employ cognitive schemes of meaning to guide our action. We have to make sense of our world in order to live in it. Meanings provide the maps that guide our action. To the extent that meanings are shared, everyone in a society has the same map. Reaching a minimal level of agreement with regard to meaning therefore becomes one of the problematics of any society.

This general theoretical perspective will be drawn on, explicitly or implicitly, throughout the book as I focus, first, on aging and dying at the societal level and, then, turn to consider the individual who is aging and dying.

Overview of the Book

Chapter Two describes historical changes and cross-societal variation in the demographic characteristics of death, showing that the relationship between old age and death is a relatively modern phenomenon. In the chapter, attention is given to the ways in which the demographic structuring of death poses problems for the society.

The demographic variability in the occurrence of death has led to different societal solutions for handling death. Although societies throughout history have dealt with death in many different ways, Chapter Three focuses on the universal features of the encounter with death and, more importantly, the extent to which common patterns in dealing with death and in the meaning of death and dying are associated with modernization and industrialization.

Chapter Four focuses on the aging individual in contemporary society. The aging, holding beliefs about aging and dying as a result of their societal membership, must accomplish their dying in the organizational and expectational milieu described in Chapter Three. Although some of the historically important debates in the sociology of aging have relevance for this dilemma of the aging and dying person, much of the theory in social gerontology is not terribly helpful. This chapter then is really a statement of the dilemma of the aging and dying individual.

Chapter Five describes the consciousness of human mortality as it becomes variously relevant to individuals across the life span. The argument is offered that the consciousness that we are mortal, while given to us in an abstract way very early in life, takes on a particular edge and importance in later life. Chapter Five also examines some of the important theoretical approaches in the sociology of aging, including various approaches in the developmental social psychology of aging. These approaches are assessed, and found somewhat wanting, as explanations of the impact on aging individuals of their growing nearness to death, and an alternative approach is considered.

In Chapter Six aging and dying is viewed as a "career" or "status passage" over which people attempt to maintain control. The thesis is presented that people are able to die under optimal conditions if they can draw on the support of others in their family or community. This discussion refers to the discussion of the bureaucratization of death and dying in Chapter Three.

Chapter Seven examines the ways in which people try to make sense of death and give meaning to it. This chapter also provides an opportunity to speculate about future changes in the patterns of aging and dying, particularly as these will be affected by the changing demographic situation. The argument is presented that this area is highly responsive to research inputs and that the policy process indeed calls for a major research thrust in this area. It is hoped that the politics of aging and dying will alter the present situation to provide better ways of supporting the aging as they face their last days.

While I have not hesitated to present facts, I believe that the present state of our knowledge in this area makes ideas more important. The book is organized so that a reader might benefit from individual chapters. However, the serious reader should recognize that the organization of topics is a guide to a sociological theory, in rudimentary form, of aging and dying.

Review Questions
for Chapter 1

1. As individuals or in group discussion, reflect on your reasons for taking this course or reading this book. Why are you interested in the topic of aging and dying? Hundreds of books that deal with death and dying have appeared in recent years. Why do you think death is so "fashionable" these days? Does such interest reflect a desire to make death meaningful? Is there a "crisis of meaning" surrounding death and dying these days? If so, why?

2. At this point, before reading further in the book, it might be useful to think for a moment and try to estimate the length of your life and the age at which you think you are likely to die. What will the last five years of your life be like? And what will society be like during those five years? One way to stimulate your thoughts in this area is to write an obituary to be published on the occasion of your death.

2

The Character
of
Death in
Society

Karl Mannheim once suggested a mental experiment in which we should imagine "what the social life of man would be like if one generation lived on for ever and none followed to replace it" (1952, p. 292). Such is the material of much good science fiction, but Mannheim's intention was to point to the consequences for our life in society of the fact that people do, in fact, die. While societies are in a sense immortal, the individuals whose shared life constitutes them are mortal. This situation leads to some of the more interesting problems with which sociologists have dealt and, more importantly, to some of the crucial problems facing humans as they organize a collective life (Moore, 1966).

Many features of social life are affected by the volume of death in a society and by its character. *Volume of death* refers to the amount of death experienced by a society—how many people, or what proportion of them, die within a given period of time. The *character of death* refers to other features of mortality, such as the typical age at which people are likely to die and the typical causes of death. Demography, the science of population, provides some useful concepts and a great deal of hard-earned data in this area.

Although our concerns are not demographic, these concepts and data provide a framework or foundation for the subsequent chapters. The intention in this chapter is therefore restricted to describing the character of death in contemporary society and placing this description in a historical and comparative context.

Some Terminology

The *crude death rate* is a very general measure of mortality that reports the number of deaths in a given period for each 1000 people. Since the number of deaths is affected by the age structure of the population, it is wise to use a more refined measure. *Age-specific death rate* is the number of deaths within a given age category for each 1000 people. The crude death rate will be higher if there is high infant mortality, as in many relatively nonmodernized societies, and, more important for our purposes, it will be higher if there are more older people in the society. Demographers frequently use *adjusted* or *standardized* death rates in order to control for the effects of the age structure of the population. This is a simple statistical technique described in any demography text, but, since our interest is precisely in the age-relatedness of death rates, we need not be concerned with adjusted or standardized rates in this book.

Life expectancy depends on mortality rates, being in a sense the converse of them. The term refers to the average number of years of life still remaining to persons at a specified age under conditions prevailing at that time. *Life expectancy at birth* refers to the average number of years an individual born at a given period might be expected to live on the basis of the age-specific death rates of the period. *Life expectancy at age 60*, for example, refers to the average number of additional years a person aged 60 at the time might be expected to live according to prevailing death rates above age 60.

Life expectancies at each age are contained in *life tables,* which are constructed by converting age-specific death rates in a particular period into probabilities of surviving to any given age. Life tables are a convenient way of summarizing prevailing mortality conditions. Since life tables are normally based on death rates of a given period, they are sometimes called *period life tables* to stress their cross-sectional, as opposed to longitudinal, nature.

Insurance companies use life tables for the practical purpose of estimating their outflow of payments to survivors. Demographers use them to understand the dynamics of population change. Life tables for the United States population at two different periods of time—1900–1902 and 1974—are given later in this chapter. According to these life tables, life expectancy at birth increased from 48.2 years in 1900–1902 to 71.9 years in 1974. The 1900–1902 life table indicates how long persons at each different age could be expected to live if they experienced the death rates for 1900–1902 the rest of their lives. In reality, death rates subsequently declined, and thus persons born between 1900 and 1902 actually experienced lower death rates during their lifetime than implied in the life table. Although some persons born between 1900 and 1902 have yet to die, we can already be sure that the average life span of persons born between 1900 and 1902 will far exceed the 48.2 years indicated in the 1900–1902 life table. Whether persons born in 1974 will actually live to be 71.9 years depends on future mortality conditions and not on those of 1974 on which the life table is based.[1]

Historical demographers sometimes construct life tables reflecting the actual mortality experience of particular cohorts of people over their life spans. A *cohort* is a defined group of people born within a specified period of time—for example, all persons born in England between 1901 and 1905. The longevity of a cohort of people can be known only by following that cohort over time until all die. This would provide *longitudinal* data. However, social gerontologists, through convenience or necessity, often work with *cross-sectional* data. In this instance, they often work under the assumption, implicit in period life tables, that the experiences of young cohorts will approximate the contemporary experiences of the older cohorts that constitute the population of a society arrayed by age at that point in time. This is clearly a hazardous procedure, about which more will be said later.

The *age structure* of a population or of a society refers to the way in which the total population may be arrayed by age. For convenience, cohorts of people, rather than individuals, are used in describing the age structure, and the result is the familiar population pyramid that gives the percentage of the population in different age groups.

The age structure of a population—whether a family, a community, or a nation-state—depends in part on the way in which mortality is arrayed (it also depends on fertility, but we are not interested in that). A substantial fall in infant mortality will of course lead to a great increase in the young population. If infant mortality rates remain at the lower level, the entire population will appear to be younger, until the first of the cohorts that had been enlarged because of decreased infant mortality reaches old age. Then the average age of the population may increase, although not necessarily. As the enlarged cohorts pass into old age, they go through the reproductive ages and, in the absence of a change in fertility, increase the number of births—thus of younger generations—in proportion to their own increased size. Decreased mortality in the later years will also increase the average age of the population.

[1] It is important to recognize that statistical expressions of life expectancy are hypothetical, since they are based on mortality conditions of a given year or period and not on the actual mortality conditions that prevail during the life time of any single cohort of people. In other words, life tables assume that the mortality conditions of the period will remain constant during the remainder of the persons' lives. This is highly unlikely. For example, life tables do not take into account future societal changes such as the introduction of new medical technologies, improvements in nutrition and in sanitation and housing, wars, famines, and so forth. Nevertheless, life tables and the life expectancies they contain provide a useful way to express the mortality conditions of a period.

The age structure of the United States and Canada is still relatively young because the "baby-boom" cohort is still young. As that "baby-boom" bulge" grows older, the age structure will become older, with a higher average age and with more people in the upper age ranges. Even now, because of recent falls in mortality rates in the later years, the population structure is older than it has been.

The Changing
Demography of Death

Death visits the old much more frequently than the young. It is important to keep in mind that this statement has not long been true. To understand the ways in which death is organized in contemporary society, we need not only a summary of the social location of death today but also a perspective on today's situation rooted in the past.

Modernization, or industrialization, which is associated with the changing demography of death, is also associated with the development of good record keeping (Goldscheider, 1971, pp. 102–117; Laslett, 1976). We have only scattered and incomplete records from earlier ages and estimates made by archeologists and historians of death rate and life expectancy. Length of life is determined, of course, by the pattern of mortality. Attempts to assess these basic demographic features of earlier societies have not been very successful (Postan, 1972, pp. 31–44), and even today it is considered impossible to estimate the average length of life for better than half the world's population, since accurate death registration does not exist in many countries (Preston, 1977). It is most difficult of all to estimate actual life expectancy at birth for historical societies, and many contemporary ones as well, since many infant deaths were or are not recorded (Russell, 1948, p. 186). However, some rather ingenious studies have been done, and they provide enough evidence for us to gain some idea of the ways in which mortality affected social life in areas of interest to us. By examining the volume and character of death in historical and comparative contexts, the North American data can be placed in perspective.

Historical changes in mortality have been so great as to earn the appellation of *mortality revolution*—a term that, in general, refers to increased life expectancy, low infant mortality, and the control of infectious diseases (Goldscheider, 1971, pp. 102–134). The composite effects of this revolution have led to what is equally dramatically called a *population explosion*. However, as Langer (1963) points out, "The growth of population is never actually explosive, and as for the current spectacular increase, it is really only the latest phase of a development that goes back to the mid-eighteenth century." *Transition* is therefore a more accurate term than *explosion*.

Following the lead of the demographer Goldscheider (1971, p. 105), data on mortality rates or life expectancy in early historical periods will not be presented in tabular form. The quality of such data is simply not good enough to merit that form of presentation, and putting numbers in a table might make them appear to be more real or exact than they really are. Also following Goldscheider, I consider it less important to achieve exactness in this matter than to convey something of a feeling for what life must have been like before the mortality revolution. In Goldscheider's blunt statement (1971, p. 104), "Mortality conditions before the Industrial Revolution were terrible." Arnold Toynbee (1968) points out that

> till recently in all societies, the West included, human beings did not dream of the possibility of defying and defeating the prodigality of Nature. Like rabbits, humans bred up to the biological limit as a matter of course, since procreation of the maximum number of children was the only known means of enabling the race to survive. . . . Parents assumed, almost as a matter of course, that only part of their numerous prodigy would live to attain adult age [pp. 154 –155].

It is doubtful that procreation was so deliberately or exclusively devoted to survival of the species (Laslett, 1971, p. 137). It appears clear that, even if procreation was unhindered by deliberate birth control on the level of the individual couple, societal-level controls were always in effect, keeping fertility well below the biological limit (Knodel, 1977). It is also generally true that the age of marriage lowered and birth of children increased following a plague (see, for example, Herlihy, 1977). Before the Industrial Revolution, birth and mortality rates were even enough that, despite fluctuations, there was little long-term population growth.

Mortality, unlike fertility, was not directly controlled in any individual or societal sense, as is often the case today. Instead, it depended on crop conditions, weather, epidemics, and the like. These occurrences, most notably the plagues in Europe, caused fluctuations. Life expectancy at birth is estimated to have varied between 20 and 40 years in the period between the 13th and the 17th centuries, rising to a range of 33 to 40 years in the 18th century for Europe and the United States (Goldscheider, 1971). The general figures prior to the 18th century may well be typical of much of European history, for quite reliable estimates of life expectancy at the height of the Roman empire, based on analysis of burial inscriptions and burial remains, give a figure of 20 to 30 years (Acsádi & Nemeskéri, 1970; Preston, 1977).

A few contemporary nonindustrial societies are still in the upper limits of the European preindustrial range. For example, in 1970 life expectancy at birth in Mali was 37.2 years; it was 41 in Botswana and in Niger and 43.5 in Zambia (Hauser, 1976). For most of the less developed nations of the world, however, life expectancy is well above the traditional preindustrial range because of the dramatic falls in mortality largely brought about by public-health improvements in recent decades.

What uncontrolled mortality meant for family life in the typical peasant society is aptly described in a statement of Fourastié (1959) about France:

> At the end of the 17th century, the life of an average father, married for the first time at the age of 27, could be schematized as follows: born in a family of five children, he would have seen only half reach the age of 15; he had himself five children, like his father, of whom only two or three would live to the hour of his death. This man, living on the average to age 52, . . . had thus seen death occur, in his direct family, . . . to about nine people, of which only one was from among his grandparents (the three others having died before his birth), his two parents, and three of his infants [translation mine].

Although Fourastié's work is one of only a small number of studies to reconstruct mortality rates and life expectancies for early societies, the situation he describes is probably quite typical of that in Western Europe, including England, and in many other parts of the world, including, let us emphasize, colonial North America. (Much of the evidence about mortality in North America is collected in Drake, 1969; Glass & Eversley, 1965; Henripin, 1957; Laslett, 1971; and Lee, 1977.)

For example, of 1000 children born during the period 1670–1699 in Andover, Massachusetts, and whose ages at death are known, 152 did not live beyond one year, another 46 died before age 10, and 225 in all died without reaching the age of 20. Epidemics made the situation much worse in the following 60 years. In the period 1700–1729, 381 of 1000 children born died before age 20; and in the period 1730–1759, 534—or more than half—died before age 20. The infant mortality rate—that is, the number of deaths per 1000 in the first year after birth—in Andover in the latter period was about 248 (Greven, 1970, pp. 188–189). This rate contrasts with rates of 9 per 1000 attained in some New England communities and generally in more favored communities in many industrialized societies today.

Andover, a healthy community by colonial New England standards (Greven, 1970, p. 22), had death rates that were about half those of Boston, where the crude death rate during the next century fluctuated between 35 and 40 per 1000 (Stannard, 1975, p. 16). Epidemics pushed the crude death rate as high as 71 in Andover and over 100 in Boston; the most vulnerable were the children. Summarizing Greven's data for the period 1640–1759, Stannard says:

> During the period as a whole, more than one child in four failed to survive the first decade of life in a community with an average birth rate per family of 8.8. Thus a young couple embarking on a marriage did so with the knowledge and expectation that in all probability two or three of the children they might have would die before the age of 10 [1975, p. 18].

This passage describes Andover, which was healthier than almost any other New England locality. In fact, New England death rates for all ages were probably lower than those of England in the 17th and early 18th centuries (Greven, 1970, pp. 21–30, 289; Laslett, 1976).

The second half of the 18th century saw accelerated change in mortality rates and, consequently, life expectancy in the industrialized societies. In most European countries, life expectancy at birth increased from about 40 years in 1840 to 45 years by 1880 to over 50 years by the end of the century. Current life expectancy at birth is in the upper sixties to mid-seventies, depending on sex (Goldscheider, 1971, p. 110). Much of the increased life expectancy is attributable to declining infant and child mortality rates. For example, mortality in the first *two* years of life in London has been estimated to have been from 300 to 400 deaths per 1000 live births during the 18th century (McKeown & Brown, 1955); and the infant mortality rate in all of England was about 150 per 1000 in the latter part of the 19th century (Goldscheider, 1971, p. 110). It was still over 100 for the United States in 1900, but had dropped to 15.4 in 1976 (Statistical Bulletin, 1978).

Against this historical and comparative background, we can now consider the interplay of mortality and age structure for the United States in this century. The Canadian situation is not appreciably different. Table 2-1 incorporates portions, for selected ages, of a life table for the United States cohort born between 1900 and 1902 and of a second life table for the cohort born in 1974. These life tables are computed by the Public Health Service under the assumption that death rates for a specific category—for example, age, sex, or race—will remain unchanged in the future. That this assumption is erroneous can be seen from the fact that, whereas 1900 life tables predicted that 740,000 of the almost 2.5 million babies born in 1900 could be expected to reach age 70, in fact about 980,000 of them did so (Brotman, 1977). That is, changes in the death rate since 1900 left almost one-third more people alive at age 70 than might have been anticipated by anyone using the 1900 life table in 1901. It is crucially important to keep this in mind when thinking of the future and also when trying to imagine what today's older people must think about the fact they are still alive. A great many people who are now considered to be old had no rational basis, when they were young or middle-aged, to expect that they would still be alive today or that they might still anticipate several years of life. By the same token, population experts and those who formulate and implement social policy had no reasonable basis on which to predict how many older people would be alive today and how many would be alive in the future.

A conservative reading of Table 2-1 tells us that overall life expectancy at birth has increased by almost 24 years. The increase has been greatest for non-Whites, although not enough to catch up to their White counterparts of the same sex; the increase has been greater for women than for men. Life expectancy has increased for people at all ages, but especially for infants and the young. Life expectancy at age 65 increased by less than four years overall. At that age, White and non-White males are equal in anticipating an average of 13.4 years more of life.

TABLE 2-1. *Life Expectancy (Average Remaining Years of Life) by Sex, Color, and Selected Ages: 1900–1902 and 1974*

Period and Age	Total			White			Other		
	Total	Male	Female	Total	Male	Female	Total	Male	Female
Average remaining years of life:									
1900–1902									
At: Birth	48.2	*	*	*	48.2	51.1	*	32.5	35.0
Age 1	55.2	*	*	*	54.6	56.4	*	42.5	43.5
5	55.0	*	*	*	54.4	56.0	*	45.1	46.0
15	46.8	*	*	*	46.3	47.8	*	38.3	39.8
25	39.1	*	*	*	38.5	40.1	*	32.2	33.9
35	31.9	*	*	*	31.3	32.8	*	26.2	27.5
45	24.8	*	*	*	24.2	25.5	*	20.1	21.4
55	17.9	*	*	*	17.4	18.4	*	14.7	15.9
65	11.9	*	*	*	11.5	12.2	*	10.4	11.4
75	7.1	*	*	*	6.8	7.3	*	6.6	7.9
85	4.0	*	*	*	3.8	4.1	*	4.0	5.1
1974									
At: Birth	71.9	68.2	75.9	72.7	68.9	76.6	67.0	62.9	71.2
Age 1	72.2	68.5	76.0	72.8	69.1	76.6	67.7	63.7	71.8
5	68.4	64.7	72.2	69.0	65.3	72.7	64.0	60.0	68.1
15	58.6	55.0	62.4	59.2	55.6	62.9	54.3	50.3	58.3
25	49.3	45.9	52.7	49.8	46.5	53.3	45.2	41.5	48.8
35	39.9	36.7	43.2	40.4	37.2	43.6	36.4	33.2	39.7
45	30.9	27.9	33.9	31.2	28.1	34.3	28.3	25.5	31.1
55	22.7	19.9	25.3	22.8	20.1	25.5	21.1	18.7	23.4
65	15.6	13.4	17.5	15.6	13.4	17.6	15.1	13.4	16.7
75	9.8	8.4	10.8	9.7	8.3	10.7	10.8	9.6	11.8
85	5.7	5.0	6.1	5.6	4.9	6.0	7.3	6.7	7.8

Increase over 1900–1902										
At: Birth	23.7	*	*	*	*	20.7	25.5	*	30.4	36.2
Age 1	17.0	*	*	*	*	14.5	20.2	*	21.2	28.3
5	13.4	*	*	*	*	10.9	16.7	*	14.9	22.1
15	11.8	*	*	*	*	9.3	15.1	*	12.0	18.5
25	10.2	*	*	*	*	8.0	13.2	*	9.3	14.9
35	8.0	*	*	*	*	5.9	10.8	*	7.0	12.2
45	6.1	*	*	*	*	3.9	8.8	*	5.4	9.7
55	4.8	*	*	*	*	2.7	7.1	*	4.0	7.5
65	3.7	*	*	*	*	1.9	5.4	*	3.0	5.3
75	2.7	*	*	*	*	1.5	3.4	*	3.0	3.9
85	1.7	*	*	*	*	1.1	1.9	*	2.7	2.7
Percent expected to reach specified ages who were born in:										
1900–1902										
Age 25	*	*	*	*	*	73.9	76.6	*	53.3	55.8
35	*	*	*	*	*	68.2	71.0	*	46.5	49.6
45	*	*	*	*	*	61.4	64.7	*	39.2	42.3
55	*	*	*	*	*	52.5	56.5	*	30.0	33.1
65	*	*	*	*	*	39.2	43.8	*	19.0	22.0
75	*	*	*	*	*	21.4	25.4	*	8.9	11.1
85	*	*	*	*	*	5.3	7.1	*	2.0	3.6
1974										
Age 25	96.4	95.6	97.4	96.8	94.9	95.9	97.7		93.7	96.1
35	95.1	93.6	96.5	95.6	91.9	94.3	96.9		89.4	94.3
45	92.4	90.3	94.6	93.3	86.9	91.5	95.3		82.7	90.6
55	86.4	82.6	90.2	87.8	77.3	84.3	91.3		71.1	83.1
65	73.8	66.6	81.1	75.6	61.4	68.5	82.7		52.9	69.9
75	52.2	41.3	63.4	54.0	38.8	42.8	65.5		30.2	48.0
85	23.3	14.6	32.5	23.9	18.9	14.9	33.4		12.6	26.0

From "Life Expectancy: Comparison of National Levels in 1900 and 1974 and Variations in State Levels, 1969–1971," by H. B. Brotman, *The Gerontologist*, 1977, *17*(1), 12–22. Reprinted by permission.

Females at age 65 can anticipate more, since they have lower death rates than males at all ages. To be absolutely clear about the notion of average life expectancy, this means that, of 100 White females born in 1974 who reach the age of 65, 50 will live to be 82.6 years or older, and 50 will not, if current mortality conditions prevail. Therefore, many women who turn 65 can reasonably anticipate living an additional 15 to 20 years.

In terms of our own interests, these data imply that an increasing proportion of people are dying in the later years. In fact, in the United States about two-thirds of all deaths in a given year are of people over the age of 60. The situation has changed a great deal since colonial Andover or preindustrial France or England.

Life expectancy continues to increase dramatically; for the average American, it increased 2.4 years between 1969 and 1976 (Walker, 1977). Because the most important cause of death is now heart disease, it is possible that this drop is largely attributable to a nearly revolutionary change in life style.

While causation cannot be argued from the juxtaposition of parallel trends, data presented by Walker (1977) certainly lead to speculation about the effects of a changing life style on mortality, especially mortality in the years after infancy and childhood. Table 2-2 contains data showing comparisons for the years 1963 and 1975. These years were chosen because, in early 1964, the United States Surgeon-General warned of the health hazards of tobacco smoking, and the American Heart Association advocated that Americans adopt a healthier diet. These recommendations seem to have been followed. The work of McKeown and his associates (McKeown, Record, & Turner, 1975) for England and that of McKinlay and McKinlay (1977) for the United States convincingly show that about three-quarters of the decline in mortality since 1900 can be attributed to control of infection. This, in turn, is affected by a higher standard of living, leading to better diet and standards of hygiene. Of these factors, improved nutrition is considered to be the most important by far (see McKeown, 1976, for the most complete statement of this work). If the trends summarized by Walker continue, the 1974 life table (Table 2-1) may prove to be as great an underestimate of life expectancy as had been the 1900 table.

On the broader world scene, Preston (1975) argues that it seems to have been predominantly broad-gauged public health programs of insect control, environmental sanitation, health education, and maternal and child services that transformed the mortality picture in less developed areas, while it was primarily specific vaccines, antibiotics, and sulphonamides in more developed areas. Vallin (1968, cited in Preston, 1975) has argued that, while medical technology can have some independent effects, no country could attain a life expectancy of more than 60 years without having made progress out of the category "less developed." Preston (1977) notes that much of this advance occurred prior to 1880. "Since then, it [the advance] seems primarily

TABLE 2-2. *Declines in Age-Specific Coronary and Cerebrovascular Mortality and Changes in Per Capita Consumption: United States, 1963–1975*

Declines in Age-Specific Mortality				Change in Per Capita Consumption[c]	
Coronary[a]		Cerebrovascular[b]			
Age	Decline (percent)	Age	Decline (percent)	Product	Change
35–44	27.2	35–44	19.1	All tobacco products	22.4% decline
45–54	27.4	45–54	31.7	Fluid milk and cream	19.2% decline
55–64	23.5	55–64	34.1	Butter	31.9% decline
65–74	25.3	65–74	33.2	Eggs	12.6% decline
75–84	12.8	75–84	21.9	Animal fats and oils	56.7% decline
85+	19.3	85+	29.4	Vegetable fats and oils	44.1% incline

[a]Current unpublished mortality figures obtained through personal correspondence with the National Center for Health Statistics, Rockville, Maryland. Calculations of declines were made after multiplying figures before 1968 (seventh revision, International Classification of Disease) by 1.1457, as recommended by the National Center for Health Statistics, to make these statistics comparable to those of the eighth revision.

[b]From the U. S. National Center for Health Statistics.

[c]Figures for calculating percentage changes were obtained from the U. S. Department of Agriculture.

Adapted from "Changing United States Life-Style and Declining Vascular Mortality: Cause or Coincidence?" by W. J. Walker, *New England Journal of Medicine*, 1977, 297(3), 163–165. Used by permission.

attributable to advances in medical knowledge and to the embodiment of those advances in government programs of death control. All nations and groups have shared in these gains, but they have been largest for the very young and the very old, for females, for urbanites, and for the most disadvantaged social groups."

Aging and the Changing Character of Death

The concentration in this chapter has been on describing changing mortality rates and life expectancy. The remainder of the chapter deals with the experience of aging under varying conditions. To keep the treatment within manageable limits, the focus will be on the social settings that have already been discussed—peasant France and England, colonial America, and the United States from the industrial transition to the present era. The discussion will also be restricted to outlining the life cycle in demographic terms.

Describing Europe in the period 1550–1660, the British historian Henry Kamen says:

> The knowledge that life would be short, and that only a relatively small proportion of the population would survive into old age, must have made the quality of life differ appreciably from that of modern Europe. Without a large complement of aged people, the Europe of 1600 was predominately a youthful one, a preindustrial society in which natural forces conspired to keep life cruelly short. Children and young people must have been everywhere more in evidence than the aged [1976, p. 15].

This statement must have applied to much of the world until this century. The relatively unstable demographic situation and the occurrence of plagues, epidemics, and famines produced great variation in the age structures among preindustrial communities and in the same community at different points in time. However, the work of Laslett and his associates (Laslett, 1976) for many communities in Europe, as well as Japan and colonial America, shows a low proportion of the population being old.

Laslett's further contribution was to show that the population structure did not change appreciably with the Industrial Revolution and that the really significant increases in the proportion of the aged population occurred only in this century. In France, the one exception, the changes had set in 50 or 60 years earlier. Thus the 1900 figures for percentage of population over the age of 65 for England and Wales (4.7), Germany (4.9), the United States (4.1), and Canada (5.1) are not appreciably different from estimates made for several English communities for years ranging from 1599 to 1698 or for the other preindustrial communities in Europe studied by the Cambridge Group for the History of Population and Social Structure; they are, however, in the upper range of those estimates (Laslett, 1976).

At the other end of the age structure, however, a great deal was happening. Although the age structure of the population did not look that different from what it looks like even today, the bottom levels of the structure required a great deal of replacement for people who died—a notion that becomes readily apparent if we look at it in terms of the typical stages of a family life cycle. In a now-classic paper, Glick set out the notion of family cycle:

> From its formulation until its dissolution, a family passes through a series of stages that are subject to demographic analyses. Typically, a family comes into being when a couple is married. The family gains in size with the birth of each child. From the time when the last child leaves home, the family remains stable in size. As the children leave home for employment or marriage, the size of the family shrinks gradually back to the original two persons. Eventually one and then the other of the parents die and the family cycle has come to an end [1947, p. 164].

Glick is describing the life cycle of the *typical* family at the time of his writing; but it is important to recognize that the pattern he describes was anything but typical in earlier eras, because death at an early age interrupted it.

Uhlenberg (1969, 1974) and Wells (1973) provide illustrative data for different cohorts of American women. Uhlenberg (1969) distinguishes among six different types of family life cycles, with one type divided into two subtypes. He then compares five cohorts of native-born women in Massachusetts to see what proportions experienced the different types. This typology is presented in Figure 2-1. Uhlenberg studied cohorts for 1830, 1850, 1870, 1890, and 1920. Of 100,000 women born in a given year, a certain number would die before age 20. Of those who died, for any cohort studied by Uhlenberg, 95% would have never married, and, indeed, four-fifths would have died before the age of 5. This first type of life cycle is called *Abbreviated*. Of those women who did live to age 20, some would never marry. The second cycle is therefore called the *Spinster* life cycle. The remainder of this cohort of 100,000 women will have married. Those who marry but remain childless constitute the third life-cycle type, the *Barren*. Those who marry and have children but die before age 55 are the fourth life-cycle type, the *Dying mother*—a term used because age 55 is the approximate age at which the last child leaves home or marries. This life cycle breaks down into two life-cycle types, depending on whether the father remains alive. If the father survives until age 57—that is, until about the age when the mother dies and when the children have left home or married—the type is called *Motherless-child producing*. If the father dies before age 57, the type is called *Orphan producing*. The fifth life-cycle type, that of the *Widowed mother*, refers to those families in which the husband dies while the children are still at home—that is, before he reaches age 57 and his wife 55—but the wife remains alive. Finally, the sixth, or *Typical* life cycle, is the one described earlier by Glick: the woman

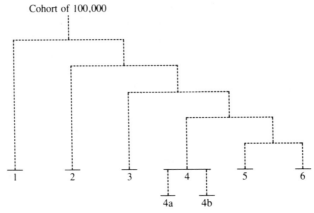

Cohort of 100,000

Type 1   life cycle: *Abbreviated;* die before age 20.
Type 2   life cycle: *Spinster;* survive to 20, never marry.
Type 3   life cycle: *Barren;* marry, remain childless.
Type 4   life cycle: *Dying mother;* have children, die before age 55.
Type 4a life cycle: *Motherless-child producing;* husband survives to 57.
Type 4b lfe cycle: *Orphan producing;* husband dies before he is 57.
Type 5   life cycle: *Widowed mother;* have children, survive to 55,
                husband dies before he is 57.
Type 6   life cycle: *Typical;* survive to 20, marry, have children,
                survive with husband alive to age 55.

FIGURE 2-1   A typology of family life cycles. (From "A Study of Cohort Life Cycles: Cohorts of Native Born Massachusetts Women, 1830–1920," by P. R. Uhlenberg, Population Studies, *1969, 23, 407–420. Reprinted by permission of the author and publisher.)*

survives to age 20, marries, has children, and lives with a surviving husband at least until the children leave home or marry.

The life-cycle experiences of different cohorts are presented in Table 2-3. Dramatic differences in typical family-life experiences are apparent. The proportion of women dying before age 20 fell by more than two-thirds—and the proportion experiencing a typical life cycle increased by almost two-thirds —from 1830 to 1920. In the 1920 cohort, many fewer mothers died while their children were still at home, and many fewer children were orphaned.

It is also clear that, while the changes were for the most part regular over the entire period, by far the most dramatic changes occurred between the cohorts born in 1890 and 1920. This finding is consistent with the work of Laslett, discussed earlier, on the age structure of the population (see also Preston, 1977). The figures in Table 2-3 strongly support the description Kett (1971) gives for family life in rural New England during the period 1800–1840. Kett describes a variety of factors that disrupted family life in almost random, unplanned ways:

> The pattern of random experience, however, could extend just as readily to the family itself. Families were constantly being disrupted by the death of one or

TABLE 2-3.   *Selected Cohort Life Cycles of Massachusetts Women*

Life-Cycle Type	Cohort: All Native-Born Massachusetts Women Born in the Year. From Every 100,000, the Number in Each Type Is:				
	1830	1850	1870	1890	1920
1. Abbreviated	35,600	31,400	30,900	26,300	10,800
2. Spinster	12,900	14,200	17,800	17,800	10,600
3. Barren	9,500	10,000	11,400	12,200	9,000
4. Dying mother	11,900	11,700	8,700	7,800	4,000
4a. Motherless-child producing	8,100	8,400	6,300	6,000	3,500
4b. Orphan producing	3,800	3,300	2,400	1,800	500
5. Widowed mother	9,100	9,800	8,600	8,500	8,500
6. Typical	20,900	23,000	22,600	27,400	57,100

Adapted from "A Study of Cohort Life Cycles: Cohorts of Native Born Massachusetts Women, 1830–1920," by P. R. Uhlenberg, *Population Studies*, 1969, *23*, 407–420. Used by permission of the author and publisher. Based on data from Massachusetts and U. S. censuses, Massachusetts Vital Registration Reports, and life tables calculated by Jacobson (1964).

both parents, not simply because of higher mortality from disease, but also because of the length of time which usually elapsed between the birth of the first and the last child. A man who fathered his first child at 25 might not father his last until he was 40 or even 45. It was a statistical probability that the father would be dead before the youngest child reached maturity. The frequency of being orphaned in the early nineteenth century had a personal as well as a demographic significance, for it meant that the plans laid by youth were subject to drastic shattering by chance [1971, p. 2].

This imagery is also quite consistent with Fourastié's description (1959) of the typical 17th-century French peasant family.

Wells (1973) provides data for 276 Quaker families in New York, New Jersey, and Pennsylvania, for whom the wife was born before 1786, and compares their family life with that of the wives described by Glick and Parke (1965). These data, which appear in Table 2-4, show that age at first marriage of colonial Quaker women and women from the ten-year cohorts beginning in 1880 and in 1920 was quite stable. However, the age of women at the birth and also at the marriage of their last child fell by over seven years. While these changes were taking place, mortality rates were falling, so that the age at which the first of the spouses would die rose from 50.9 to 64.4 years.

The effect of mortality on family life is indicated by the fact that one of the spouses would, in the typical Quaker case, die about ten years before the last child had married, whereas, typically, the first parent from the 1880–1889 cohort would not die until one year after the last child had left home. By the 1920–1929 cohort, the two spouses could anticipate living together for 12.2 years after the last child had left home. The so-called empty nest could now be

TABLE 2-4. *Median Age of Wives at Stages of the Family Life Cycle*

Stage of the Family Life Cycle	Wives Born		
	Before 1786	1880–1889	1920–1929
1. First marriage	20.5	21.6	20.8
2. Birth of last child	37.9	32.9	30.5
3. Marriage of last child	60.2	56.2	52.0
4. Death of first spouse to die	50.9	57.0	64.4

Note: As measured by the interquartile range, the distribution around the median at the age at first marriage, the age of the mother at the birth of her last child, and the duration of marriage seem to have been much the same from one group to another.

From *The Family in History: Interdisciplinary Essays,* by T. K. Rabb and R. I. Rotberg (Eds.). (Harper Torchbooks, 1973.) Copyright © 1971 by the Massachusetts Institute of Technology and the editors of the *Journal of Interdisciplinary History.* Reprinted by permission of Harper & Row, Publishers, Inc.

considered a typical stage of the family life cycle. The experience of the death of a spouse was now likely to occur in later life, after the children had left home.

Uhlenberg (1969) also presents data on changes in cause of death over the period 1856–1865 to 1945 for Massachusetts—data that we can probably take as typical for those periods in North America in general. The overall death rate was 17.9 per 1000 in 1856–1865 and fell by 32% to 12.2 by 1945. Tuberculosis was the leading cause of death in the earlier period, but, by 1945, the death rate for tuberculosis had declined 91.2%. The death rates for typhoid fever, diphtheria, measles, scarlet fever, whooping cough, diarrhoea, and enteritis all declined by more than 97%. As Uhlenberg says, "The control of contagious and infectious diseases, above all tuberculosis, through improved sanitation, better living conditions, public health efforts, and medical advances led to the very different survival patterns recorded for the different cohorts" (1969, p. 416).

While the life-cycle data of Uhlenberg and Wells refer to the family life-cycle experiences of women, it is useful to think of the impact of those life cycles on different family members, as Kett (1971), for example, has done when describing the situation for youth. Parents no longer anticipate that one-third to one-half of their children will die before the age of 10. On the contrary, they anticipate that *none* of their children will die before they will.

Neugarten (1977) has recently pointed out that this assumption is not always warranted. Given the differential mortality between men and women, there is a reasonable chance that a male first child will die before his mother. Infant mortality rates are, on the whole, so low in industrialized societies as to pose no serious threat in the consciousness of prospective parents. A comparison of census documents of today with those of earlier decades will reveal that little treatment, if any, is given to the category *orphan* now, whereas this used to be an important classification.

Children do not think much about the death of their parents while they themselves are young; and the utter terror of the prospect of an early death that was used by adults as a means of exercising social control over Puritan children is no longer present. Death, which used to be *unpredictable* because it might come at any stage of the life cycle, now rarely comes in a random fashion, rarely in early stages of the life cycle and rarely in two-generation households. The volume of death has decreased, as crude death rates and age-specific death rates have decreased for all ages, especially in infancy and childhood. The character of death has changed too, since now it is less frequently caused by epidemic and infectious disease. (The contemporary causes of death will be discussed in Chapter Three.)

Implications

Having attempted to illustrate different relationships between mortality and the age structure of a society as experienced by individuals passing through it, I would like now to emphasize some general points that are relevant to the sociology of aging and dying in contemporary society and, therefore, to our considerations in subsequent chapters.

The contrast provided centers around generalizations about *before* and *now*. The variability in death rate in different societies at different times is quite high, as is variability in age structure. This point is made explicitly by Laslett (1976) and by most of the historical demographers on whom I have drawn. In considering the variability, however, one needs to keep in mind the contrast between contemporary industrialized societies—such as the United States, Canada, and much of Western Europe—and much of the preindustrial European world and the relatively nonmodernized world of today.

In comparison to our own society, then, it is probably reasonable to assume the following about preindustrial and nonmodernized societies:

1. The volume of death was much greater. Death rates were not just higher; they were massively higher than at present.
2. Although death rates were higher at all ages, they were most dramatically higher at the birth, infancy, and childhood stages of the life cycle.
3. Death was therefore associated primarily with the young.
4. Although the age structure of the population was not on the whole dramatically different from that today, there was a somewhat younger average age, a higher proportion of very young children, and a lower proportion of older people. Preindustrial society was much more a child-centered society than is today's society. Thus Laslett estimates the English population, between 1574 and 1821, to be 43% "unmarried resident offspring, irrespective of age" (1969, p. 217).

5. Because death occurred so massively, and mainly to the young, it was much more frequently thought about by people at all ages than is the case today.
6. The causes of death were much less predictable than they are today. Famine and plague were not factors that could be anticipated in any reasonable manner.
7. Death was, and was considered to be, much less under the control of human beings than it is today. Death was, so to speak, an outsider. As an outsider, death was both unpredictable and difficult to comprehend.

This list is not exhaustive, and similar lists are available elsewhere (for example, Kastenbaum & Aisenberg, 1972, pp. 192–193). It should suffice to tell us that both aging and dying are different today than they were in preindustrial society. It should also be clear that the contrast is between contemporary society of only about the past century and a pattern that lasted for several centuries.

Preindustrial, as I have indicated, is not the correct term to describe the contrasting societal types, for *the dramatic changes occurred not with industrialization but some time afterward* (Laslett, 1976). They occurred as an accompaniment to declining fertility, the growth of medical technology, and, most important, the rising standard of living with its improved nutrition, sanitation, and other related factors, such as better housing conditions.

In presenting this contrast, I have hinted at some of the implications of changing mortality not only for the age structure but also for family life. There are other implications for individuals and for their life in society. In the next chapter we return to Mannheim's and Moore's problem of the consequences for social life of the fact that humans are mortal. We should be better prepared to understand these consequences by our recognition that it is not just the *fact* of mortality but the *character* of death that is consequential.

The cases on which I have drawn to establish this contrast were selected not just as a background against which to illuminate the present. The argument, unfortunately, has to be somewhat more complex. In some respects, the *differences* between our own and earlier societies are relevant. In others, the *newness* of the contemporary situation is the key to understanding. In still other respects, the *legacy* from the past is the important factor in understanding the social aspects of aging and dying today.

Review Questions
for Chapter 2

1. *Mannheim's suggestion that we think about what it would be like if nobody died has been taken up in many works of science fiction. You might read or discuss some of these works and how they describe the ways in which the social system is affected by immortality.*

2. *A good way to get an idea of the changing demography of death is to visit a cemetery. Head for the oldest section, and examine the dates of birth and death on the gravestones. You will find several cases of families in which many children were born but few survived the first few years. For comparison, examine newer sections of the cemetery. While you are at it, observe different styles of ornamentation and decoration of headstones, mausoleums, and the like. Serious investigation will also give you an idea of family histories from generation to generation. Can you find any "black sheep" who were not buried in the family plot? What evidence can you find of social-class differences among the dead?*

3. *Trace out your own genealogy, noting number of persons born in various generations, their ages at marriage, widowhood, and death. Interview your parents, grandparents, and other older members of your lineage to obtain data, and examine family Bibles to see if they include handwritten information.*

4. *While you are interviewing older members of your lineage, ask them about their perceptions of death now, and when they were young. Treat them as anthropological informants describing the rituals and the social organization of death in an earlier age, or perhaps in other countries from which they immigrated.*

3

The Social Organization of Death and Dying

This chapter describes the development of the social and cultural context in which today's aging person will enact his or her own process of dying. The varying patterns of mortality and age structure described in the previous chapter pose what can be called "problems" for the society—problems that members of the society try to solve in various ways. In this chapter I will refer to an *institutionalization* of death and dying, by which I mean the development and continuance of patterned ways of acting toward death and dying and of shared meanings about death and dying.

The Societal Problematics of Death and Dying

Sociologists often speak as though societies had problems. This is a loose way of speaking, because societies do not *have* anything. From a sociological perspective, they *are* something. The term *society* refers to members of a defined collectivity, or group of people who share patterned interaction. Controversy exists about how exactly a boundary might be drawn to distinguish a group who interact a great deal within their collectivity and yet who, in the kind of world we live in, are likely to have at least some minimal interaction with other collectivities. Commonsensically, however, we can think of societies as groups of people, be they tribes or nation-states, who are linked together through direct and mediated interaction.

A useful technical definition of a society is "A group of human beings sharing a self-sufficient system of action which is capable of existing longer than the life-span of an individual, the group being recruited at least in part by the sexual reproduction of the members" (Aberle, Cohen, Davis, Levy, & Sutton, 1950, p. 101).

This is not the only possible or worthwhile definition of society; however its usefulness for our purposes should be immediately apparent. If the group did not live longer than the life span of the individual, if everyone in society died, there would, rather obviously, be no society left. It should be apparent from the material reviewed in the previous chapter that this was by no means a trivial issue in many of the societies of the past and indeed in some of the societies in today's world; life in peasant England or France and in colonial New England was indeed precarious.

This definition of society calls attention to the relationship between individual mortality and the *survival* of a society; and we can broaden our focus to include the relationship between mortality and the *character* of the society. Having established in the previous chapter that the character of death can vary greatly in different societies, we turn at this point to the consequences of this character for the ways in which individuals organize their life in society.

Many sociologists (for example, Aberle et al., 1950; Levy, Jr., 1952; Parsons, 1951, pp. 26–36) have found it useful to devise lists of tasks or functions that must be performed if a society, as defined above, is to continue to exist. A society can cease to exist for a number of reasons. By definition, the biological extinction of all members implies the cessation of the society, as does the complete dispersion of all members through mass exodus. Loss of motivation to interact would destroy the patterned interaction that constitutes society. Failure to direct interaction, at some minimal level at least, toward common purposes would lead to the "war of all against all" that the classical political philosophers called the antithesis of society. Finally, a given society can become completely absorbed or assimilated into another society, so that the distinct interaction patterns lose their identity (Aberle et al., 1950).

Our own concern is primarily with the implications of the possibility of biological extinction, although under conditions of extreme precariousness, all of these elements would or could enter into a sociology of death and dying. For example, some scholars see the era of the plagues as one in which the sense of community became eroded under the massive threat of horrible death;

and they trace the growth of individualism to this era (Ariès, 1974, see especially pp. 27–39; Ziegler, 1969, Chap. 17). Lifton notes a similar process of individualism among survivors of Hiroshima (1967, pp. 44–46).

There is little point in repeating any of the lists of so-called "functional requisites"—or "prerequisites"—that ensure the survival of a society. Clearly a balance between deaths and births must be attained if any society is to survive. Some division of labor may also be presumed to be necessary, if only on the grounds of sex and age. Neither males nor infants can bear children, and the very old have less ability than the young to undertake arduous physical labor. In any society age is at least one basis on which roles are assigned (Eisenstadt, 1956, pp. 21–24). Aberle and associates argue that "whatever the society, activities necessary to its survival must be worked out in predictable, determinate ways, or else apathy or the war of each against all must prevail" (1950, p. 105). Role differentiation necessitates communication in order to coordinate activities. At a more general level, some sharing of meaning must occur if people are to be able to attain any routinization of their collective activities. There must be some agreement about what "is" and about what "ought to be" in order for any common or shared definition of the situation to exist. Otherwise each individual would live in his or her personal world, and it would be impossible to work with anyone else for the collective good. As indicated in Chapter Two, there must be some continuity between the generations, some passing on of the cultural heritage to the young, so that the "immortal" positions may continue to be filled when they are vacated by death. Moreover, if the patterned activity in a society is not to become highly rigidified, there should be some means to ensure that positions do become vacant (Levy, Jr., 1966, p. 441; Mannheim, 1952). Death is therefore convenient, and substitute procedures, such as retirement, may develop to make this process more stable and predictable.

Although this argument relies heavily on Parsons (1951) and his students (Aberle et al., 1950; Levy, Jr., 1952) and has a decidedly "functionalist" tone, its generality becomes apparent in the words of Marx, who discusses the conditions under which a particular capitalistic form of society can survive:

> The proprietor of labour power is mortal. If such proprietors are to appear permanently on the market, and the unceasing demands of capital require this, then must that amount of labour power which is lost to the market in consequence of wear and tear or death be continually replaced by at least an equal amount of new power [Marx, *Capital*, Vol. 1, Chap. 6; excerpted in Eastman, 1932, p. 37].

More generally, Marx's view of the process of civilization was that the basic explanation of human history was to be found in the need for people to preserve themselves. Acting on the material environment, people produced themselves as human beings and produced a social and human world: "We must begin by stating the first presupposition of all human existence, and therefore of all history, namely, that men must be in a position to live in order to be able to make history" (Marx, 1845–1846; excerpted in Bottomore, 1956, p. 60). The general point is that individual and social survival are intertwined. This point is valid when approached from various theoretical stances; in fact, the point is so crucial that it needs to be approached in as many different ways as possible.

Death brings a halt to an individual's activities, but it also interrupts the normal, ongoing routine of life in a society. Where a society's population is small and the sheer volume of death is very high, and where death takes individuals who are highly involved in the normal routines of everyday life, it is possible that the society can suffer a kind of systematic shock to its social relations and its system of beliefs. This shock will be greater than that experienced in larger societies with lower death rates, in which death comes more frequently to those who are less intimately or elaborately involved in the affairs of the society. How death affects an industrialized society can be better understood by taking a comparative view. I will again refer to the preindustrial European and Colonial examples discussed in Chapter Two but will first examine the case in which this argument has been most fully developed—the relatively nonindustrial or premodern societies customarily studied by anthropologists.

Death and Integration of Societies

Much of the myth and ritual discussed in anthropological accounts of nonmodernized societies centers around death and dying. This observation indicates the importance of death to people in societies in which death is a frequent occurrence. Since not many people in such societies lived to be very old, these accounts give less information about aging and the aged than we would find useful. Therefore, the focus here will be on the central tradition of research in this area and on studies that explicitly deal with the problematics of death and dying and, even then, on only a few classical works.

A number of anthropologists and sociologists have argued persuasively that the importance of death ritual in many societies is related to the precariousness of the society. The historian David Stannard summarizes one of the most comprehensive general studies in this area, that of the English anthropologist V. Gordon Childe (1945), who analyzed archeological evidence about funeral practices over a 50,000-year period:

> As societies become more settled and more culturally and materially stable . . . there is a marked tendency for funeral customs and burial rituals to become less elaborate and less extravagant; conversely, such customs and

rituals seem to be most elaborate and most extravagant during periods of social and cultural instability [Stannard, 1977, p. 122].

Childe also found that sepulchral monuments are generally most imposing in societies that are least stable. Both patterns are of interest to Stannard because, while he and Childe admit exceptions to them, the Puritan case that Stannard has studied (see Chapter Two) fits this pattern quite nicely. Despite the original emphasis of the first Puritans on an avoidance of elaborate ceremonial at the time of death, during periods of societal stress and instability, the Puritans adopted a highly elaborate funeral ritual and abandoned their unadorned style of headstones and burial markers (see, for example, Coffin, 1976; Tashjian & Tashjian, 1974).

The most important point made by many sociologists and anthropologists is that the funeral ritual serves the living more than it serves the dead. Robert Hertz, a student and associate of Durkheim, emphasized the social character of the treatment of death in society. Taking the position that societies think of themselves as immortal and that society imparts life onto its members, Hertz argued:

> Indeed, society imparts its own character of permanence to the individuals who compose it: because it feels itself immortal and wants to be so, it cannot normally believe that its members, above all those in whom it incarnates itself and with whom it identifies itself, should be fated to die [1960, p. 77].*

The death of any member, but particularly of important members, is therefore seen as threatening to the survival of the society in its immortal character. "Thus, when a man dies, society loses in him much more than a unit; it is stricken in the very principle of its life, in the faith it has in itself" (Hertz, 1960, p. 78). The ritual treatment of death in almost all societies thereby serves to make of death "not a mere destruction but a transition" (Hertz, 1960, p. 48).

Hertz had begun with the problem of trying to explain why the "double funeral" is such a common phenomenon in so many societies. Double funerals are those that occur in two stages. In many Christian societies, a wake or prayer service will precede a formal funeral service and burial (see, for example, Vallee, 1955), and in the Dayak societies described by Hertz, "the body of the deceased, while awaiting a second burial, is temporarily deposited in a burial-place distinct from the final one" (Hertz, 1960, p. 30).

The corpse is then temporarily in a transitional state, which can last up to two years in Dayak society but which might be only a few days in a North American funeral ceremony. During this period the body is considered in danger from evil spirits, and the soul is also considered to be hovering some-

---

*From *Death and the Right Hand*, by R. Hertz. Copyright 1960 by Cohen and West. (Translated by Rodney and Claudia Needham.) This and all other quotations from this source are reprinted by permission.

where in the vicinity of the body. Only after the second funeral is the soul considered to be at rest. The society has been shocked at the death of one of its members, and the ritual, which brings together all members of the community, serves to send the soul on its way to the other world. This is usually a world of continuing life, although often not of immortality for the soul (Davidson, 1971). "Death is not a mere destruction but a transition: as it progresses, so does the rebirth; while the old body falls to ruins, a new body takes shape with which the soul—provided the necessary rites have been performed—will enter another existence, often superior to the previous one" (Hertz, 1960, p. 48). In this manner, a society of the dead is established, by which the society of the living regularly recreates itself" (Hertz, 1960, p. 76).

The period between the funerals is a transitional period, a rite of passage (van Gennep, 1960) both for the soul of the deceased and for the survivors. During this period the normal social obligations of the survivors are suspended, and ritual behavioral prescriptions, as well as the support from other members of the community, help the survivors through the time of crisis. As the rite progresses, the survivors are helped to behave "appropriately," until, at the end of the rite, they resume their everyday activities along the lines of behavior that they had followed before the death.

Jack Goody has reviewed Hertz's argument and that of many other sociologists and anthropologists, and his summary is useful:

> Like other members of the same school, Hertz displays a tendency to reify society [to treat society as if it were real and capable of doing things on its own], a tendency that makes for certain misunderstandings. But we may eliminate this difficulty by putting his general point in a slightly different way. Beliefs in an afterlife appear to be related to the basic contradiction that exists between the continuity of the social system—the relative perpetuity of the constituent groups and of their corpus of norms—and the impermanence of its personnel. This conflict between the mortality of the human body and the immortality of the body politic is resolved, in part at least, by the belief in an afterlife. A future existence is postulated as a supplement to man's earthly span, a Land of the Dead as a counterpart to the Land of the Living [1962, p. 27].

The general argument of Hertz has become widely accepted. As Goody (1962, p. 27) points out, van Gennep's (1960) treatment of the rites of passage, which extends the notion of ritual passage to include all major points in the life cycle and also situations outside the life cycle, adds little to Hertz's analysis.

Malinowski (1948, pp. 48–49), like Hertz and van Gennep, called attention to the basic similarities in the mourning customs of most world cultures. Although he postulated an instinctive fear of death (1948, p. 50), which has no support in research (Anthony, 1971; Goody, 1962, p. 22), his major contribution was to examine the social functions of mourning customs. In Malinowski's words:

> A small community bereft of a member, especially if he be important, is severely mutilated. The whole event breaks the normal course of life and shakes the moral foundations of society. . . . Death in a primitive society is . . . much more than the removal of a member. By setting in motion one part of the deep forces of the instinct of self-preservation, it threatens the very cohesion and solidarity of the group, and upon this depends the organization of that society, its tradition, and finally the whole culture [1948, pp. 52–53].

Goody's own research (1962) on the LoDagaa of West Africa, in addition to being the most thorough theoretical treatment of inheritance to be found anywhere, provides a more recent example of the social function of mourning customs. Two communities of the LoDagaa, similar in many other respects, have different systems of property ownership. In one community, the LoWiili, all property is inherited through the male or paternal side; in the other community, the LoDagaba, immovable property, such as land, passes through the male line, but movable property, such as cattle, passes through the female line. As Goody points out, "The crucial features of any system of relatively exclusive rights . . . seems most likely to be displayed when these rights are transmitted from one individual to the next, a process that is made inevitable by the inescapable fact of death" (1962, pp. 10–11). It is also here that the possibilities for conflict are likely to be highest. In LoDagaa society, as in most nonmodernized societies, the funeral is a key device for effecting the transfer of property and other rights (for our own society, see Rosenfeld, 1979; Sussman, Cates, & Smith, 1970). The differential complexity of the inheritance system between the two communities provided a natural laboratory in which to examine the social functions of funeral behavior in this regard. Tension focusing on the transfer of rights varies between the two communities of LoDagaa. The dead retain most of their property rights after their deaths and continue to hold many of them as ghosts, until an entire series of funeral rites is held. "The process of transmission is never complete, since the dead ancestors continue to belong to the same corporation as their living descendants; indeed they are its most important members" (1962, p. 328).

While it is not necessary to go into the details of the differences in funeral rites between the two communities of LoDagaa, it is important to note that Goody was able to discuss differences that are most meaningfully understood in relation to the different systems of inheritance. Elaborate funeral rituals may then be seen as a way to minimize the conflict and threat to the stability of the community occasioned by the death of an important, property-owning member.

Counts (1976–1977) describes essentially the same processes for the Kaliai of New Britain, Melanesia, which suggest the near-universality of the general functions served by funerals. Among the Kaliai, too, death is seen not as the end of all experience but as transition between different life states —a transition that takes time. Counts (1976) points out that "death requires time for the severing of social relationships in the normal world. The separation process may either precede or follow the event of bodily death" (p. 368).

The Kaliai have a conception of the "good death" that parallels very closely the notion of "disengagement" postulated as optimal preparation for death by many contemporary gerontologists. The good death seems to be an ideal that the Kaliai seldom realize. Most of them die because of the presumed malevolence of some being, which violates the right to the good death. The good death follows longevity, occurs with the acquiescence of the dying person, and takes enough time to allow for the severance of social relationships. The Limbu of Nepal (Jones, 1974) and the LoDagaa have a similar ideal conception of the good death (Goody, 1962, pp. 208–209). When the Kaliai realize that death is approaching, they try to ward it off. The time thus gained is spent bringing social relationships to a close. In the idealized good death, the dying person "called all his kinsmen to gather around him, disposed of his possessions after repaying the obligations owed by him and forgiving any obligations of others to him, and then informed those gathered that it was time for him to die" (Counts, 1976–1977, p. 370).

The significance of the good death in Kaliai is that *there are no mortuary rites* for a good death. But, since there are virtually no good deaths in Kaliai, there are almost always funerals. The Limbu have a modest funeral for the good death in old age but elaborate rites for unexpected and violent deaths (Jones, 1974). The general pattern is, therefore, analogous. The funeral ceremonial, as in the case of the LoDagaa and, more generally, in societies such as those described by Hertz, Malinowski, and others, serves as a substitute for processes of "making things right" that might have occurred in life. The ceremonial smooths the transition from one social state to another as a segmental member of a society is lost.

The good death in Kaliai is one in which the individual times withdrawal from society to coincide with actual biological decline and cessation. The individual ceases to be a social being at the same time that he or she ceases to be a living biological being. Because funerals are given for social beings—for members of the community or society—no funeral is given for the nonsocial being. In this respect, it is important to note that in Kaliai (Counts, 1976–1977), in LoDagaa (Goody, 1962, p. 52), and in most similar societies (Hertz, 1960, p. 76), including Western peasant societies (Shorter, 1977, pp. 172–173; Vallee, 1955), the death of an infant or child goes unnoticed or is accompanied by little, and private, ritual. As Counts puts it, "For the Kaliai death becomes a social event signalling the time-consuming transformation process only for those persons who have become fully social beings. Thus the death of very young children who have not been integrated in the web of society is an essentially private event" (1976–1977, pp. 368–369). In Kaliai, children are not considered fully human until they are able to discuss dream life with their parents. Hertz notes that deaths of children, strangers, and slaves "arouse no emotion, occasion no ritual" (1960, p. 76). Hertz reviews the implications of this attitude for the aged:

> In various Australian tribes, old people who, because of their great age, are incapable of taking part in the totemic ceremonies, who have lost their aptitude for sacred functions, are buried immediately after death. . . . This is so because, due to the weakening of their faculties, they have ceased to participate in social life; their death merely consecrates an exclusion from society which has in fact already been completed, and which every one has had time to get used to [1960, p. 85].

In general, the literature, mostly anthropological, concerning death ritual and belief in the so-called "primitive" societies suggests a great concern for death among the people. In cases that appear to be exceptions to this generalization, such as the ancient Israelites or traditional Eskimo of the Eastern Arctic (Carpenter, 1954; Guemple, 1969), concerns for the survival of the society as a whole probably obscured individualistic concerns. Gatch (1969, in Shneidman, 1976) reminds us that an emphasis on the individual is a peculiarly modern Western tradition. For example, the dying patriarch Abraham was concerned not for himself but for the preservation of the existence of his people. On his deathbed, he commanded his servant to get a wife for his son Isaac so that the patriarchal line could be continued. Gatch says of the scriptures:

> There is no attempt (indeed, it is not possible) to speak in individual terms for Abraham, for the Hebraic mind does not conceive of the situation as we do. There is no way to separate Abraham from the clan he produced . . . his personality is indistinct from that of the tribe. Thus, one can only speak anachronistically of his death as an end since, even dead, Abraham continues to be an important part of the corporate personality [p. 47].

Gatch also claims that the Old and New Testaments, on the whole, offer no theology of death and afterlife. Instead, both Testaments speak of a *people* or a *kingdom,* rather than of individuals, and of resurrection as the restoration of that people or kingdom. This conclusion is particularly surprising and important, given the uses of scripture by later Christians to provide an understanding of death; but it helps us to understand the colonial American situation, as we will shortly see.

As an added complication to an understanding of death, ritual, and society, note Radcliffe-Brown's (1965) disagreement with the formulation emphasized here. Radcliffe-Brown takes issue with Malinowski—a major contributor to this discussion. Whereas Malinowski has emphasized the importance of religious ritual as a means of dealing with the problems death causes in a society, Radcliffe-Brown argues that religious ritual *creates* anxieties about death. He points out that

> in our fears or anxieties, as well as in our hopes, we are conditioned by the community in which we live. And it is largely by the sharing of hopes and

fears, by . . . the common concern in events or eventualities that human beings are linked together in temporary or permanent associations [1965, p. 81].

Homans (1941, in Lessa & Vogt, 1965; see also Leming, 1977) has argued persuasively that Radcliffe-Brown's position is complementary to that of Malinowski:

> Malinowski is looking at the individual, Radcliffe-Brown at society. Malinowski is saying that the individual tends to feel anxiety on certain occasions; Radcliffe-Brown is saying that society expects the individual to feel anxiety on certain occasions. But there is every reason to believe that both statements are true [p. 126].

If in our life in society we develop mythological beliefs that arouse anxiety and employ ritual to develop, dramatize, and reinforce these beliefs and the concomitant anxiety, the ritual also serves to reduce the anxiety; while doing so, it brings together the members of that society and binds them more closely to one another. In sum, this dialectical process contributes to societal cohesion.

Death is then both a societal and an individual concern in relatively nonmodernized societies. Most researchers have seen this concern as flowing from the precariousness of such societies and from the ease with which societies of such a small scale and so exposed to capricious death can be disrupted. Funeral ritual and mythological systems are major ways to preserve societal integration under such circumstances.

A survey of this kind cannot go into great detail about any one society. It is, however, particularly important to emphasize that the survival of the society as a whole was not the only concern of these peoples, nor were funeral ritual and mythology the only mechanisms for preserving societal stability. To so assume would both simplify the case and commit the serious fallacy of attributing a great deal of social engineering skills to these people. It is almost certainly the case, for example, that the development of funeral practices in the societies described was not deliberately planned as a means of preserving social integration. As far as we know, no LoDagaa ever sat down and decided that the best way to manage the conflicts caused by a complicated kinship and succession system was to invent a particular kind of funeral. However, we are not so much interested in the origins of these practices and beliefs as we are in their consequences. It seems to be the case that, in society after society, common problems were caused by the frequent occurrence of death. Over centuries, and indeed millenia, certain general types of practices surrounding death and dying seem to have been useful in dealing with these problems. The origin of these practices is not so important for us to understand (and probably it could never be discovered in any case) as the way in which they have worked.

Funeral practices and beliefs about the dead are not the only phenomena that have been affected by the character of death. Goody (1962), who focuses on the institutions of inheritance, also discusses a great many other features of life in LoDagaa and in similar societies that are affected by the character of death. The discussion that follows, however, focuses on the character of death in the preindustrial peasant society first discussed in Chapter Two. Although a more complex society than those that interested Hertz, Malinowski, and Goody, this was basically a rural society of peasant households and tiny villages (Laslett, 1971, especially Chap. 1) and can be thought of as more similar in most respects to the societies just discussed than to industrial society of today. As suggested in Chapter Two, it was a society in which individual life and societal survival were no less precarious than they were in the relatively nonmodern societies just discussed.

Death, Family, and Community in Preindustrial Society

Pressat (1972, p. 71) argues that a population will not continue to survive with a sustained average crude death rate of above 45 to 50 per 1000. This is because the upper limit of the birth rate appears to be around 45 to 50 per 1000. Pressat also estimates that the average crude death rate in the era before statistics were systematically kept was about 30 to 35 per 1000. Preston (1977) claims that crude death rates in Africa, Asia, and Latin America averaged about 38 per 1000 in the second half of the past century but declined to about 17 per 1000 by 1960–1970. The conjunction of this decline in mortality with crude birth rates that remained constant at a little over 40 per 1000 produced the so-called population explosion.

In preindustrial Europe, if the average crude death rate in earlier times was close to the upper limit of 45 to 50 per 1000, the impact of plagues and epidemics such as the Black Death becomes more obvious. In normal times, the population would just barely reproduce itself, making small gains in numbers. Departures from normality could seriously threaten a society. As Kamen argues, "It only needed a disaster—say, a war or an epidemic—to tilt the balance heavily in favour of death. Even without such disasters, in normal conditions in the early seventeenth century something like two live births were necessary to produce every adult human" (1976, p. 18). That all of this was a relatively unpredictable phenomenon had consequences that lead us to question the supposed stability of preindustrial society.

Laslett (1971) reports that a 17th-century English village had an unexpectedly high turnover in population. In two communities studied, "people were moving to and fro, society was changing, whole households were coming and going" (p. 156).* Although this change went on "quite independently

*From *The World We Have Lost* (2nd ed.), by P. Laslett. Copyright 1971 by Charles Scribner's Sons. Published in the British Commonwealth by Methuen & Co., Ltd. This and all other quotations from this source are reprinted by permission.

of the level of birth-and-death rates," Laslett claims that it can be demonstrated that this movement of people is intimately connected with the low expectation of life. "In fact," Laslett says, "every feature of preindustrial society could be shown to fit in with this somewhat unexpected characteristic of peasant society, and especially the migratory activities of servants" (p. 156).

Laslett's argument, which should be consulted in detail, is that the high death rate resulted in the development of a highly flexible household type—including immediate family and, usually, servants—in order to accommodate the lack of certainty that a given individual would be alive for very long. The servants in most households might well be children orphaned by the death of a neighbor. In a society in which the death of a child was "a matter of consequence, for it always must be remembered that the actual work on most of the plots of land was done by the working family, the man, his wife, and children" (Laslett, 1971, pp. 72–73), servants were workers and, in fact, functional equivalents of children.

This was a world, Laslett informs us, in which "everything temporal was tied to the human life-span" (1971, p. 8). The head of a family and household might run a bakery, which would cease to exist on his death, since, if the baker died at the typical age, his sons would most likely be too young to take over the business. "Or," Laslett tells us, "an apprentice might fulfill the final function of apprenticehood, substitute sonship, that is to say, and marry his master's daughter, or even his widow" (p. 8). The household and the family were therefore organized flexibly, in order to account for death, because, since almost all activities took place within the family, it was here that "there was an unending struggle to manufacture continuity and to provide an expectation of the future" (Laslett, 1971, p. 8).

Even for the upper classes, whose mortality rate was lower, the unpredictability of death posed problems:

> Complicated arrangements then existed, and still exist in England now, which were intended to make it easier for the noble family to give the impression that it had indeed always persisted. Such, for example, were those intricate rules of succession which permitted a cousin, however distant, to succeed to the title and to the headship. . . . Nobility was for ever [Laslett, 1971, p. 9].

Nobility could be forever, of course, only if the continuity of the lineage could be maintained. Since direct succession over several generations was virtually impossible because of the probability of death before reaching the childbearing years, the notions of succession and lineage had to be loosened as an accommodation:

> That familial, patriarchal system which dominated and gave structure to pre-industrial society, had succeeded in maintaining permanence in spite of the shortness of life, the fluctuations of prosperity, the falling in of leases, the wayward habits of young folk in service, and the fickleness of their employers. The institutions of the old world must be looked upon in this way, as

expedients to provide permanence in an environment which was all too imper-
manent and insecure [Laslett, 1971, p. 157].

More generally, Laslett continues:

> The respect due to the old and experienced, the reverence for the Church and
> its immense, impersonal antiquity, the spontaneous feeling that it was the
> family which gave a meaning to life because the family could and must
> endure, all these things helped to reconcile our ancestors with relentless,
> remorseless mortality and mischance. . . . An unchanging, unchangeable so-
> cial structure may well be essential to a swiftly changing population [Laslett,
> 1971, p. 157].

Drawing on material from peasant France, Shorter (1977) emphasizes
that it would be a mistake to use the term *family* in its current meaning, which
emphasizes positive feelings and affection, to refer to the "family" of the past.
Laslett, of course, has attempted to counter the common assumption that most
people in the past lived in extended families. He argues that the nuclear family
was very widespread in earlier times (see especially Laslett, 1971). Shorter
(1977) shares Laslett's views about family and community to a great extent
and tells us a bit more about the treatment of death. He characterizes the
traditional pattern of dealing with death as a community affair involving family
and neighbors in a collective ritual that united individual and society: "In
birth, marriage, and death . . . the surrounding community was present,
intertwining itself about the grief and passion of individuals, separating them
from their immediate families, drawing them into a larger world of social
interaction" (p. 218).

Family life, as portrayed by Shorter, was primarily an economic, not
an emotional, affair even at the time of death:

> So much more firmly did economics rather than emotion bind together the
> peasant couple that when the wife fell ill, her husband commonly spared the
> expense of a doctor, though prepared to "cascade gold" upon the veterinarian
> who came to attend a sick cow or bull. That was because, in the last analysis, a
> cow was worth much more than a wife [1977, p. 57].

And, as in the societies discussed earlier in this chapter, the death of infants
and children was hardly noted at all. At the spiritual level, infant death meant
a soul proceeding directly to heaven: "On the human plane infant death is
almost a banal accident, which a subsequent birth will recuperate" (Shorter,
1977, p. 173).

The death of mature adults involved people beyond their immediate
families. Everyone who could hear the bells toll was to say a prayer for the
deceased, participating at least minimally in the death ritual. Neighbors would
circulate in the village and in distant villages to notify relatives of the death.
The whole village would attend the wake, which was sometimes quite a rowdy
affair with laughter and dancing (for a literary example, see Uris, 1976). In
France, a postburial meal would be served the community by the family of the

deceased, and dinner would often conclude with an attempt to arrange a new marriage for the surviving spouse (Shorter, 1977, pp. 213–218).

It seems to be generally the case that individual and society linkages were the focus of concern surrounding mortality for all the relatively non-modernized societies considered so far, including preindustrial France and England. Not only was individual fate closely linked with the prospects and occurrence of death within the immediate family, but whole structural arrangements for aggregates of people were linked to general trends and patterns of mortality. Important examples of this attitude in the classical sociological area of stratification and mobility can be found in property ownership (class issues) and occupational careers (stratification issues).

Preston (1977; see also Habakkuk, 1972, p. 27; McInnis, 1977) explains the more general linkages among mortality rates, property ownership, and family formation:

> There is one aggregate-level linkage between death and birth rates that deserves mention because of its apparent importance in pre-industrial Europe. In a spatially limited system where land is the basis of wealth and accession to land the prerequisite for marriage, the rate of marriage, and hence childbearing, will depend upon the rate at which land becomes available, hence on mortality [p. 172].

Laslett (1976, 1977) argues, however, that in more cases than has usually been thought, including Ireland (Arensberg, 1937; Streib, 1976), land would pass to the son before the death of the father. While both patterns could be found, the implications for tension within family units are quite obvious.

Officers in the Royal Navy of Great Britain and in the Royal Canadian Navy preserve a set of traditional toasts, one for each day, that are offered in the wardroom (officers' mess). In one of these, dating back centuries, the officers toast to "a bloody war or a sickly season." Here the relationship between individual and social fate is explicitly recognized. A bloody war or a sickly season will lead to the death of large numbers of senior officers, creating vacancies that will enhance the careers of those who survive.

Speaking of changes in mortality rates in general, Preston argues:

> It is clear that the origins of persons in the occupational structure at any point are affected by these mortality changes. Simply stated, the same occupational structure will produce, one generation hence, a higher proportion of persons who originated in lower classes when mortality is low than when it is high. . . . By reducing the average origin status of the labor force, mortality declines have almost certainly enhanced upward social mobility in this century [1977, p. 170].

Not only the demographic creation of vacancies but also people's interpretation of it influenced the relationship between mortality and mobility. As noted earlier, when mortality rates are high, there will be many vacancies created at higher levels of the social structure. Seeing opportunities, people may marry earlier and have children in the hope that the children will have better opportunities (see Habakkuk, 1972, pp. 27–28).

These observations should be placed in the context of a society in which life expectancy at birth was much shorter than it is now. Consider the great length of time that many North American youth of today spend in school, including college and graduate school. Even in light of today's normal expected life expectancy, many people, especially students, think that this amount of time is too large a slice of life. In colonial America, as seen in Chapter Two, a person marrying at the typical age could not anticipate very many years with spouse and children. An adult life of a reasonable duration would have to be started at a relatively young age. The prolonged adolescence that many people experience today would not have been reasonable or practical in former times in North America. Conversely and in general terms, only when average life expectancy rises to levels beyond those customarily found in relatively nonmodernized societies can the privilege of an extended period of socialization for adult roles be granted to more than a few.

The earliest generation of American colonists had a great struggle to survive as a people, but the overall level of health of the population, as discussed in Chapter Two, was quite high and certainly higher than that in the England that they had left. By the fourth generation, however, there was a rise in mortality rates, at least in Andover, Massachusetts—a case that has been admirably documented by the historian Philip Greven.

The demographically stable situation in much of New England, especially the small agricultural towns, made them "excellent places in which to realize the goals of order, hierarchy, and the closely knit community" that had been the dream of their Puritan founders (Greven, 1970, pp. 270–271). This stability was to persist until about the middle of the 18th century.

Greven (1970, pp. 222–258) remarks that an increase in mortality, particularly in infancy and childhood, among the fourth generation of settlers in Andover, Massachusetts, must have led to a "heightened sense of the impermanence of life itself," which was probably associated with the increasing autonomy that parents began to give their children at that time. This growing autonomy is reflected in the transmitting of estates to sons and in the setting up of the sons in independent livelihood. In this period and for this community, then, one effect of the changing character of death was to loosen the ties binding the generations.

The scope of this book does not permit me to examine the situation in New England, or in Andover in particular, in any more detail. The important lesson is to note the intertwining of demographic and social changes. Subtle, and even quite marked, changes in such fundamental social patterns as those surrounding inheritance, child rearing, and the quality of family life may be viewed as accommodations to the gross pattern of demographic changes in death rate. Laslett's general argument that the institutions of preindustrial Europe may be viewed as an attempt to provide some stability in the face of capricious death seems to apply in large measure to early North America as well.

If the early settlers of North America were seeking some kind of stability, a major device through which they sought it was religious belief (Tashjian & Tashjian, 1974, p. 14). With this observation, the emphasis shifts from the social to the cultural domain (see Chapter One). In turning to the area of shared belief, I will continue to use pertinent examples from selected cases to make general points, avoiding detailed descriptions of all aspects of aging and dying in any one society. The concrete examples will, however, be largely from North America and will provide the context for the detailed account of aging and dying in North America that is the subject of the rest of the book.

Death and the Problem of Meaning

Without death, the problems of passing on meaning from generation to generation would be greatly reduced. People would be born into a society, learn and create meanings, and share them with others. If people lived forever, their memories would preserve meanings. In a very general but nonetheless important sense, then, death poses problems for the continuity of society while at the same time it expands the potential for change in meaning over the span of the generations. But there is another, and more fundamental, way in which the necessity of making sense of death itself becomes problematic for society. The strong version of this argument is found in the work of Berger and Luckmann, who argue:

> The experience of the death of others and, subsequently, the anticipation of one's own death posit the marginal situation par excellence for the individual. . . . Death also posits the most terrifying threat to the taken-for-granted realities of everyday life. The integration of death within the paramount reality of social existence is, therefore, of the greatest importance for any institutional order [1967, p. 101].

Like many other scholars, Berger and Luckmann view death as terrible and terror-filled, at least potentially. In any society, they argue, meanings must be provided to reduce this terror by legitimating death:

> All legitimations of death must carry out the same essential task—they must enable the individual to go on living in society after the death of significant others and to anticipate his own death with, at the very least, terror sufficiently mitigated so as not to paralyze the continued performance of the routines of everyday life. . . . Such legitimation . . . provides the individual with a recipe for a "correct death." Optimally, this recipe will retain its plausibility when his death is imminent and will allow him, indeed, to "die correctly" [1967, p. 101].

Setting aside for the moment the extent to which death is inherently terrifying, we can nonetheless observe that in every society some set of meanings exists to "explain" death. Berger and Luckmann argue that no system of meanings can survive unless it provides a way to render death sensible or understandable; that is, unless death can be, in their term, *legitimated*. Although many authors assume that the need to explain death is the basis for the origin, or social invention, of religions, this is an untestable assumption. Whatever its origin, religious belief plays an important role in providing an explanation for and interpretation of death in all societies, perhaps being supplemented by nonreligious interpretations only in the contemporary world. Berger (1969) views religion as a major way in which the integration, or solidarity, of a society might be maintained.

Death is viewed as the limit or the boundary of the individual's participation in society. Berger would argue along the same lines as Hertz and other scholars, such as Mary Douglas (1966, pp. 96–97) and Victor Turner (1967, Chap. 4), that it is at the point of death that the very nature of society—its cohesiveness or integration—is most likely to be threatened. Although not the only one, death is perhaps the most serious threat to the taken-for-granted image that a people have of their society and their life in society (for an excellent perspective on this point, see Geertz, 1966). It is, therefore, in one sense possible to agree with Berger that

> every human society is, in the last resort, men banded together in the face of death. The power of religion depends, in the last resort, upon the credibility of the banners it puts in the hands of men as they stand before death, or more accurately, as they walk, inevitably, toward it [1969, p. 51].

As the fate of "Everyman," death requires explanation. It is possible to say this without assuming that death without explanation is terrifying. In fact, the explanations given for death often provide its terrible character. In reviewing the changing meaning of death, it is well to treat death as an inherently neutral event, with its meaning socially constructed. At the same time, the positions taken by many scholars of death cannot be understood without realizing that, perhaps because these scholars shared the meanings of their own culture, many of them view death as inherently terrifying.

The most significant contemporary interpretation of changing attitudes toward death in the Western world and one that does not assume death to be inherently terrifying has been put forth by Philippe Ariès (1974, 1975, 1977). Ariès' analysis traces out the changing meaning of death in terms of a typology of attitudinal and behavioral clusters (see Table 3-1). These attitudes are summarized by Ariès as follows:

> The first, the oldest, the longest held, and the most common one, is the familiar resignation to the collective destiny of the species and can be summarized by the phrase, *Et moriemur,* and we shall all die. The second, which appeared in the twelfth century, reveals the importance given throughout the

Attitudinal Type	Approximate Dates	Aspects of Behavior and Meaning
1. Tamed Death	Before 1200	"We shall all die." Death is forewarned. The individual controls death ritual. Death is familiar and taken for granted. Death is among the living.
2. One's Own Death	1200–1700	"I shall die." God's judgment is individualized. An individual's biography is a balance sheet. The "art of dying" emerges. Deathbed scenes are dramatized. Horror of bodily decomposition appears.
3. Thy Death	1700–late 1800s	"You shall die." Death is seen as romantic and erotic. Death is a break with the living. The family becomes more involved. Fear of the death of the other increases.
4. Forbidden Death	Late 1800s but especially 1900s	Emotion is contained or avoided. Physicians assume control of dying. Death and mourning become private. There is a cultural denial of death and of the honoring of the dead.

entire modern period to the self, to one's own existence, and can be expressed by another phrase, *la mort de soi,* one's own death.

Beginning with the eighteenth century, man in western societies began to give death a new meaning. He exalted it, dramatized it, and thought of it as disquieting and greedy. But he already was less concerned with his own death than with *la mort de toi,* the death of the other person, whose loss and memory inspired in the nineteenth and twentieth centuries the new cult of tombs and cemeteries and the romantic, rhetorical treatment of death [Ariès, 1974, pp. 55–56].*

With *Tamed Death* the individual was usually forewarned. Abrupt deaths, such as might be caused by the plague, were treated as exceptions. And when forewarned, the individual did not seek to deny his or her impending death. Rather, preparations would be made, in ritual context. Sorrow was expressed that life must end, one's relations with others were made right, and then attention was turned to God. All this was organized *by* rather than *for* the individual, and it involved family, including children, friends, and neighbors.

*From *Western Attitudes toward Death: From the Middle Ages to the Present,* by P. Ariès. Copyright © 1974 by The Johns Hopkins University Press. This and all other quotations from this source are reprinted by permission.

Although ritualistic, the ceremony, according to Ariès, was simple and untheatrical. By calling it *Tamed Death,* Ariès calls attention to the fact that death was familiar and taken for granted. By contrast, he sees contemporary death as "wild" (Ariès, 1974, pp. 1–14; 1975).

Also, in this period the "city of the dead" was alongside the city of the living; the cemetery was an essential part of the church, the center of the community (Ariès, 1974, pp. 14–25). People were therefore as familiar with the dead as they were with the idea of their own death. This attitude, Ariès claims, was subtly modified, beginning around the 11th and 12th centuries. At this time a change occurred in Christian belief, which introduced a notion of individual judgment at the time of death. Up to then, the Last Judgment had implied the rising of God's people at the time of the Second Coming of Christ. Now judgment was *individualized* and linked to the individual biography. During the 13th century, the individual judgment at the moment of death supplanted the Last Judgment in importance: "Each man is to be judged according to the balance sheet of his life. Good and bad deeds are scrupulously separated and placed on the appropriate side of the scales" (Ariès, 1974, p. 32). Initially, this balance sheet was maintained after death, in the period between death and the Last Judgment. For this reason, indulgences—favors to speed entry into heaven granted at the intercession of the living—had a place in this system. By about the 15th and 16th centuries, the final judgment was moved forward to the time of death. And final judgment included an assessment of how the dying individual reacted to the balance sheet of his or her life:

> The dying man will see his entire life as it is contained in the book, and he will be tempted either by despair over his sins, by the "vainglory" of his good deeds, or by the passionate love for things and persons. His attitude during this fleeting moment will erase at once all the sins of his life if he wards off temptation or, on the contrary, will cancel out all his good deeds if he gives way [Ariès, 1974, pp. 36–37].

Ariès infers these changes from the art of the period, including the inscriptions that accompanied it, and from other writings. This was the period that saw the introduction of books on the art of dying, the *artes moriendi.* As Ariès points out, while dying is still a collective ritual, those surrounding the dying person—including God, demons, and mythological figures, as well as earthly religious and lay people—are spectators watching to see how an *individual* life is assessed and concluded: "The iconography of the *artes moriendi* joins in a single scene the security of a collective rite and the anxiety of a personal interrogation" (1974, p. 37). Ariès (p. 38) notes that, as this view of death and individual responsibility became widespread, the belief grew that at the time of death an individual's entire life flashed before his or her eyes. It is significant that this belief is still widely shared, as we shall see in Chapter Six.

During the period of *One's Own Death,* the deathbed scene was still under control of the individual, but it had taken on a much more dramatic character. At the same time, beginning in the 14th century, but especially in the 15th, the imagery of the horror of bodily decomposition following death reached a height. The interpretation of this phenomenon is contentious. Significantly, Ariès does not attribute the imagery to the horrors of death from plague but argues that it reflects a horror of death related to a love of life —individual life. Decomposition and decay were sometimes, in this period, also portrayed as features of old age and taken as signs of failure (1974, pp. 42–44). Also during this period, beginning around the 13th century, individually marked graves replaced anonymous sites, first in the case of important people, then also for commoners. The 14th century saw the introduction of the death mask—a realistic portrait of the deceased individual. The memory of the deceased, as an individual, was provided for through picture and inscription. Ariès sees these developments as tied to the growth of individualism (he is not alone in so interpreting them): "In the mirror of his own death each man would discover the secret of his individuality" (1974, pp. 51–52).

Beginning in the 18th century, the meaning of death changed once more. Between the 16th and 18th centuries, Ariès claims (1974, pp. 56–58), themes in art and literature concerning death assumed a more erotic tone. Thanatos became linked with Eros. There are scenes of death raping the living, and love becomes associated with death:

> Like the sexual act, death was henceforth increasingly thought of as a transgression which tears man from his daily life, from rational society, from his monotonous work, in order to make him undergo a paroxysm, plunging him into an irrational, violent, and beautiful world [Ariès, 1974, p. 57].

Death came to be thought of as a "break" (1974, p. 58). As the century wore on, eroticism became less flagrant and death became simply beautiful. The ugliness of the death's-head on tombstones was replaced by the beauty of angels or cherubs ascending to heaven (for England, see Morley, 1971; for the United States, see Coffin, 1976; Curl, 1972; Douglas, 1975; French, 1975; Stannard, 1977, pp. 167–187; Tashjian & Tashjian, 1974).

Wills lost their religious connotations and became wholly legal means for transmitting estates. While this might be interpreted simply as a decline in the importance of religion, as argued by the French historian Vovelle (1973, in Ariès, 1974, pp. 64–65), Ariès sees the change in wills as related to the changes in the family noted earlier in this chapter. As the family became more affectionate, feelings could be more readily transmitted orally than had formerly been the case. This change involved the family and spectators more than had been the case during the period of One's Own Death. In fact, so pronounced did this participation of others become that Ariès calls it "hysterical" mourning.

Funerals and cemeteries became more elaborate and ostentatious, reaching the point later satirized by Evelyn Waugh in his book *The Loved One* and symbolizing an increasing difficulty for people to accept death. But the death that is feared, Ariès argues, is no longer the death of the self; it is the death of the other, *Thy Death* (1974, p. 68). A new cult of the dead developed in which the survivors sought to maintain the presence of the dead:

> Now people wanted to go to the very spot where the body had been placed, and they wanted this place to belong totally to the deceased and to his family . . . the burial concession became a certain form of property, protected from commerce, but assured in perpetuity. . . . Memory conferred upon the dead a sort of immortality which was initially foreign to Christianity [Ariès, 1974, p. 72].

Ariès points out (1974, pp. 73–76) that this was a private cult, but also, from the beginning, a public one. Designers of the 18th century planned cemeteries as parks and museums as well as graveyards. Here famous people and national heroes were buried. Arlington Cemetery in Washington, and even Washington itself, epitomizes this development.

Finally, Ariès argues, in the United States a fourth kind of attitude toward death emerged—*Forbidden Death*. Originating in an attempt by the family to comfort the dying person and to assume part of the burden of dying, it led to lies and dissimulation and, ultimately, to a new attitude:

> One must avoid—no longer for the sake of the dying person, but for society's sake, for the sake of those close to the dying person—the disturbance and the overly strong and unbearable emotion caused by the ugliness of dying and by the very presence of death in the midst of a happy life, for it is henceforth given that life is always happy or should always seem to be so [Ariès, 1974, p. 87].

Death became hidden, the place of dying was changed from the home to the hospital, control over the dying passed from the dying person and his or her family to the doctor and health professionals, and the art of a good death became a matter of technology. Mourning became private and much less elaborate, while overall supervision of the funeral came increasingly under the control of a growing funeral industry. Embalming was now common, allowing display of a "lifelike" body. Graveside visits all but disappeared, and death became, in Geoffrey Gorer's (1965) phrase, a "taboo topic."

Ariès (1975) argues that, while commercial exploitation by the funeral industry has had some influence on the development of North American funeral customs, the real meaning of these customs "is the denial of the absolute finality of death and the repugnance of physical destruction without ritual and solemnity" (p. 154). Addressing the common practice of embalming and displaying the body, Ariès says:

> The idea of turning a deceased person into a living one in order to pay tribute to him one last time may seem to us to be childish and ridiculous. . . . It is, however, proof of a rapid and precise adjustment to complex and contradictory feelings. It is the first time that a society has in a general way honored its dead while refusing them the status of death [1975, p. 156].

Of necessity, Ariès' description of changing attitudes toward death overgeneralizes (see, for example, Garrity & Wyss, 1976). His writings in English translation are broad in sweep and miss the fine-grained detail of some of the studies that he cites (Vovelle, 1973) and of his untranslated monograph (1977). More important is Ariès' failure to tie changes in culture to changing social conditions and, specifically, to the changing character of death. As a general overview, however, Ariès' portrait has not been matched.

Against this background we can now consider the interplay between the changing character of death and the meaning of death in America. Marcuse (1959) views attitudes toward death as ideology: "The traditional notion of death is a sociopolitical concept which transforms nasty empirical facts into an ideology. . . . Both fear of death and its repression in the acceptance of death as sanctioned necessity enter as cohesive factors into the organization of society. The natural fact of death becomes a social institution" (p. 73). As the Catholic church cultivated fear of death in the times of the plagues in order to advance its own control over individual life and over the secular, political domain as well, the meaning of death has more generally—although perhaps sometimes less deliberately—served to accommodate the political realities of the era. As Marcuse puts the case:

> The cohesion of the social order depends to a considerable extent on the effectiveness with which individuals comply with death as more than a natural necessity . . . on their agreement to sacrifice themselves and not to fight death "too much." Life is not to be valued too highly, at least not as the supreme good. The social order demands compliance with toil and resignation, heroism, and punishment for sin. The established civilization does not function without a considerable degree of unfreedom; and death, the ultimate cause of all anxiety, sustains unfreedom [1959, p. 74].

The meaning of death can be such as to demand a subjugation of the significance of individual life, including its culmination in death (as in Ariès' One's Own Death) for the perpetuation of society and constituting, in a sense, a sacrifice to ensure the continuity of the society.

Davidson interprets the relationship between individual death and the character of a society in a similar fashion, especially with regard to Puritan New England and New France (French Canada). He first makes a distinction between *telos*, "the Greek word for end as purpose of destiny or fulfillment of design, and *finis*, the Latin word for end as termination or cessation" (1971, p. 417). Like many anthropologists, he sees mythology as a cultural resource on which individuals as individuals and as societal members can draw to reaffirm their identity. He argues that individuals are basically motivated to seek some sense of meaning through which to transcend their mortality and achieve *telos*, a sense of purpose that transcends individual death. Note that Davidson is not claiming a universal tendency to seek to transcend *finis*—to seek immortality. A common way in which *telos* can be sought is through the unity of individual and social purpose, which is reaffirmed through the mythological ordering of individual biography and societal survival over time.

Both New France and New England were conceived as attempts to maintain, or restore, a "people of God"—the one, an undiluted Catholicism; the other, a purified Anglicanism. The people of New France, as their European Catholic forebears, remembered the dead. The prayers of the living could, according to their beliefs, aid the dead, most of whom were waiting in that transitional postdeath state of limbo. By the second generation, however, a general orientation to the dead was intertwined with a conception of the birth of their new society: "The focus of mission shifted from establishing the paradigmatic settlement to remembering the fathers who had transplanted the paradigm; . . . the graves of the cemeteries became the symbols of a destiny of remembrance" (Davidson, 1971, p. 421).* From that time and to this day, the descendants of those habitants take as their motto *je me souviens,* which translates most accurately as "I do remember." This motto unites the memory of the "faithful departed" with the preservation of what is now a threatened culture and society in a larger sociocultural milieu (Davidson, 1971).

Warner's (1961, 1962) description of the treatment of death and the dead in Yankee City (a city founded by Puritans in 1635) shows a parallel theme. He describes Memorial Day celebrations as part of a "cult of the dead" (1962, Chap. 1), and he sees the cemetery as a "city of the dead" that reproduces and symbolically preserves the social structure of the living (see especially 1961, Chap. 5). For example, and in keeping with what we know about relatively nonmodernized societies, "Those unfortunates who die as children have secondary places within the family plot. Their stones are small, commensurate with the 'length' of their lives and the size of their small bodies" (1961, p. 179). Warner was even able to find traces of individual social mobility by studying transfers of bodies from one part of the cemetery to another of a higher social status (1961, p. 183).

The relationship between social structure and aspects of funeral ritual and burial continues to be one of the most firmly established findings of research in this area. Although the lower classes pay proportionately more of their earnings for funerals, the absolute amount spent increases with increasing socioeconomic status (see Bynum, 1973; Pine & Phillips, 1970; Kalish & Reynolds, 1976, pp. 46–49 for a discussion of American ethnic group differences). In summary, the treatment of the dead became a symbol of the hierarchical nature of the society, and the ritual surrounding death and the dead became a reaffirmation of the kind of society toward which the people were striving and a means of strengthening the historical ties of the people.

Like colonial New France, late-17th-century New England was a precarious frontier society, but even more precarious was the rigid belief system

*From "Histories and Rituals of Destiny: Implications for Thanatology," by G. W. Davidson, *Soundings,* 1971, *54*(4), 415–434. This and all other quotations from this source are reprinted by permission.

of the Puritans who dwelt there. It was a society that depended on a small number of the original settlers as moral or spiritual leaders. The Puritans felt themselves under siege in a society that was rapidly growing, urbanizing, and secularizing; in this context, "The Puritans intensely felt the death of a Saint to be a devastating blow to the dwindling circle of concerned survivors" (Stannard, 1977, p. 133).

As a people of God, the Puritans held a covenantal tie with God—a tie, Davidson (1971) argues, that, like the covenant of the ancient Israelites, was with a *capricious* God. This model was perhaps quite appropriate to account for their encounters with death. Davidson points out that for the Puritans, as for the French Canadians, the death of the individual was closely tied to reaffirmation of societal identity:

> For both peoples, despite their competing and radically different missions, the death of individuals was the occasion when the progress of the mission was assessed. Judgment of the individual was judgment on the whole people. In the rituals of an individual's dying and burial were means for the people to discover, remember, and repeat this mission. In the destiny of his people the individual found transcendence beyond his own mortality [1971, pp. 426–427].

That death came primarily to the young in Puritan New England was not ignored in the religious advice given to children. Stannard tells us: "From the moment they were old enough to pay attention children were repeatedly instructed regarding the precariousness of their existence. The sermons they listened to, the parents who corrected them, the teachers who instructed them, and eventually the books they read all focused with a particular intensity on the possibility and even the likelihood of their imminent death" (1977, p. 65). For example, the *New England Primer,* from which children learned the alphabet, instructed children that "T—*Time* cuts down all / Both great and small; X—*Xerxes* the great did die, / And so must you & I; Y—*Youth* forward slips / Death soonest nips" (cited in Stannard, 1977, p. 65).

This preaching also emphasized the possibility that the child was not of the elect and that death would produce a terrifying and horrible separation from parents and loved ones. A common image was indeed that the father would join God the Father in passing judgment on an errant child, thereby joining in condemning the child to hell (Stannard, 1977, pp. 61–71). None could be certain of salvation, according to Puritan beliefs (Stannard, 1977, pp. 73–75; Weber, 1958, Chap. 4), so the prospect of death brought both uncertainty and terror over possible damnation. The belief in the horrors of hell was not a mythology for children only. In this era, both common people and well-educated individuals on the whole believed in a hot and horrible hell peopled with devils and the damned.

In summary, as Stannard (1977, p. 76) argues so persuasively, the Puritans viewed death as both punishment and reward; and they thought of death much of the time. Death was, then, important, but the meaning of death was ambivalent (see also Tashjian & Tashjian, 1974, Chap. 1). In contrast to our own age, both the occurrence of death and the preoccupation with it assumed dramatic importance early in the life cycle. This ambivalence is perhaps responsible for the varying interpretations that scholars put on the meaning of death for the Puritans; some scholars argue that the blessings of death were uppermost in Puritan minds, and others stress the Puritans' fear of death. In any case, it was ambivalence, not ambiguity. As Stannard again so eloquently says, "Unlike Bacon, they did not fear death merely 'as children fear to go in the dark'; they feared it because they knew precisely what to expect from it" (1977, p. 89).

Drawing on dissonance theory and related cognitive approaches in social psychology, Stannard (1977, p. 93) argues that New England cultural beliefs could not forever contradict in this manner; one element of the belief system had to change to accommodate the other. By the late 18th century, attitudes had changed. For the later Puritans, under the influence of romanticism, thoughts of death were accompanied by a longing for it. The angel ascending to heaven replaced the death's-head. As infant mortality declined, Puritan children were told by their parents not to worry about and not to think about death, because death came to the old (Stannard, 1977, p. 189). We may well imagine that this admonition influenced attitudes toward both death and the old.

Stannard argues that "the twentieth-century American adult moves into a world of death avoidance and denial, a world in which social compartmentalization is so thorough that only the deaths of his very closest loved ones touch him at all" (1977, p. 189). This reflects the growth of Forbidden Death to replace the romantic Thy Death in Ariès' typology. Some support for Ariès' interpretation comes from examination of an unusual source of data.

Hendrix (1977) has made ingenious use of folk ballads to outline changing American attitudes toward death. The folk ballad is an important source of data on culture because, being by definition a narrative song transmitted mostly by word of mouth, it portrays the point of view of its carriers: peasants and rural and uneducated people. The imagery of death found in those ballads popular enough to survive and eventually be written down is more likely to indicate the feelings of the mass of common people than would the writings of the literate elite.

Hendrix points out that ballads deal with the unusual, stressful, and problematic rather than with the typical or common events in life. Ballads, like rumors, "play some part in the efforts of men to come to terms with their ever-changing world" (Shibutani, 1966, p. 183). The research that folklorists have done in collecting and dating ballads can be used to classify ballads chronologically into three major groups. These groups correspond to the classification scheme of the dominant conceptions of death outlined by Ariès (1974).

A sample of ballads from three periods was content-analyzed and coded according to major themes. Death themes occurred as a focus in these ballads with greatly varying frequency according to the historical period (see Table 3-2. There was a great increase in the proportion of ballads focusing on death in the group originating after about 1850. In no historical period did many of the ballads deal with natural or nonviolent death. As Hendrix puts it, "Ballad characters mostly get killed in battles and fights, cattle stampedes, log jams, train wrecks, ship wrecks and storms at sea, in snow storms, and in fires and floods. These deaths are not those of the aged, but mostly of younger adults and occasionally children" (1977, p. 9).

A detailed analysis, based on whether death was treated as a problem or as the outcome of the problem, shows that death was more likely to be defined as a problem, particularly in family relationships, in native American ballads dating from Ariès' Forbidden Death period than in the earlier periods. "Typically, in the recent ballads, death is sudden and unexpected. It is usually a problem for the survivors, rather than the character who dies" (Hendrix, 1977, p. 10). There is also an increase in the expression of emotion about death, which, significantly, occurs primarily between the first and the second ballad groups. Hendrix concludes that "death has become increasingly a problem for survivors, and . . . it has become a problem that has no culturally defined resolution. Hence, the survivors can do little more than express their shock and grief through emotional outburst" (1977, p. 10).

That the emotional response to death increased in the historical period preceding that in which the problematics of death increased gives some credence to Ariès' analysis. Death became a more emotional phenomenon in the period that Ariès called the period of Thy Death (1700s and early 1800s); it became more of a problem, although equally emotional, in the subsequent Forbidden Death period, which began in the late 1800s. The increasing concern with death in the Forbidden Death period, Hendrix plausibly argues, is consistent with Ariès' formulation, since "to forbid death does not resolve the problem. . . . An attempt to sweep death under the cultural rug may create more dilemmas and problems than it resolves" (1977, pp. 11–12).

Hendrix also points out that the emphasis on death as a problem coincides very closely with the increase in the longevity of the population. We are left, then, with the puzzling conjunction of a declining death rate (especially at younger ages), presumably fewer deaths of a violent nature, more people than ever before dying in later life and yet, paradoxically, a more problematic and emotional preoccupation with death expressed in ballads about the violent deaths of the young.

We should expect death to be problematic in the period of the later ballads, because the social character of death changed dramatically and became located, for the first time, primarily in later life. It is possible, although we are clearly lacking the evidence to know for sure, that Americans were using the only meanings available to them in their culture to deal with the

TABLE 3-2. *Death Themes in American Ballads in Different Historical Periods*

Conception of Death (Ariès)	Ballad Group	Sample Number of Ballads	Percentage of Ballads with Death as Major Theme		
			Nondeath	Murder/War	Accident/Neutral
1. Tamed Death (before 1100)	None				
2. One's Own Death (1100–1700)	Traditional British (origin 1300–1700)	106	81	16	3
3. Thy Death (1700–late 1800s)	British Broadsides (origin 1700–early 1800s)	114	87	5	8
4. Forbidden Death (late 1800s but especially 1900s)	Native American (origin late 1800s–early 1900s)	120	52	24	23

Note: Chi-square value is significant beyond the .05 level.

Adapted from "Death Themes in Anglo-American Folk Balladry," by L. Hendrix. Paper presented at the meeting of the American Sociological Association, Chicago, 1977. Used by permission.

problematics of death. Their meanings might have reflected the heritage of the earlier period of colonial history, when an unpredictable death visited primarily the young. This interpretation is consonant with one made by Parsons (1963; Parsons & Lidz, 1967) in one of the major, and controversial, sociological interpretations of the meaning of death in contemporary American society.

Parsons and Lidz have challenged the common assumption that ours is a death-denying society, arguing instead that the American orientation toward death reflects "a mode of acceptance appropriate to our primary cultural patterns of activism" (1967, p. 134). These writers view death as a "natural" phenomenon at the biological level and argue that people living in a scientifically oriented society, such as ours, could not reasonably deny this fact.

The demographic changes discussed in Chapter Two are seen by Parsons and Lidz as defusing the potential for fear of death, as death has become less capricious and most people can anticipate living a long life. Rather than the young, it is the aged who constitute a group "institutionally placed so that, in some sense, it must rather directly confront the problem of inevitable death" (Parsons & Lidz, 1967, p. 136). In vivid contrast to the situation in the past,

> The problem of the *meaning* of death is coming . . . to be concentrated about death occurring as the completion of a normal life cycle. . . . This central, irreducible problem is becoming disentangled from the problem of adjusting to deaths that occur earlier in the life cycle, particularly in infancy and early childhood, which was much more general in the premodern period [1967, p. 137].*

Not only death but also the pain and suffering that might have accompanied it in former periods have been largely controlled. The very notion of a "natural death," Parsons and Lidz stress, stands in contrast to the view in many primitive societies that all deaths are unnatural (see Chapter Two for the discussion of the "good death" among the Kaliai). In summary, they argue that "we should view the modern . . . orientation toward death as a component of a much broader orientation system which emphasizes dedication to activity that can be expected on rational grounds to maximize human control over the *conditional* elements of the life situation" (1967, p. 139; for a similar argument, see Howard & Scott, 1965–1966). This control, they note, cannot be extended to the inevitable fact that death occurs, but it does characterize our attitude toward the timing of death and the way in which it should occur (see also Parsons, 1963, and Parsons, Fox, & Lidz, 1973). As Cassell (1974) has more recently put it, in North America "death is a technical matter, a failure of technology in rescuing the body" (pp. 31–32).

Parsons and Lidz maintain that death has always been a matter affecting the immediate family. With the larger scale of society today, the indi-

*From "Death in American Society," by T. Parsons and V. M. Lidz. In E. S. Shneidman (Ed.), *Essays in Self-Destruction*. Copyright 1967 by Jason Aronson, Inc. This and all other quotations from this source are reprinted by permission.

vidual is a smaller unit in the society, and there is no reason for people beyond the relatively close family to be concerned with an individual's death. The death of the individual is therefore no longer a problem for the society, as it used to be when societies were smaller. There is therefore no highly elaborate ritual as in the past.

Do Americans deny death? Parsons and Lidz focus on the open-casket wake, which occurs in about nine out of ten funerals and which is seen by many as a sign that Americans do deny death. Briefly, the wake "centers about the presentation of the deceased to his former associates. Typically, the corpse is not only embalmed and placed in an expensive, often ornate, casket, but also 'restored,' decorously dressed-up, sorrounded by an elaborate floral display, and perhaps posed in a 'lifelike' manner" (1967, p. 155). Rather than interpreting the presentation of the body in a lifelike manner as a denial of death, Parsons and Lidz (1967) argue that "there seems to be a strong tendency in our individualistic, activistic society to want the deceased to appear in a manner that makes his former capacities recognizable" (p. 155). Second, they argue that this form of presentation involves "an important extension of the 'control' orientation toward the suffering component of the death complex. . . . An effort is made not to exacerbate the problem of mourning, perhaps particularly by not calling attention to the suffering, loss of capacity, or mutilation which the deceased underwent in dying" (p. 156). Parsons and Lidz see this form of presentation as an attempt to make grieving and mourning easier and to expedite the work of mourning, so that the bereaved can soon get back to the normal routines of life.

Vanderlyn Pine's interpretation of the practice of viewing the body is somewhat different (1975, pp. 135–137). For Pine, the value of viewing the dead body (and he does see this practice as valuable) lies precisely in its representation of the *end* of activity: "It is an important aspect of the funeral to present a dead person in a manner that will elicit a memory of that person as a dead body." To remember a person as dead is, Pine argues, more realistic, since the person is, after all, dead. In regard to Parsons and Lidz's second point, it is possible that presenting a body that has been restored so as to appear lifelike and normal can help the bereaved avoid thinking of mutilation (as in the case of accidental death) or bodily decay; but it is hard to see this approach as anything other than an attempt to avoid some of the aspects of death.

There is no convincing evidence that viewing the body, and the related practice of embalming, in any way assists the grieving process by decreasing its intensity or duration, despite unfounded claims by supporters of the funeral industry (see, for example, Jackson, 1957; Raether & Slater, 1977). What is clear, however, is that these practices enhance the financial status of the undertakers.

Pine (1969; Pine & Phillips, 1970) argues that some expenditure on the part of survivors is a universal feature of funeral practices in all cultures. He also believes that expenditure becomes particularly important as a kind of "secular and economic ritual of payment formerly performed by more religious customs and ceremonies" (Pine & Phillips, 1970, p. 416), which is helpful to the bereaved. Parsons and Lidz (1967), however, point out that, while the funeral has become more elaborate and costly during the past century, the ritual actions of participants have hardly changed at all. They therefore argue that changes in funeral style cannot be considered as reflecting any great changes in attitudes toward death. Instead, they probably reflect the fact that the funeral director is someone who, although striving to be a professional and be accepted as such, is nonetheless a businessperson (for an excellent and highly sympathetic treatment of these dilemmas, see Pine, 1975; for less sympathy, see Ariès, 1974, 1975).

Parsons sees our treatment of death and the dead as congruent with the more general sociocultural organizational features of North American society. Robert Blauner, in an analysis that has become a modern classic in the sociology of death, takes a similar view:

> Modern societies . . . have largely succeeded in containing mortality and its social disruptiveness. Yet the impact of mortality on a society is not a simple matter of such demographic considerations as death rates and the size of the group. Also central is the manner in which a society is organized, the way it manages the death crisis, and how its death practices and mortuary institutions are linked to the social structure [1966, p. 379].*

To describe the contemporary North American complex of beliefs and practices surrounding death and dying, Blauner employs the term *bureaucratization*. When he says that death is bureaucratized, Blauner means that the treatment of death has come to be removed from the family and placed in the hands of experts and specialized institutions. Thus we see the development of a massive funeral industry and an increased proportion of persons dying in hospital settings rather than at home. These bureaucratic means of dealing with the dying and the dead may, however, be efficient for some purposes:

> This separation of the handling of illness and death from the family minimizes the average person's exposure to death and its disruption of the social process. When the dying are segregated among specialists for whom contact with death has become routine and even somewhat impersonal, neither their presence while alive nor as corpses interferes greatly with the mainstream of life [Blauner, 1966, p. 384].

This treatment of death and the dying is not surprising, since virtually all aspects of our lives are bureaucratized. However, there are additional aspects to the bureaucratization of death and dying that are of central importance when we focus on the dying of the aged. Blauner repeats the argument, reviewed earlier in this chapter, that one way of minimizing the impact of

---

*From "Death and Social Structure," by R. Blauner, *Psychiatry,* 1966, *29*(4), 378–394. This and all other quotations from this source are reprinted by permission.

death in a society is to reduce the importance of those who are most likely to die. We saw that this was the case with children and infants, who, in many societies, were neither treated as fully human nor accorded elaborate funerary recognition at death. Blauner points out that a devaluing of the aged can have the same effect:

> The disengagement of the aged in modern societies enhances the continuous functioning of social institutions and is a corollary of social structure and mortality patterns. Disengagement, the transition period between the end of institutional functioning and death, permits the changeover of personnel in a planned and careful manner, without the inevitably disruptive crises of disorganization and succession that would occur if people worked to the end and died on the job [1966, p. 383].

Here then is where aging and dying come together in contemporary society. The institutionalization of retirement is a means of handling the problem of succession to office posed by death. The notion of compulsory retirement, because it fails to take into account the actual ability of an individual to maintain an active role in the society, represents a bureaucratic solution. Retirement in the occupational domain is only a case of the general phasing out of the individual from the society in anticipation of death. Let us be clear that such a phasing out of the individual appears to have been the idealized drawing to a close of the life cycle in most societies of the past—a prelude to the good death. The difference is that now bureaucratic means are used to decrease and ultimately sever the ties that link the individual to society. Our treatment of the dying and the dead and our treatment of the aging and the aged can be seen as one complex of social and cultural patterning. The institutions through which the aging are treated are linked to those through which the dying are treated, and the meanings we hold about the aged are related to the meanings we hold about the dead. Both Kalish (1976) and Streib (1976) argue, as only one example of this attitude, that the negative evaluation of the aged in our society stems from the fact that we associate them with death.

Neither Parsons nor Blauner can, however, fully account for the *meanings* that death and dying have in contemporary society. This is because culture, as something handed down from the past, continues to bear meanings from earlier eras. As Ariès emphasizes in his own work, the changing attitudes toward death are modifications on a theme rather than a series of unrelated attitudinal clusters. The key to understanding the meanings of death in contemporary North America is in understanding the historical development of these meanings. The character of death, as indicated by its location in the age structure and the changing causes of death (see Chapter Two), has changed most markedly in the last century. Only within the past century has death come to be located primarily in old age. Death in old age is something relatively new as a typical event, and so is death that does not greatly threaten the very survival of the society. Death that takes time, as in the case of death from chronic illness, stands in contrast to the typically quick deaths of earlier ages (Lofland, 1978).

If the contemporary meaning of death is to be understood, the religious legacy of the past must be added to the general bureaucratization of society emphasized by Blauner and to the general growth of activism and scientism as values in American society. This legacy can best be described as one of *ambivalence* (Dumont & Foss, 1972). At least from the time of the Black Death, one shade of death's meaning has continued to be its swiftness and capriciousness. The Four Horsemen of the Apocalypse (war, strife, famine, and pestilence) took on particularly vivid meaning in that era, and death as a sign of God's judgment became part of the meaning complex. That these meanings could find a place in the culture of early North America is probably attributable not only to a continuing preservation of religious belief but also to their appropriateness in accounting for the death of infants, children, and persons still active in the prime of life. There were other meanings: death as a blessed release from a life of toil and suffering, death as reunification with the departed already in heaven, and death as erotic ecstasy. Although some of these meanings could easily be utilized to construct a meaningful death in old age, in general it may be said that the meanings of death that persist to this day are meanings constructed and used to account for the death of the young.

The good death in old age has been the rarity, and one that we have, in a sense, been ill equipped to make sense of. As Gorer (1965b) and others (Michalowski, Jr., 1976) have pointed out, much of the imagery of death relates to violent death: "live" death in war, brought to us on television news, death by gunshot on crime shows and in movies, and fantastic death and re-birth on cartoon shows. What Gorer has called a "pornography of death" can be interpreted within the "forbidden death" theme of Ariès.

Furthermore, the secularization of society has greatly weakened death's religious meaning, creating something of a vacuum. This seculariza-tion is apparent for the deaths of both the old and the young and may well be a major reason for the growth, within the past 20 years, of the "death and dying" field of scholarship (Kalish, 1976). Resort to religion and religious functionar-ies is still the common way to deal with death in our society, even by unbe-lievers, for few alternatives for dealing with death exist. Religious phraseolo-gy provides words to speak when we do not know what to say. At the same time, the new location of death and the rise of secularization create new demands on individuals to render death meaningful, particularly death as the completion of the life cycle. That these attempts vacillate between efforts to render death and dying more "natural"—as in the "death with dignity" move-ment—and efforts to hide or deny death—as in contemporary hospital and funerary practice—is evidence that a new set of meanings appropriate to a new social character of death has not yet emerged. Parsons' characteriza-tion, although by no means recent, still holds for today:

Until a new symbolic structure which gives more meaning to the ultimate outcome for the individual of the positive moral responsibilities of an achievement-oriented ethic has become formulated and institutionalized, continued oscillations between "hell-fire and damnation" fundamentalism—and perhaps its intellectual equivalent, existentialist "despair"—and the sugary sentimentality of "positive thinking" are to be expected [1963, p. 65].

Finally, the difficulties in constructing meanings that will render death "sensible" and legitimate have been exacerbated by one technological development—the bomb. I have suggested that many societies provide a symbolic mechanism for uniting the destinies of the individual and society, and I have shown briefly (following the work of Davidson, 1971) how this has been the case in French Catholic Canada and English Puritan New England. This mechanism facilitates a kind of "symbolic immortality" through which the individual is able to anticipate some continuance after biological death.

Robert Lifton has attempted to construct a general theory of death and immortality in relation to the possibilities of total extinction from nuclear holocaust (Lifton, 1967, 1969, 1971). Rejecting Freud's (1957) oft-quoted conviction that it is not possible for us to imagine our own death, Lifton (1971) argues:

I believe it is more correct to say that our own death—or at least our own dying—is not entirely unimaginable but can be imagined only with a considerable degree of distance, blurring, and denial; that we are not absolutely convinced of our own immortality, but rather have a need to maintain a *sense of immortality* in the face of inevitable biological death; and that this need represents . . . a compelling urge to maintain an inner sense of continuous symbolic relationship, over time and space, to the various elements of life. Nor is this need to transcend individual biological life *mere* denial [p. 173].

Lifton points out that a sense of immortality may be gained *biologically* through establishing family continuity; *theologically,* through belief in afterlife; through one's creative *works or human influences;* or through being *survived by nature* itself. These dimensions become criteria through which life is evaluated and which are in a sense tested by death.

The possibility of total annihilation by nuclear war destroys or seriously weakens the possibility of gaining a sense of immortality by any of these modalities. Total nuclear war will leave no descendants, no works, and only a greatly changed nature; it will be so horrific as to strain the credibility of a belief system based on a benign or heavenly afterlife. This is not mere speculation, for Lifton bases his reasoning on research with survivors of the Hiroshima disaster (1967; 1971, p. 183). In a similar manner, Morgenthau (1967) argues: "The significance of the possibility of nuclear death is that it radically affects the meaning of death, of immortality, of life itself. It affects that meaning by destroying most of it, . . . by depriving it of its individuality . . . [and] by making both society and history impossible" (p. 74).

Here again is the possibility of death "out of control," more capricious and infinitely more terrifying than even the plagues. As Morgenthau argues, we are only dimly conscious of the threat of nuclear annihilation—although those old enough to remember the era of nuclear bomb shelters or the tension surrounding the Cuban missile crisis may feel differently—and so this theme has not had a dramatic impact on our daily lives. As an additional threat to the meaning of life and death, however, nuclear annihilation only compounds the problem already discussed of how to construct a new system of meanings to deal with "normal" death—that is, with the process of aging and dying.

Implications

I have argued that death poses "problems" for the social organization of any society and that individuals band together to create patterned interaction (institutions) and to construct meanings (culture or belief systems) to deal with these problems. A major organizing principle for this chapter has been the concept of the social character of death. In societies in which death visits mainly the young and those active in the adult years, the impact of death is likely to be very high and mechanisms for maintaining the integration of the society will develop. The impact of death will in fact be felt through all the institutions of the society. Conceptions of death and of the ideal death will also be influenced by the age at which most people in a society die and by the way in which death comes. Thus, some facets of the meaning of death even in today's society may be traced to the imagery of death that developed during the era of the great plagues.

I have stressed that the major features of the social character of death were relatively constant until the very recent past. In all societies, until about 100 years ago, death came much more frequently to the young than to the old, and death was much less "under control" than it is now (although the possibility of uncontrolled nuclear death is also with us). In our own society many aspects of death and dying are predictable and under technical guidance, although the ultimate fact that everyone shall die still demands that individuals find some set of meanings to understand their own mortality. The cultural legacy from the past provides some meanings, but in general the meaning of death has overtones of an earlier era.

Death and dying have become both private and bureaucratic. Death and dying are affairs of the family and of bureaucratic practitioners, such as funeral directors and hospital and nursing-home staff, in contrast to being affairs involving the entire community. Perhaps it could not have been any other way in a massive, urbanized, and bureaucratic society such as ours. As a general theme, linking social interaction and culture, it may be said that the individual has, in many respects, lost control of his or her own dying, which is instead a managed process. The ways in which the dying and the dead are treated and the meanings given to dying and death are human and social creations. However, they gain a life of their own and can be viewed as a *context* in which the individual must fashion his or her own dying. In this chapter that context has been described as one heavily influenced by the past and ill adapted to the radically new association of death with the aged, who live in a more secular and scientific era than was formerly the case. Our institutions and beliefs have yet to be adapted to the current—and dramatically new—situation. In Chapter Four the aging and dying individual is placed in this context.

Review Questions for Chapter 3

1. *What is the North American conception of "the good death"? Is there more than one conception of the good death? Examine conceptions of the good death that appear in movies, drama, and fiction. Look for variations by setting and social era.*

2. *Select a contemporary North American religion and examine the meanings it provides for death and the ritual it provides to accompany death. Is there a parallel to the "double funeral" described by Hertz?*

3. *Can you detect concerns about death and dying in nursery rhymes, fables, classical children's stories, and so forth? How might these concerns relate to the character of death in the historical period in which such cultural manifestations arose?*

4. *We have observed that death causes vacancies and that filling these vacancies represents a problem for society. One way of finding out more about the "vacancy theme" is by attending to historical accounts as well as to fiction or drama. The theme is prominent, for example, in discussions of the relationship between the long-lived Queen Victoria and the Prince of Wales, in analyses of power in the U. S. Senate, in analyses of the succession problem in the Soviet Union and China, and in all the many classical murder mysteries that involve inheritance, such as* Kind Hearts and Coronets.

5. *If you have never done so, attend a funeral in a religious tradition that is familiar to you and one in a tradition that is unfamiliar to you (if you can do so gracefully and unobtrusively). Also, visit a funeral home and inquire about funeral arrangements. Then consult your local Memorial Society or other consumer group in the funeral area. Examine costs of funerals and legislation governing funerals and disposition of bodies in your jurisdiction, and compare the perspectives of funeral-industry representatives with those of consumer and religious groups.*

4

The Aging and Dying Individual

In all societies, death poses problems both for individuals and for the society. The demographic "shape" of the population structure and of death, along with other sociocultural phenomena, contributes to the development of sociocultural responses to death. The response to death is never individual, for the individual is never completely divorced from society: "Death gives rise to personal emotional responses, which initiate culturally oriented responses and reactions" (Pine, 1972, p. 150). These responses in turn provide the framework within which individuals must do their own dying.

It is important to emphasize that the cultural and societal responses are organized by humans for both personal and social reasons. In this chapter the focus is on the individual living and dying within the social and cultural setting whose origins and character were described in Chapter Three.

The others who impinge on the career of the dying individual enact roles that are in some sense "scripted" by the patterned ways of dealing with death and dying that characterize a society. This statement does not, however, imply a deterministic view of the processes of aging and dying. It would greatly distort what actually occurs if we were to assume that there is one aging and dying role, or even a set of roles, that shapes the course of aging and dying. There are shared meanings and expectations about aging and dying, but these should be viewed as part of the setting in which individuals fashion their own life course. The issue of "determinism" will be with us through much of the remainder of this book. My own position is that individuals are partly free and partly constrained in their actions but that, ultimately, individuals are free. An individual can always exercise an option if an option is available (Berger, 1963, pp. 122–150). In this chapter we will be searching through some of the theoretical approaches to the social psychology of aging and dying to gain an understanding of the perspective of the individual. Many of the positions reviewed assume the highly deterministic view that all behavior is caused by external factors. My own view is that people not only *react;* they *act.*

Facts do not speak for themselves; when we speak of facts we, of necessity, rely on processes of interpretation. Something is considered to be an "event" when we focus on it and manage to persuade other people that it is an event. In the social sciences, interpretation is strongly influenced by the theoretical framework. Theoretical approaches to understanding death and aging and dying must be examined in the light of their premises or interpretive systems, explicit or implicit.

The first part of this chapter considers clinical research on dying patients. Then the chapter examines attitudes toward death and dying as measured in survey research. Against this background, three related approaches to understanding aging are considered, all of which focus on the concept of aging as role behavior or enactment and none of which gives a significant amount of attention to the dying of the aged. Next, the chapter reviews developmental approaches to understanding aging, because these approaches, more than any others, have taken the dying of the aging into account. Finally, having critically reviewed these approaches, I draw from them what appears useful for a nondeterministic, interpretive understanding of aging and dying.

The Fear/Denial Assumption in Clinical Thanatology

It is not productive to assume, before considering the evidence, that death is inherently fearful. Most research on attitudes toward death and dying makes precisely that assumption and thereby oversimplifies a complex set of phenomena. A more reasonable starting point is to assume that death is a matter of concern for most people, and more so as people come to anticipate that they will themselves die soon.

We may well imagine a fundamental difference between the young and the aged in their concern about death. As Munnichs has noted:

> We can as little imagine youth without a future as old age with one. Now this feature of old age ought to be most prominent when an old person is confronted or confronts himself with the last phase of old age, i.e. death. The experience of death, that is to say, to realize and to know that life comes to an end and adjustment to this fact, might possibly be considered the *focal point of the mentality of the aged* [1966, p. 4].

Awareness that time is running out becomes more salient with increasing age. As the social psychologist Vischer (1967) wrote in his own old age, "Slowly or suddenly we realize under the pressure of the circumstances to which we, as aging people, are exposed, that we can no longer plan in terms of unlimited time, because we have now drawn near to the end" (p. 64).

Do people fear death? As people age and come closer to their own death, do they fear it more or less? When gerontologists and clinicians who work with the sick turn to thanatological concerns, these questions are often asked. A review of attitudinal and clinical studies of death and dying demonstrates that investigators have been hindered by sampling problems, by a lack of conceptual clarity about the particular measurement task, and by assumptions derived from the theoretical perspective in which many of them work. Although extended discussion of these problems may be found in several sources (Donaldson, 1972; Dumont & Foss, 1972; Lester, 1967a; Marshall, in press; Munnichs, 1966; Vernon, 1970; Williams, 1966), we can briefly summarize the problems here. Since some of the early and very unsophisticated studies continue to be cited or reprinted (see, for example, Fulton, 1976), it is necessary to refer to them as well as to some more recent work.

Attitudes toward death and dying have been measured in many ways. Many clinicians use projective tests such as the Thematic Apperception Test (TAT) or sentence-completion measures. Subjects may be asked to tell stories about a picture that deals with a death theme or that is ambiguous in its visual stimuli, or they may be given sentence fragments that have vague death-related connotations and asked to complete the sentences. The stories or sentences will then be thematically coded within a set of categories.

The influence of the researcher's conceptions on this process is most evident when data are coded after they have been collected, as is often the case in clinical research. It is important to recognize, however, that an investigator also relies on commonsensical or theoretically grounded categories when constructing responses to fixed-choice questionnaires. The problem of fit between scientific categories and the categories used by people from whom the data are gathered is the same in either case. An investigator may well end up forcing the respondents' projective data into categories that are inappropriate; and respondents who are asked to complete multiple-choice questionnaires may well have to distort their attitudes in order to answer the questions.

Research on attitudes toward death and dying suffers from this problem, and so does attitudinal research in general (see Cicourel, 1964, pp. 7–38; Denzin, 1970, pp. 98–106). Thus it may be said that the clinician is part of the measuring device; but it is also important to remember that there is a human element in the classification process and in measurement itself (Hays, 1967, pp. 5–6).

The influence of theoretical preconceptions on coding schemes is apparent in an interview study of geriatric patients that used both direct and indirect questions and a word association test in assessing attitudes toward death (Christ, 1961). A "fear of death" scale was constructed, employing judgments of clinicians. Failure to make a will and not having previously talked about death or dying were both interpreted as indicative of fear of death. It is possible, of course, that this inactivity might instead be taken as indicative of lack of concern with impending death, absence of possessions or descendants, or a predisposition to keep one's thoughts to oneself.

Becker and Bruner (1931), in an early paper, had suggested that, in considering the individual's attitude toward death, "there are three possible emotional tendencies that are important: joy or gladness, indifference, and horror or fear" (pp. 828–829). Like many investigators since, Christ ignored this suggestion in classifying responses to impending death as either fear or denial. He assumed death to be both a salient and a highly threatening concern for old persons.

Jeffers, Nichols, and Eisdorfer (1961) coded responses to the question "Are you afraid to die?" asked of volunteers aged 60 and over. According to these researchers' classification scheme, an individual could admit fear, be ambivalent, or not admit fear; in the latter case denial was considered to be an important attitude (for a similar coding scheme, see Kalish, 1963). Since only 10% of their subjects admitted being afraid to die, Jeffers and his associates had to interpret the negative responses to their single indicator. They found certain factors associated with a declaration of no fear of death: a tendency to read the Bible more often, greater belief in a future life, reference to death with more religious connotations, fewer feelings of rejection and depression, higher scores on full scale and performance IQ, and more responses on the Rorschach (a projective test). To treat these factors as consonant with an interpretation of denial is surely a "leap of faith" based on a view of death as traumatic. This leap is grounded in the "clinical impressions and experience of the present investigators, who have had extensive study and contact with not only the . . . subjects . . . but also with other groups of older persons" (Jeffers et al., 1961, p. 55). What the investigators are saying is that they know the minds of their subjects better than the subjects themselves.

Cappon (1962) also valued his own position over that of the people whom he interviewed. He constructed a questionnaire to compare attitudes toward death among normal, physically ill, and psychiatric patients. As an example, he then took an affirmative reply to the statement "I avoid consulting doctors at all costs" as indicative of a *latent* fear of death. It is obvious that such a response might just reflect attitudes toward doctors. On the other hand, "I am easily driven to consulting doctors on the average of more than three times a year" reflects, Cappon says, *overt* fear of death; we can see that agreement with that statement might reflect hypochondria. "I am very concerned with my aging" is held to indicate overt fear of death, while "I am glad to be growing older" supposedly indicates latent fear of death. Cappon is willing to take the respondent's word in some instances. He takes the affirmation "I am very worried about dying" as indicating overt fear; but then he scores "I am quite concerned about dying" as indicating no fear and "I rarely think about dying" as indicating latent fear.

Cappon's coding scheme makes absolutely no sense unless the questions are placed within a psychoanalytic framework of assumptions—that expressed mild fear of death is "normal" and that expressions indicating low awareness of finitude, or low concern about it, are determined by mechanisms of denial or reaction formation. For Cappon there *has to be* fear of death, by virtue of psychoanalytic theory. Where he does not find it, he invents it by fiat of his coding categories.

These rather dated examples admirably exemplify the problems that remain in current clinical approaches. Levin and Kahana (1967), in introducing a collection of readings on aging that represents the psychoanalytic tradition, state "Regardless of one's theoretical orientation, one cannot but conclude that there is something instinctive in man which is directed toward self-preservation and which gives rise to fear in the face of death" (p. 17). Similarly, Payne (1967) sees the child as inevitably coming to fear death and to bear this fear, at least at the unconscious level, throughout life. He says "The infantile contributions to the fear of dying are reawakened by the regression induced by illness and by the threat of danger" (p. 122).

Most contemporary psychoanalysts and social scientists have rejected Freud's (1948) theory of a "death instinct"—a universal tendency of all living matter to "return to the peace of the inorganic world." However, they have often kept the related notion that the human cannot conceive of his or her own death (see Dumont & Foss, 1972, p. 25; Eissler, 1955, p. 34). This notion is related in psychoanalytic thought to the mechanism of denial, a mechanism that is particularly important in the work of Kübler-Ross (1969). It is critical to understand the denial mechanism and its theoretical framework in order to address the question of whether impending death is important for older people. This is because, if a notion of denial is invoked, a statement that death is of little or no concern can be and has been interpreted as an expression of fear—but fear denied. We will focus on the work of Kübler-Ross because it is, without question, the formulation that has had the greatest impact not only in clinical settings but also in popular culture.

As early as 1966, Elisabeth Kübler-Ross used the phrase "denial, repression, and reaction formation" to characterize dying in contemporary bureaucratized settings (Kübler-Ross, 1966). In a book that continues to be a best-seller (1969), she developed a view of the dying process as involving five stages, the first of which is *denial*. Her belief is that "the fear of death is the most inescapable fear of human beings and the most unavoidable one" (1966, p. 1), and the answer to that fear seems always to begin with denial. She refers to a "basic knowledge that, in our unconscious, death is never possible in regard to ourselves. It is inconceivable for our unconscious to imagine an actual ending of our own life here on earth" (1969, p. 2).* In addition, still roughly following the lead of Freud, she says that "in our unconscious mind we can only be killed; it is inconceivable to die of a natural cause or of old age. Therefore, death in itself is associated with a bad act, a frightening happening" (Kübler-Ross, 1969, p. 2).

From the psychoanalytic perspective, the subconscious is given primacy over phenomenological experience and consciousness. As with the clinical formulations already discussed, there is no *empirical* resolution to this problem. (Dumont & Foss, 1972, pp. 78–79, illustrate such difficulties.) Whether one is labeled *unconcerned* or *fearing-but-denying* with respect to impending death is a matter of interpretation. The warrant for the psychoanalytic view is a *theoretical* warrant that relies on the acceptance of a particular paradigm (Kuhn, 1970).

Kübler-Ross (1969, p. 34) claims:

> Among the over two hundred dying patients we have interviewed most reacted to the awareness of a terminal illness at first with the statement, "No, not me, it cannot be true." This initial denial was as true for those patients who were told outright at the beginning of their illness as it was true for those who were not told explicitly and who came to this conclusion on their own a bit later on.

Denial is thought of as a defense mechanism that "functions as a buffer after unexpected shocking news, allows the patient to collect himself and, with time, mobilize other, less radical defenses" (1969, p. 35).

Kübler-Ross postulates that dying occurs in a series of stages. The second stage, after denial, is *anger,* at which point the patient says, in effect, "Why me?" Following anger is a relatively brief stage in which the patient attempts to secure a bit more time by *bargaining,* for example, by offering prayers. The fourth stage is *depression:* "When the terminally ill patient can no longer deny his illness, he cannot smile it off anymore. His numbness or stoicism, his anger and rage will soon be replaced with a sense of great loss" (1969, p. 75). This is a kind of "preparatory grief" in anticipation of final separation from the world. At this stage, death should be contemplated and the depression and grief "worked through." When this has occurred—and it almost always does—the individual enters the fifth and final stage, *accept-*

---

* From *On Death and Dying,* by E. Kübler-Ross. Copyright © by Elisabeth Kübler-Ross. (New York: Macmillan Publishing Co., Inc., 1969.) Published in the British Commonwealth by Tavistock Publications, Ltd. This and all other quotations from this source are reprinted by permission.

ance. Kalish (1976) describes this stage: "The dying individual's sense of loss diminishes as his attachments diminish in importance. That this stage closely resembles the concept of disengagement is not generally recognized" (p. 486; see also Kalish, 1972).

In Kübler-Ross' formulation, death is *never* a matter of indifference. One cannot be unconcerned about impending death. Moreover, one cannot be positively disposed toward it without something of a struggle, a "working through." Thus, when Kübler-Ross does not find fear, she finds denial. Her theoretical framework does not allow her to find unconcern. Methodologically, however, we may question this classification.

Let us first note that the entire stage formulation describes events following the announcement of "bad news." An alternative interpretation to Kübler-Ross' view is that the "unexpected shocking news" might be difficult to assimilate and that what she calls *denial* might in fact be a description of the cognitive problem of assimilating novel cognitions into a long-held cognitive set (see Weisman, 1972, p. 61; see also Chapter Five of this book). This possibility bears close scrutiny particularly in the light of the young age of many of Kübler-Ross' subjects. Many, if not most, of the patients interviewed by Kübler-Ross, being young, could not reasonably be expected to think of death as an imminent personal possibility. Among the over 200 terminally ill patients who provided the material for the book *On Death and Dying,* Kübler-Ross found only three who attempted to deny death until the last. All three were middle-aged (1969, p. 36). The fourth and last patient described explicitly in the chapter on denial was only 28 years old (1969, p. 38). Any actual assimilation of knowledge that their cases were terminal must have been difficult, given the massive weight of the reasonable expectation that people typically live longer than that. Young age can also provide a reasonable explanation for the anger and bargaining that Kübler-Ross describes. What young person would not be angry—or seek to bargain for more time to fulfill commitments (Weisman, 1972, pp. 110–111)?

Nor is it clear that the patients had objective knowledge of their terminal status, for indeed "we are talking about dying with patients who are not actually dying in the classical sense of the word" (Kübler-Ross, 1969, p. 23); some of the patients "were not told explicitly" (p. 34), nor "do [we] always state explicitly that the patient is actually terminally ill" (p. 41).

One must wonder how much Kübler-Ross and her colleagues participate in the creation of what she would call *denial* and might instead be called *uncertainty.* Weisman, whose own patients seem to have an average age of about 60, points to the pervasiveness of this very practice in the clinical care of the dying:

> The most tenacious, invidious misconception is that death and fear are inseparable. Some clinicians go so far as to assert that anyone who fails to show marked anxiety is denying fear of death. . . . This is a tendentious fallacy. The doctor finds a patient who seems relatively calm, even though he is facing

death. He then concludes that "denial" is the reason for the equanimity! Without conceding that harmonious acceptance of death without denial is possible, the doctor then goes on to foster even more denial [1972, pp. 32–33].

We are all, of course, dying all the time, but that fact is not highly relevant to most of us most of our lives. At least at one stage of a patient's illness or an individual's aging, what an observer may call *denial* may be thought of as a construction of reality by the observer using the term. "From the inside, people do not recognize that they have denied a reality, whether it is a perception or a meaning" (Weisman, 1972, p. 62). The signs of impending death might simply be unclear, and the individual might be in ignorance or confusion. The first stage in coming to terms with death, then, is the recognition of personal impending death and the acceptance of its relevance. This important prerequisite to our understanding of the meaning of dying to the dying themselves is clouded by the denial concept.

Survey Research on Attitudes toward Death and Dying

Although the denial concept is given much attention in clinical research and care, the emphasis of those employing questionnaires or structured interview methodologies has been on the measurement of fear. Several attempts have been made to move beyond single-indicator measures (for example, the simple question "Are you afraid to die?") to the construction of indices or scales that measure death fear through several questions. These types of measures yield data more reliable, on the whole, than the clinical data previously discussed. Unfortunately, few of the highly developed measures have been used with older populations or over a wide age range, and therefore this research effort is of little use for our purposes. Research using single indicators is, by contrast, much more useful, as should become apparent shortly. The major problem with most scales and indices, however, is their single-minded attention to the fear of death. Almost all such measures focus on either death fear or death anxiety; very few treat this fear as multidimensional.

Two early exceptions to this unidimensional approach, which also pay some attention to age differences, are the research of Swenson (1961) and that of Diggory and Rothman (1961). Swenson (1961), studying various groups over the age of 60, presented them with a checklist of death attitudes, asking for agreement or disagreement, and a forced-choice rating scale. Item-cluster analysis of the checklist yielded two clusters, which resulted in a four-fold typology of death attitudes:

1. negative
2. actively evasive
3. passively evasive
4. positive or forward looking

Swenson's research represents a significant advance in coding procedures. He was not committed by his theoretical approach to finding pervasive fear of death among his aging subjects. He, in fact, found no clustering of attitudes that could be called *fear of death*. Swenson concludes:

> It is apparent that the aged person does not often admit to a fear of death. In fact, either he looks forward to death or tends to be evasive in his contemplation of the experience of death. Investigators postulating a relatively common "fear of death" in the persons they study probably have resorted to subjective or indirect inferences [1961, p. 52].

Diggory and Rothman (1961; see also Diggory, 1966, pp. 381–415) made explicit their assumption that death is feared; they, therefore, investigated the different ways in which it is feared. They gathered questionnaires from an opportunistic sample, of which less than 20% were over the age of 55, and asked them to rate a number of statements about various fears of death. Thus, restricting the respondents by excluding the possibility of *no fear*, they arrived at the following typology:

1. fear of dissolution of the body
2. fear that all experiences will end
3. fear of the pain of dying
4. fear of an unknown future
5. fear of affective consequences for survivors

Diggory and Rothman recognize that other fears may be more salient than the fear of death. They do not, however, concede that death might not be feared by some respondents. Despite this limitation, and the limitations of relying on precoded responses, their study is valuable in demonstrating that investigators who have discussed a "fear of death" have not been treating a unidimensional variable.

Only very recently has this multidimensionality been recognized; therefore, we have no firm knowledge based on multidimensional measures of death fear applied to age-diverse samples. For example, Nelson and Nelson (1975; also Nelson, 1977) use a sophisticated factor-analytic technique to isolate four dimensions of death anxiety: death avoidance—an unwillingness to be near the dead or to touch them and a reluctance to experience situations reminiscent of death—death fear, death denial, and reluctance to interact with the dying. However, although Nelson and Nelson have an age-diverse sample (of males only) from a general population, they have yet to describe age differences.

One of the most widely used, and better validated, indices to measure death anxiety is the Death Anxiety Scale (DAS), constructed by Templer (1970, 1971a, 1971b, 1972; Templer & Dotson, 1970; Templer & Ruff, 1971; Templer, Ruff, & Franks, 1971). This index measures verbalized death anxiety, sometimes referred to as *fear of death* by the author. There are 15 items in the index, such as:

> I am very much afraid to die.
> I fear dying a painful death.
> I feel the future holds nothing for me to fear.

Agreement or disagreement with items like these yields a score for each individual, and average scores have been calculated for several groups of subjects. There are sound reasons to believe that the measure provides a good index of nonverbalized, as well as verbalized, death anxiety (Templer, 1971a).

In one of the studies employing the measure, questionnaires were sent by mail to 250 retired persons. Despite a very low response rate of only 30%, it is worth noting the findings, since this is one of the few instances in which a well-validated measure of death anxiety has been applied to older subjects. In this case the average age of the 75 respondents was 69.7 years, with a range of 51 to 92 years. Mean score on the DAS for this sample was 4.25, which is considerably lower than the mean score for any other group to which the measure has been applied. Psychiatric patients, preselected because they were clinically judged to have high death anxiety, had a mean score, by contrast, of 11.62; and several samples of adolescents and college undergraduates scored in the 5 to 6 range (Templer & Ruff, 1971). In a more recent study (Nehrke, Bellucci, & Gabriel, 1977–1978), one nursing-home sample had a mean score of 4.08. Swenson (1961) had also found the institutionalized elderly to be less fearful of death than those in the community. This is a finding that we will consider in greater detail in Chapter Six.

We have considered only a small number of studies, but there are not many more of use. In general, we could hope for larger samples, greater use of multidimensional measures that include not only several dimensions of death anxiety or fear but also several dimensions of indifference, acceptance, and positive attitudes toward death. It is regrettable that so many measures, not considered here, have been developed and used only with college student populations. This is a frequent criticism in the area of psychometrics, but it is especially valid when we consider that death is so directly related to age.

As our interest is precisely in the age relatedness of attitudes toward death, we will now focus on two studies, based on large and carefully drawn samples, which allow for age comparisons. One is a national study conducted by John W. Riley, Jr. (1970; Riley & Foner, 1968), and the other is a Los Angeles study conducted by Kalish and Reynolds (1976), which focuses on ethnic as well as age variability in attitudes toward death. Although both studies employ single indicators instead of more complex scales or indices, they do capture several different dimensions of attitudes toward death and dying and thereby provide a good context for our subsequent discussion, much of which will be based on the cumulative results of numerous less ambitious research endeavors.

As we turn to these data, we should bear in mind that they have a dual reality. Let us consider Riley's finding (1970) that 53% of adult Americans agree with the statement "Death always comes too soon." At one level, this finding gives us information about individuals. We can infer that 53 of 100 individuals believe—or at least claim to believe—that death *always* comes too soon. This is a statement *about individuals.* The finding also represents *sociocultural reality,* in that any given individual lives in a social context in which better than half of his or her associates share the belief that death always comes too soon. This social fact may validate the individual's belief about death, or, if the individual is one of the 47% of adult Americans who do not agree with the statement, it may eventually lead the individual to change his or her belief. Since our focus in this chapter is on the individual, the important point is that the individual will grow older and die in the context of this shared belief.

A large study that directly asked respondents whether they were afraid to die is that of Kalish and Reynolds (1976). Their question, put to 434 respondents from four ethno-racial groups (Black Americans, Japanese Americans, Mexican Americans, and Anglo-Americans) living in Los Angeles County, was worded as follows: "Some people say they are afraid to die, and others say they are not. How do you feel?" Striking age differences emerged. The data, broken down by ethnicity, sex, and age appear in Table 4-1. The most important finding is that few people of any age say that they are afraid or terrified of death. Those in the youngest age category (20–39) are most likely to say that they are afraid and least likely to say that they are unafraid or eager to die. It is important to recognize the location of most death fear in younger-age groups in light of the overresearching of this age group in the many studies of attitudes toward death and dying. We have little research to go on to discover what death means to older people, but, if the Kalish and Reynolds sample is typical, there is much less fear of death among the old than among the young. There are no sex differences in response to this question, although other investigators, working with young samples, generally find females more fearful of death than males (Feldman & Hersen, 1967; Templer, Ruff, & Franks, 1971; Thorson, 1977).

In a larger and controlled study of another Los Angeles multi-ethnic sample, Bengtson, Cuellar, and Ragan (1977) asked more than 1200 respondents "How afraid are you of death: Not at all? Somewhat? Very much?" As in the Kalish and Reynolds study, sex, race, and social class were not significantly associated with responses to this indicator of death fear. Only age (the respondents were all over age 45) was significantly associated with fear of

TABLE 4-1.   *Fear of Death, By Ethnicity, Age, and Sex*

Item No.	Question/Response	Ethnicity				Age			Sex	
		B.A.[a]	J.A.[a]	M.A.[a]	A.A.[a]	20–39	40–59	60+	M	F
088	Some people say they are afraid to die and others say they are not. How do you feel?									
	Afraid/terrified	19	31	33	22	40	26	10	27	26
	Neither afraid nor unafraid	28	13	13	24	21	20	17	22	16
	Unafraid/eager	50	50	54	53	36	52	71	47	56
	Depends	3	6	1	2	3	3	2	3	2
Chi-square significance:					(.05)			(.001)		(n.s.)

[a]The ethnic groups were Black Americans (B.A.), Japanese Americans (J.A.), Mexican Americans (M.A.), and Anglo-Americans (A.A.).

From *Death and Ethnicity: A Psychocultural Study*, by R. A. Kalish and D. K. Reynolds. Copyright 1976 by the University of Southern California Press. Reprinted by permission.

death, and expressed fear fell dramatically with increased age. There was a slight tendency for females to express more fear than males. However, the most important finding of this survey is that very few people (4%) said that they were "very afraid" of death, while 63% said that they were "not at all afraid" (Bengtson, Cuellar, & Ragan, 1977, p. 79). A second major finding of this study is the failure to predict responses to this direct question of death fear in terms of major demographic variables. Even the combined variables of age, race, sex, and socioeconomic status accounted for only about 5% of expressed fear of death (p. 83).

As part of continuing research sponsored by the Equitable Life Assurance Society, a nationwide sample of 1482 adults was surveyed under the direction of John W. Riley, Jr. Among other questions, some of which we will consider in later chapters, respondents were asked whether they agreed or disagreed with five statements about death and dying. The numbers, in each of five age groups, of those who agreed with each statement are given in Table 4-2.

Age differences are not great in these data. Most adult North Americans agree that death is sometimes a blessing, and almost as many state that death is not tragic. Older people are more likely than those younger to think of *death* as a long sleep and to view *dying* as involving suffering. However, few people of any age associate the process of dying with suffering. The difference

TABLE 4-2.   *Beliefs about Death and Dying in a National Sample*

Statement	Percent of Respondents Who Agree with Statement				
	Age 30 and under	Age 31–40	Age 41–50	Age 51–60	Age 61 +
a. Death is sometimes a blessing.	88	88	86	92	91
b. Death is not tragic for the person who dies, only for the survivors.	78	81	83	84	85
c. Death is like a long sleep.	46	54	53	64	62
d. Death always comes too soon.	51	45	65	60	51
e. To die is to suffer.	13	10	13	18	18
Total respondents = 100%	(348)	(389)	(280)	(211)	(249)

Note: The respondents were told "People's beliefs and attitudes toward death are, of course, quite varied. I'll read you a few statements, and you tell me whether you agree or disagree with each one."

From *Aging and Society: An Inventory of Research Findings* (Vol. 1), by M. Riley and A. Foner. Copyright 1968 by the Russell Sage Foundation. Reprinted by permission.

in the proportions of various age groups who agree with the statement "Death always comes too soon" is interesting enough to call for longitudinal analysis.

Although this set of data is the largest and most representative ever gathered, we still do not know whether to attribute the patterns to a process of aging, to the historical period in which different cohorts of people formed their views, to the differential exposure of cohorts over the life cycle to historical experiences, or to intergenerational relations. For example, the smallest proportion agreeing that death always comes too soon is found for people aged 31–40, while the largest proportion agreeing is in the cohort ten years older. Is agreement with the statement increased by the likelihood that persons in the latter category have experienced the death of their own parents? Is it, alternatively—although not in contradiction—heightened awareness, because of age and the experienced death of one's parents, of one's own mortality?

One could argue that experiencing the death of parents increases concerns about death in a period when one's own life is highly valued. The ensuing decades allow preparation for death and release from the hold on life until, for those in the oldest age category, there is again considerable agreement that death does not always come too soon—that it sometimes comes on time or even too late. One could make that argument, and, in fact, I will do so in Chapter Six; but the argument cannot be made conclusively on the basis of cross-sectional data, because the differences for various cohorts may relate to events other than the processes of aging.

Riley's survey was actually carried out in 1963. Respondents who, at that time, were aged 41–50 had been aged 21–30 in 1943, at the height of World War II. One could plausibly argue that so many of them felt that death always comes too soon because, in part at least, they lived through a period when millions of their own cohort died too soon in war. This *cohort* hypothesis, which competes with an *aging* hypothesis, could be tested if we had data on which of the cohort were veterans or had lost brothers or sisters during the war, for it could be argued that these people would more readily endorse the view that death comes too soon; but such data are lacking. What we are left with, in the absence of the ability to separate aging from cohort and historical experiences, is not an explanation but only a description of the beliefs of people of various ages measured in 1963. We can move a bit toward an explanation, however, by considering some of the correlates of those attitudes.

Although many people believe that the aged *should* fear death more than the young, a number of studies have shown older people to be less fearful or anxious or, conversely, more accepting of death than young people (Bengtson, Cuellar, & Ragan, 1977; Kalish & Johnson, 1972; Kalish & Reynolds, 1976; Riley, Jr., 1970; Sharma & Jain, 1969; Templer & Ruff, 1971). Other studies that do not explicitly compare age groups have found little fear of death among the aged (Hochschild, 1973; Jeffers, Nichols, & Eisdorfer, 1961;

Marshall, 1975a; S. Matthews, 1979; Swenson, 1961). As Kalish and Johnson summarize:

> That older people are less fearful of death and dying is not part of contemporary folklore and many aware persons might hypothesize directly the opposite, based upon their observations of the frequency with which the elderly discuss death. Apparently, older persons find death and dying more salient, and they discuss it more; but they do not appear to find it more stressful or frightening. Perhaps, having lived their allocated time, death is less of a punishment than it might be for someone who feels that life still owes him additional time [1972, p. 53].

There may be other reasons. Negative attitudes toward death have been found to be associated with negative attitudes toward aging and the aged (Kalish & Johnson, 1972). Since older people feel more positively disposed toward themselves than young people do toward the aged, the relationship between attitudes toward aging and death is likely to be affected by a strain toward cognitive congruence or balance. In other words, if death and old age are associated, then positive attitudes toward old age may lead to more positive attitudes toward death.

Yet another reason for the age differences in attitudes toward death is found in the work of Diggory and Rothman. They found that subjects aged 55 and over ranked fear that all their plans and projects would come to an end less highly than younger subjects. This pattern can be reasonably interpreted in terms of the utility of the self: "What one would lament most about his own death is loss of the specific activities in which he is most involved or feels to be most important" (Diggory & Rothman, 1961, p. 206). Kalish and Reynolds (1976, pp. 208–209) asked the questions used by Diggory and Rothman in a modified format in their study of ethnicity and death in the Los Angeles area. As a possible reason why a person would not want to die, the statement about plans and projects was endorsed as important less often with increasing age.

The negative association between age and fear of death may be partly spurious. Riley (1970) found age to be less important than education in relation to attitudes to death: "Older people are a little more likely than younger to agree that 'Death is like a long sleep,' or that 'Death is sometimes a blessing'; but there is little indication that such attitudes constitute a general set of views which change with age and which condone a passive acceptance of death" (pp. 38–39). Within each age category in his national sample, however, Riley found higher education associated with a reduced fear of death.

We can only speculate with regard to the future about the joint impact of aging of individual cohorts and the higher education of successive cohorts. At present, the young are more anxious or fearful concerning death than the old, despite their generally higher educational levels. If aging has independent effects, then each cohort will become progressively less fearful of death, and, because of the higher educational level, each successive cohort should start off less fearful. Perhaps the future will be a time when the assumption that all people are very afraid of death will be even more demonstrably false than it is today.

Kalish (1976) suggests three general reasons why the old might fear death less than the young. First, because the value of life is generally considered to be low in old age and because older people tend to share in this evaluation, the costs of giving up life might be lower. Second, it is possible that, when people reach the age that is typically reached in their society, they do not feel cheated by death but rather feel that they have been given a just length of life. Third, people may become socialized to accept their own death: "By the time the elderly person faces his own death, he has dealt with death sufficiently often, perhaps even rehearsing his own death, that he has been socialized to death" (Kalish, 1976, p. 490).

To speak of socialization implies a somewhat deterministic model in which "teachers" inculcate attitudes and meanings in people as they age. In contrast, I will argue that there is little socialization for impending death, just as there is little socialization for any other aspect of later life (Rosow, 1974). However, people do on the whole manage to work out accommodations to the exigencies of aging, including the basic fact of impending death, and probably all of the reasons enumerated above play some part in such accommodations.

We do not want to fall into the trap of assuming that people hold only one attitude toward death at any given time. As Kalish notes, "It is not unusual for one person to undergo several different, often contradictory, feelings about his death within a fairly short period of time—or even simultaneously" (1976, p. 489). Although some people fear death, the weight of research evidence suggests that this fear is not universal and that many other things, such as dishonor, pain, and loneliness, are feared more (Kalish, 1976; Diggory & Rothman, 1961). The important pattern is the general tendency for the fear of death to diminish with increasing age. While at least a significant minority, if not a majority, of young people express fear of death, only a minority of old people do so. This is a gross generalization but one strong enough to suggest that some processes of aging—as opposed to cohort or historical effects—probably have something to do with these changes.

Activity-Theory, Disengagement-Theory, and Role-Theory Interpretations of Aging and Dying

At the risk of oversimplification, I will now summarize three closely related theoretical approaches to aging and dying: activity theory, disengagement theory, and role theory. Although advocates of these approaches often argue with one another, the approaches can be treated as roughly similar in contrast to other, especially developmental and interpretive, perspectives, which are discussed later.

That little support exists for any notion that older people fear death greatly does not obviate our earlier contention that impending death must be of no little concern to most older people, given their increasingly close proximity to it. As Vischer (1967) argues, gerontologists should "try to assess how people react to the experience of seeing their future foreshortened, how this experience affects their general experience of life and their fundamental condition and which internal resources they have at their disposal for dealing with this experience" (pp. 64–65).

Let us, following Munnichs, call this generally age-related recognition of impending death *awareness of finitude,* which refers to the individual's estimate of the amount of time left before he or she dies. A brief examination of the major paradigms within social gerontology will show that awareness of finitude has largely been neglected and that, where it is mentioned, it has been given brief conceptual and empirical consideration.

Activity theory has long guided both sociological research and practice. As an unsystematized set of research and practice assumptions, activity theory rests on a root metaphor of a continuing equilibrium between the aging individual and society. Thus, Palmore, summarizing the approach, argues that "the majority of normal aging persons maintain fairly level amounts of activity and engagements" and that maintaining or developing high levels of activity "is usually necessary for successful aging" (1969, p. 58). Nothing is said of death or awareness of finitude in Palmore's summary nor in a more recent attempt to systematize the theory (Lemon, Bengtson, & Peterson, 1972).

As Lemon, Bengtson, and Peterson indicate, the major argument of activity theory "is that there is a positive relationship between activity and life satisfaction and that the greater the role loss, the lower the life satisfaction" (1972, p. 511). Interaction, whether formal or informal, involves individuals in role behavior with others. In this sense, activity theory—and disengagement theory as well—is a kind of role theory. The formalization of activity theory by Lemon, Bengtson, and Peterson links age-related loss of role relationships with loss of the activity that has provided support for the identity of the aging individual. The ultimate result of role loss, in this analytical chain, is decreased life satisfaction. Lemon, Bengtson, and Peterson tested this theory with a fairly small and atypical sample of White, mostly middle- and upper-middle-class applicants for a retirement village and found little support for it.

The many studies employing activity theory, including those somewhat supportive of it, need not concern us here (see, for example, Maddox, 1970; Palmore, 1968; Palmore & Luikart, 1972). Our only concern is to point to the restrictions of a theory that has been the focus of so much gerontological research. Activity theory, like much gerontology, is a kind of social psychology of happiness. The dependent variable is happiness, morale, adjustment, or life satisfaction. Activity theory in particular is based on an image of an individual seeking to maintain feelings of self-worth or morale through continuing high levels of activity with others. It postulates as normal those persons who continue to be productive (Kuypers & Bengtson, 1973; Marshall & Tindale, 1978–1979). The adjusted American is the "rugged individualist" who participates actively in the system (Bengtson, 1973, p. 43).

We may safely conclude that activity theory has no place in its assumptive framework for death—the end of activity. Nor does it have anything to say about awareness of finitude. Indeed, the theory is criticized for precisely this neglect by Cumming and Henry in their major formulation of disengagement theory.

Disengagement theory is an explicit reaction against activity theory. Deriding the activity theorists for their emphasis on continuing high levels of functioning, Cumming and Henry observe:

> An extension of this implicit theme of continuing usefulness is the feeling that the life span must, in order to be successful, undergo steady expansion. . . . Studies based on such an assumption are unlikely to deal with the idea of death. . . . The death of old people is a slipping away. If it is believed to be a good thing to remain tightly bound to the fabric of life, death must be a tearing away [1961, p. 18].

Disengagement theorists fault the activity theorists for their neglect of death. However, death is relevant for Cumming and Henry only in a narrowly defined way. They continue: "Death is a logical preoccupation for those who are going to die, and it seems reasonable that those who are approaching death should give some thought to it, *as well as to how their departure will affect the people with whom they have close ties*" (1961, pp. 18–19; italics mine).

In fact, it is the latter consideration, rather than the putative thoughts about death, that has received attention by the disengagement theorists. Since its initial formulation in 1960 (Cumming, Dean, Newell, & McCaffrey, 1960), disengagement theory has been elaborated (Cumming & Henry, 1961) and revised (Cumming, 1963, 1975; Henry, 1964). The disengagement concept, originally conceived as an "inevitable mutual withdrawal" between the individual and society and "resulting in decreased interaction between an aging person and others in the social systems he belongs to" (Cumming and Henry, 1961, p. 14), has been differentiated to separate social disengagement (interaction in role relationships) from psychological disengagement (the extent to which the individual is preoccupied or involved with people or events in the external world) (Havighurst, Neugarten, & Tobin, 1963).

Cumming (1975) has recently argued that disengagement theory was not originally intended as a theory to predict morale. Nonetheless, the great bulk of research on disengagement theory, as on activity theory, has been devoted to finding optimal patterns of aging (Havighurst, Neugarten, & Tobin, 1963). Whereas activity theorists and disengagement theorists agree that role relationships are lost with aging, activity theorists see the individual as motivated to replace lost role activities, and disengagement theorists see this process as voluntary (Havighurst, Neugarten, & Tobin, 1963).

Here, as has often been pointed out, we find a developmental strain in this largely functionalist argument. Willingness to disengage is seen as intrinsic to the aging individual:

> Social withdrawal is accompanied by, or preceded by, increased preoccupation with the self and decreased emotional investment in persons and objects in the environment; and that, in this sense, disengagement is a natural rather than an imposed process. In this view, the older person who has a sense of psychological well-being will usually be the person who has reached a new equilibrium characterized by a greater psychological distance, altered types of relationships, and decreased social interaction with the persons around him [Havighurst, Neugarten, & Tobin, 1963, in 1968, p. 161].

This reduction in role relationships eases the exit of the individual from the society. As a mutual process, it is, at the same time, society's way of solving the problem of passing people through positions (see Chapter Three) and the individual's way of preparing for his or her own exit from the society. The successfully aging individual will voluntarily accede to this process of phasing out, or being phased out, of the society. (For formal statements of this theory, see Bromley, 1970; Damianopoulos, 1961; see also Hochschild, 1975; Markson, 1975; Rose, 1964; Spence, 1975.)

The phasing-out process, according to disengagement theorists, is preparatory for death and is initiated by age-related awareness of mortality: "If the individual becomes sharply aware of the shortness of life and the scarcity of the time remaining to him, and if he perceives his life space as decreasing, and if his available ego energy is lessened, then readiness for disengagement has begun" (Damianopoulos, 1961, p. 216).

In his discussion of this postulate, Damianopoulos argues: "It seems probable that disengagement would be resisted forever if there were no problem of the allocation of time, and thus no anticipation of death. Questions of choice among alternative uses of time lead to curtailment of some activities. Questions of the inevitability of death lead to introspective reflections on the meaning of life" (1961, p. 217). Disengagement, then, is seen as correlated with awareness of finitude. However, neither Cumming and Henry nor any other disengagement theorists have clearly explicated a theory of awareness of finitude beyond the simplistic inclusion of awareness of finitude as a "starting mechanism" that leads to "readiness to disengage" (see especially Damianopoulos, 1961, pp. 216–217).

If activity theory is based on a root metaphor of continuing equilibrium, disengagement theory is based on a root metaphor of equilibrium that is lost and then regained. This equilibrium involves a stable pattern of social relationships. Both theoretical schools focus on equilibrated social role relationships and their association with life satisfaction variables. Disengagement theory tantalizingly hints at other aspects of the meaning of experiencing awareness of impending death but never spells them out.

If we set aside for the moment the empirical validity of disengagement theory, we can at least conclude that, for our purposes, it represents an advance over activity theory in that it at least acknowledges that aging and dying are linked phenomena. Interestingly enough, as we will see in subsequent chapters, very little of the empirical research employing disengagement theory focuses on this link; and, when it does so, it appears to assume that the only important aspects of aging and dying are connected with vacating one's roles. In this sense, disengagement theory is a social psychology of leave taking, of saying goodbye.

Role theorists also address the phenomenon of vacating roles. They are interested in role *change,* viewed as role *exit* (Blau, 1973, pp. 210–245) or role *loss* (Cavan, Burgess, Havighurst, & Goldhamer, 1949; Phillips, 1957). These terms are used almost interchangeably, although they have different connotations. *Exit* implies a focus on unidirectional change, ignoring role entry; the assumption is, of course, that aging brings fewer entries and more exits. The term *loss* connotes a negative evaluation of such changes. As Rosow says, "The later years approximate social 'failure' in many respects . . . the aged commonly move on to fewer and emptier roles" (1976, p. 469). The end result of the role shedding that accompanies aging is presumably to leave the individual in the dying role; but little has been made of this obvious extension of role theory.

Blau (1973) points out that the life course can be viewed as a series of role entrances and exits, with the individual possessing the most roles in the peak activity years of adulthood. However, "Before old age, the *sequential ordering* of institutional social roles operates to obscure the recurring phenomenon of role exit" (1973, p. 227). In old age the number of role exits increases, and the two major age-related ones, retirement and widowhood, are involuntary (1973, p. 243). Blau argues that declines in morale in later life are directly related to cumulative role exits (1973, p. 236). Since involvement in social roles supports identity, role loss can jeopardize individuals in later life not only through the particular crisis of an individual loss but also through a reduction in an individual's social support system in a more general sense. This theory is thus formally identical to activity theory as formulated by Lemon, Bengtson, and Peterson (1972).

The relationship of role-theory approach to disengagement theory is also quite obvious. Only the *voluntarism* of disengagement theory is rejected. Rosow makes this link:

> While disengagement theorists have arbitrarily interpreted the shrinkage as a function of a normal social psychological process, they have not articulated this view with a coherent theory of adult development. Yet there are more

economic explanations of reduced social participation: role loss and devaluation . . . social decline and failure are invidious, and as a consequence, people frequently restrict their public participation [1976, p. 469].

Rosow's interpretation leads to a concept of "social death," in which the individual loses social standing in the eyes of others and is placed in a situation similar to that of old people in some relatively nonmodernized societies (see Chapter Three). According to Kalish (1966), "Social death occurs when an individual is thought of as dead and treated as dead, although he remains medically and legally alive. Any given person may be socially dead to one individual, to many individuals or to virtually everyone" (p. 73). Social death is therefore, in disengagement-theory terms, full social disengagement and, in role-theory terms, complete rolelessness.

One additional contribution of role theory to a sociology of aging and dying should be noted. Rosow takes the position that ideally people ought to be *socialized* to old age. He views adult socialization as "the process of inculcating new values and behavior appropriate to adult positions and group memberships" with resulting "new images, expectations, skills, and norms as the person defines himself and as others view him" (Rosow, 1974, p. 31). Rosow argues that socialization for old age is problematical because of the devalued position of the aged in North American society, the ambiguity of norms for the aged role, the dearth of formal socialization mechanisms (there are few people teaching others how to be old), and the low motivation that people have to be socialized into the role (Rosow, 1974, pp. 117–118). In other words, aging individuals have neither the opportunity nor the incentive to learn or to internalize expectations for old age. Although Rosow does not discuss death or a "dying role," his argument would also apply to those aspects of aging. If dying is one of the important behavioral sequences of old age, it might be argued that this aspect of the aging role is highly problematic. This argument has, in fact, been made by Riley and associates (1969) and by Marshall (1975a).

At the risk of oversimplification, we can try to summarize the approaches of activity, disengagement, and role theory as follows:

1. In all three approaches, loss of roles is viewed as inevitably associated with aging.
2. Whereas disengagement theorists view age-related role loss as a process in which the aging individual normally cooperates voluntarily, activity and role theorists stress the external features of this process; for them, loss of roles is something that happens to older people.
3. The evaluation of role loss varies among the three approaches. Disengagement theorists see reduced role relationships as functional—beneficial to the individual in allowing more time to prepare for death and to the society in facilitating the passage of people through positions. Activity and role theorists view reduced role engagement as lessening the

effectiveness of the individual's support systems and as the cause of crises leading to reduced morale or adjustment.

4. While activity theorists act as if the aging individual were not dying, disengagement theorists and role theorists restrictively view death and dying as aspects of aging. The potential value of treating dying as age-related role behavior has not been tested in the major work within these traditions.

5. Role theorists have themselves, however, paid little attention to the processes of exiting; instead, they have focused on the fact of progressive role loss and the consequences of loss for morale.

Although disengagement theory and activity theory are not always seen as variants of role theory, they do rely on an identical conceptualization of the individual as role player, as, in a sense, nothing but a bundle or summation of roles (Neugarten & Datan, 1973). This position has recently been criticized as overly deterministic (Breytspraak, 1975; Gubrium & Buckholdt, 1977; Marshall, 1978–1979). For example, Neugarten and Hagestadt criticize many role theorists for taking the "victim approach" in focusing on loss. They argue (see also Marshall, 1978–1979; Turner, 1962) that opportunities for "role making" continue to be available throughout the life course and that "the subtle changes that occur in age status as the individual moves through the periods of adulthood are not to be understood by mere enumerations of his formal roles" (1976, p. 40).

Kiefer (1974) has argued that, to speak of a psychological process of disengagement, one must make an assumption that an individual is separate and distinct from his or her roles. In his research on three generations of Japanese Americans, Kiefer found that such a distinction was foreign to the Japanese:

> Behind the Westerner's perception of himself as purposefully engaged in and thus potentially disengaged from his intimate social relations lies a long history of philosophic individualism and a personal biography that includes early independence training and the self-conscious acquisition and dismantling of many relationships. . . . The issei [born in Japan] however, cannot disengage from his social roles because he is those roles [1974, p. 207].

Kiefer points to the cultural specificity of disengagement theory, but his criticism is equally applicable to the variants of role theory. It is crucial to remember that sociologists use the concept of role as an analytic device. It is an abstraction used by sociologists in many ways (Komarovsky, 1973; Rosow, 1976) but not always relevant to those in whom the sociologist is interested. So, while a sociologist might be very concerned that roles for the aged are not clearly defined (for example, Rosow, 1974) or that being aged is to occupy a "role-less role" (Burgess, 1960), older persons might not be aware that there is a "role" for the aged or care whether there is or not (Marshall, 1978–1979).

Developmental theories in the social psychology of aging generally include implications of the finite aspects of human nature; as a result, they are more satisfactory for our purposes than many of the approaches just discussed. The focus in this section will be on the work of Erikson, Neugarten, Butler, and Levinson, because this work has particular importance as a well-integrated developmental social psychology of aging and dying.

It is possible to list certain assumptions in a "strict" developmental model to which various theorists adhere more or less faithfully (see Baltes, 1977):

1. Individual change is best viewed as a *sequence* of stages.
2. Change occurs in *one direction only*, from earlier to later stages without reversing direction.
3. The differences between stages are *qualitative*.
4. These changes are *universal*, species characteristics.

There is greater agreement on the applicability of these characteristics for the description of early childhood development than for the description of later life (Baer, 1970; Neugarten, 1966, 1973; Schaie, 1973). Cognitive and psychosexual development in the first decade of life seems to progress universally through sequences of qualitatively different stages that build on one another, as work within the Piagetian and Freudian traditions suggests. With increasing age, biological influences become less important; thus gerontologists seeking to extend the developmental framework must adopt a broader conception.

This broader conception of human development does not assume biological determinism or the inevitability of developmental change. It does, however, continue to assume that at least some of the changes in human personality and behavior that occur over the life course can be described as "an *orderly progression* with the passage of time" (Neugarten, 1966, p. 63). For Neugarten, although not for all developmental theorists, these changes are also thought of as *adaptive,* either to biological changes (for example, bodily decline or decreased energy) or to external social events.

Neugarten finds in middle age an increased focusing on the self and a withdrawal of psychological investment in the outer world. She views these changes as *developmental* because they precede the biological and social losses of aging. This growing "interiority" has set in by the mid-forties, before great decrements in health status or physiological abilities and before such major crises of aging as widowhood and retirement. Growing interiority is then *preparatory* for later crises, but it is not *adaptive* in the sense of being purposive. Rather, it is an inner psychological regularity of the life cycle that happens to the individual (Neugarten, 1970a). Since the later years will bring reduced involvement with the outer world, this interiorization allows "an emphasis upon introspection and stocktaking, upon conscious reappraisal of the self" (Neugarten, 1970a, p. 77) that is preparatory for old age.

Neugarten, Crotty, and Tobin (1964) found in a sample of 100 upper-middle-class and well-educated middle-aged persons that they had come to perceive time differently. They had begun to think of how much time was left to live rather than how much time had elapsed since their births, and they had become more aware that time is finite, that they would die:

> The change in time-perspective is intimately related to the personalization of death. Death in middle age becomes a real possibility for the self, no longer the magical or extraordinary occurrence that it appears in youth. In women there is the rehearsal for widowhood which becomes characteristic . . . ; and in men there is the "sponsoring" issue with regard to young associates as well as with regard to one's children, an issue we called "the creation of social heirs" [Neugarten, 1970a, p. 78].

Neugarten's formulation is very much in accord with that of Erik Erikson (1959, 1963), who argues that, at about this period of life, individuals experience a developmental crisis in which they must seek a balance between what he calls *generativity* and *ego stagnation*. By *generativity* Erikson does not mean producing a new generation—this occurs earlier, in the twenties —but initiating and teaching the new generation, bringing them to full responsibility as adults, in preparation for the subsequent task of withdrawal. It is in this period, Erikson argues—and Neugarten would agree—that the individual developmental task coincides with the wider species-survival task of passing the torch. In terms of our earlier discussion of the succession of generations (see Chapter Two), this is the time when the occupant of a position begins to deal with his or her own replacement.

Daniel Levinson and his colleagues (1978) incorporate Erikson's position in describing a "mid-life crisis" that occurs around the ages of 35 to 45. Levinson also draws on the work of Freud, Jung, and other psychoanalytically inclined theorists and, especially like Jung, he gives great importance to the recognition of mortality, which, he asserts, typically becomes important in this period of the life course. Levinson's formulation is important also because it forms much of the foundation for Gail Sheehy's best-selling book *Passages* (1977), which presents a popularized developmental social psychology of the life course. Levinson's empirical base is restricted to 40 men, varying only slightly in social class; but additional work of his associates suggests, he claims, that women in their mid-thirties seem to go through developmental periods similar to those of men.

Like Neugarten, Levinson sees the mid-life period as one of self-appraisal and reflection. Levinson argues (1978) that "a man at around 40 is not simply reacting to an external situation. He is reappraising his life. He makes an effort to reconsider the direction he has taken, the fate of his youthful dreams, the possibilities for a better or worse life in the future" (p. 32). What distinguishes this type of reflection from the reflection that, many developmental theorists argue, occurs at an even later stage, is that it occurs within the context of a future. The past is being appraised and evaluated, but this process of reflection occurs in a context of future plans and possibilities. For Levinson, Erikson, and Neugarten, the individual during this period will ideally invest energy into the future rather than passively accepting it. To be passive is to stagnate, to engage in no more than the routines of work and necessary living activities. The unsuccessful pole of the developmental crisis of mid-life, for all these theorists, is associated with an unhealthy preoccupation with the self.

According to Levinson, during the mid-life transition a man becomes more aware of the relationship between individual living and dying and the survival of the species:

> He comes to grasp more clearly the flow of generations and the continuity of the human species. His personal immortality, whatever its form, lies within that larger human continuity. He feels more responsibility for the generations that will follow his own. . . . He also understands more deeply that he is a drop in the vast river of human history [1978, pp. 217–218].*

Because of this concern, he strives to leave a *legacy:* "A man's legacy is what he passes on to future generations: material possessions, creative products, enterprises, influence on others" (1978, p. 218). Levinson's acknowledged intellectual debt to Robert Lifton (1971; see also Chapter Three of this book) is clear; he agrees with Lifton and with most scholars who, drawing on psychoanalytic foundations, argue that everyone has a desire for some form of immortality.

Now let us turn to the next, and last, developmental stage for this group of theorists. Neugarten and Levinson give variants of Erikson's formulation of a final identity crisis, in which the developmental task is to come to an acceptance of life as a whole as that life draws to a close.

The eighth, and final, identity crisis stems from a choice in the final assessment of one's life. This crisis is precipitated by a heightened awareness of one's finitude (Erikson, 1959, pp. 98–166). Viewing life as a whole and as nearing completion, the individual is faced with accepting that life as one that has been lived. The outcomes of this crisis are characterized by the two polar opposites of integrity and despair. The person characterized by integrity feels satisfied with his or her life and accomplishments and accepts responsibility for that life, both in its accomplishments and in its failures. As Erikson puts it, integrity "is the acceptance of one's one and only life cycle as something that had to be and that, by necessity, permitted of no substitutions" (1963, p. 268). Despair, on the other hand, characterizes the individual who feels unhappy

*From *The Seasons of a Man's Life,* by D. J. Levinson et al. Copyright 1978 by Alfred A. Knopf, Inc. This and all other quotations from this source are reprinted by permission.

and depressed about his or her life as a whole and who emphasizes its failures. While the person who has achieved integrity will accept impending death, the person characterized by despair will not and, consequently, will fear death: "Despair expresses the feeling that the time is now short, too short for the attempt to start another life and to try out alternate roads to integrity" (1963, pp. 268–269).

Peck has noted that, by contrast with the earlier stages, the eighth stage in Erikson's framework "seems to be intended to represent in a global nonspecific way all of the psychological crises and crisis-solutions of the last forty or fifty years of life" (1968, p. 88). Breaking the period after age 30 into the two broad categories of middle age and old age, Peck then delineates three types of concerns in old age: concerns with the transition from work to retirement and the need to establish alternative valued activities and self-attributes; concern with decrements in health and the constraints that these decrements place on activities; and coping with impending death.

Peck argues that the Chinese and Hindu thinkers, as well as some Western thinkers, demonstrate that a positive adaptation to impending death is possible, and he argues further that "such an adaptation would not be a stage of passive resignation or of ego-denial. On the contrary, it requires deep, active effort to make life more secure, more meaningful, or happier for people who will go on after one dies" (1968, p. 91).

Neugarten and her associates (1964) have conducted the most extensive research to evaluate whether Erikson's developmental theory can be applied to later life and have found the theory wanting. This research is reviewed in Chapter Five, where it is argued that Neugarten's approach has not given a conclusive test of Erikson. More recently, Neugarten (1970, 1972) has expressed interest in a related formulation of Robert Butler.

Butler (1963) begins with the commonly held observation that many old people reminisce a great deal, or "live in the past." Unlike many, however, Butler does not view reminiscence as maladaptive or equated with psychological dysfunction; instead, he sees it as part of a life review,

> a naturally occurring, universal mental process characterized by the progressive return to consciousness of past experiences, and particularly, the resurgence of unresolved conflicts; simultaneously, and normally, these revived experiences and conflicts can be surveyed and reintegrated. Presumably this process is prompted by the realization of approaching dissolution and death, and the inability to maintain one's sense of personal invulnerability [1963, p. 66].

Butler views the life-review process as universal in that he sees it as biologically rooted. However, personal and environmental circumstances can play their part in reinforcing the biological determination of the process. The process is both adaptive and constructive: "Such reorganization of past experience may provide a more valid picture, giving new and significant meanings to one's life; it may also prepare one for death, mitigating one's fears" (1963, p. 68).

The importance of Butler's concept of the life-review process is that it may describe the way in which the reorganization of the self, postulated by people such as Neugarten, Levinson, and Erikson, occurs. Butler's own evidence is clinical, but others have tested and modified his approach in research that is reviewed in Chapter Five.

Although Levinson's research base does not as yet extend beyond the mid-life crisis years of his subjects, he does trace out in a preliminary way what he feels are subsequent developmental transitions. He sees a developmental stage, beginning about age 60, in Erikson's terms of a resolution between integrity and despair; but he tentatively suggests yet another stage at the very end of the normal life cycle, which these days he places at about age 80 (Levinson et al., 1978, pp. 33–39).

> What does development mean at the very end of the life cycle? It means that a man is coming to terms with the process of dying and preparing for his own death. At the end of all previous eras, part of the developmental work was to start a new era, to create a new basis for living. A man in his eighties knows that his death is imminent . . . he lives in its shadow, and at its call. To be able to involve himself in living he must make his peace with dying [1978, p. 38].

Whereas Levinson has seen the mid-life transition as a time of concern for one's successors and for the continuity of the species, he sees the sixties as a time for assessing one's contribution to society; in the eighties, "he has only the self. . . . He must come to terms with the self—knowing it and loving it reasonably well, and being ready to give it up" (1978, p. 39).

The four developmental theorists we have reviewed are in considerable agreement with one another in their portrayal of the changes individuals undergo with respect to their mortality. For these theorists, one important feature of the second half of the life cycle is preparation for death. Their contribution will be assessed in Chapter Five, when the research evidence is examined. It is important at this time, however, to point to one theoretical problem of great importance: the individualistic and psychologistic emphasis throughout these works.

It is easy to see the limitations of the developmental approach by placing the putatively normal developmental life course in historical context. What does the generativity and desire to leave a legacy imply in terms of the normally expected life cycle experienced in colonial America, or preindustrial England or France, or Kaliai? We saw in Chapter Two (Table 2-3) that, in 1830 in Massachusetts, 36 of every 100 women died before reaching the age of 20 and that another 12 died before age 55. It is difficult to see the changes of a mid-life transition as relevant for this group of women. Certainly the reality of mortality and finitude must have been impressed on anyone living before this century much earlier than these theories imply and from external rather than internal sources. And yet these developmental approaches assume that the primary sources of the changes they postulate as occurring in mid-life, and also later in life, are intrinsic to the individual. This assumption is tied to the argument that human development through the life course occurs as a set of universal stages characteristic of the human species.

The failure of most people in world history to live long enough to experience Erikson's eighth identity crisis—the concern for generativity and being productive—as well as the emphasis on a reappraisal of individual identity, should warn us of the restricted applicability of these approaches. If, as argued in Chapter Three, an emphasis on the individual is a peculiarly Western and modern concern (Gatch, 1969) and if individualism emerged, as Ariès argues (1975), around 1200 in our Western world, then the growing interiority and self-focusing of mid-life and the more intense coming to terms with the self as mortal of later life postulated by these theories are unlikely to be primarily inner, intrinsic phenomena. To argue that they are implies a dramatic lack of fit between universal human nature and the sociocultural organization of societies of most peoples living in most eras of human history.

This is not to deny the applicability of the developmental approach to our own society, which does emphasize values related to individual productivity, legacy, and generativity and which exalts the individual quest for integrity. I do, however, suggest that the extent to which the data concerning the ways in which individuals come to view themselves over the course of their lives (especially in relation to their finite fate) can be organized according to developmental stages will coincide with the social and cultural organization of aging and dying in our society. If, in other words, people age and die in ways suggested by these developmental theorists, it is because of a mistaken assumption that patterns common in our own society are historical, cultural, and biological universals.

Chapter Five reexamines these approaches in the light of data. In that chapter I will attend in particular to the importance of *awareness of finitude,* arguing its relative independence from both chronological age and developmental stage. The processes of coming to terms with self and with mortality can be seen as adaptive to the increasing relevance of impending death, which is usually age-related. These processes can be seen as social-psychological rather than as biopsychological realities, in a specific sociocultural milieu. The universal claim of developmental theory is lost, and much insight is gained into the social psychology of aging and dying.

An Interpretive Understanding of Aging and Dying

The first section of this chapter was a review of the research tradition in clinical thanatology. Almost all this research has been concerned with younger dying persons, mostly people in later stages of terminal illness. Since most people in our society who die are not young, this research tradition has little demonstrable usefulness for understanding aging and dying in the later years. Most younger people have little concern for their own impending death. As we have been reminded through Tolstoy's classical novella *The Death of Ivan Ilych*, the prospect of death is something quite foreign, distant, and abstract to the young. It is, therefore, quite plausible that young people who are told that they are dying will not readily acknowledge the veracity of this fact. The first stage in coming to terms with death is to recognize that death is a personal possibility.

We saw that people of any age will readily answer questions about their attitudes toward death and that some investigators have shown ingenuity in measuring anxiety about or fear of death and dying. Less attention has been paid to measuring other possible attitudes toward death and dying, and in any case the old have seldom been asked questions relating to such possible attitudes. What little evidence we do have suggests that the old are less fearful and more accepting of death than the young. But we really have no way of telling whether age differences reflect changes associated with aging, such as developmental changes, different ideas about death and dying learned by different cohorts of people, or historical experiences with death-related connotations, such as a major war. Research is lacking that would allow us to separate one such possible cause from another.

If we are willing to make the assumption that there are real age-related changes that are not artifacts of simple cohort changes, we then have to explain why increasing age is associated with changed attitudes and behavior toward death and dying. Two points need explanation: the *increased concern about death* that accompanies advancing age and the *decreased fear of death* (or, conversely, the increased acceptance of it). The third section of this chapter reviewed three closely related theories that might account for age-related changes in the ways in which death is taken into account, and the following section considered another major attempt to explain such changes.

In the course of the discussion about the three theories, I introduced a formal concept, awareness of finitude, to refer to the individual's estimate of the amount of time left before death. Of the theoretical approaches discussed, only disengagement theory explicitly incorporates such a concept. However, whereas disengagement theorists argue that thoughts of death should increase with aging and death's approach, they, in fact, give little attention to this aspect of aging and dying. Rather, they center on the shedding of role relationships and focusing on the self. Disengagement theory is, in fact, a role-theory variant of developmental theory, sharing with the approaches discussed in the fourth section a postulate of a turning toward the self, a stock-taking on one's life as a whole that is prompted by awareness of finitude. Disengaging from role relationships is seldom voluntary, especially in the important role losses of retirement and widowhood (Shanas et al., 1968, pp. 280–285); similarly, giving up roles is not always associated with feelings of loss and lower morale.

The role theorist Phillips (1957) is wrong in asserting that thinking of oneself as old and thinking about death, both of which are associated with role loss, lead of necessity to maladjustment. Here the developmental theorists make a valuable contribution in affirming the normality of decreased role involvement, changing self-conceptions, and more thoughts of death over the last half of the typical life course.

We may parenthetically note that Blau's interpretation of Erikson's eighth identity crisis in role-theory terms incorrectly assumes that continuity of role relationships, in a way postulated as important by activity theorists, is the key to achieving ego integrity (Blau, 1973, pp. 100–114). Erikson and the other developmental theorists we have discussed do not hold, as does Blau, that continuing high levels of role activity are required for good human development in the latter half of the life course. Rather, they put forth variants of the general theme that the fortunate aging individual will change over the later years to become more accepting of the self as an aging and dying person. The self, ideally, is validated by others over the entire life course. This observation does not imply that normal or healthy human development requires validation of one stable self throughout life; instead, it implies an ever-changing sense of self that realistically incorporates finitude when this concept becomes relevant in the later years.

I noted in the third section of the chapter that role theorists have paid little attention to the *processes* of moving through roles, focusing instead on the *fact* of role exit or loss and arguing negative consequences for morale. Developmental theorists, when they have gotten beyond the individual to consider social processes, have taken a similar view of role (Marshall, 1978–1979). While focusing on internal psychological processes, they have paid little attention to external social processes.

There is no such thing as an "aging and dying role," and using the abstraction *role* to describe aging and dying is of little analytical value if by *role* is meant any stable set of expectations for the behavior of someone occupying a status position. We can accept the role theorist's assertion that expectations for behavior are important without having to assume that the social world, or the "social system," is nothing but a network of such expectations and that the "role-lessness" of the aged necessarily places them at a disadvantage.

We are on safer ground if we assume that an individual will go through life, for the most part, meaningfully. He or she will prefer to behave in ways that "make sense," and meanings that make this sense will be sought where they are available—directly from others and indirectly from the cultural resources of the society. It is not necessary to assume that a given individual will have one definition of self or one view of self-as-dying. It is not necessary to assume that a person must be either afraid of death or unafraid. It is possible to be both afraid and unafraid. Equally important, it is not necessary to assume great agreement among the members of a collectivity with regard to definitions of self as aging and dying or great stability about such agreement.

I argued in Chapter Three that meanings about death and dying, as any other kind of meaning, are best viewed as human and social creations. I also argued that the historical legacy of our evolving culture has left us with a very unclear and contradictory set of meanings for death and dying. If we are able to find any order or patterning at all in the ways in which people age and die, this orderliness is not likely to be massive. As we use the theoretical approaches discussed in this chapter to examine what is known about aging and dying and to stretch the data to theorize about the numerous gaps, we must be prepared for diversity.

As a perspective to guide us through the rest of the book, I would argue, then, that we assume the following points:

1. Individuals will seek to render their lives, including their aging and dying, more meaningful than meaningless.
2. The process of meaning construction and utilization is at root a *social* process.
3. Individuals continually negotiate with one another to work out some sense and semblance of order, including a provisional, but ever-changing, agreement as to who they are, were, and will be.

I share the developmental theorist's concern for identity and would invoke an image of the aging and dying individual as one who searches for meaning, who constructs an identity composed of many selves, and who seeks to direct his or her interaction with others in ways compatible with this sense of identity as it changes over time. This does not imply that the changing situation of the aging and dying person is entirely of his or her own making. Not only the brute external facts affecting mortality rates or health status but also the equally solid realities of other people and their own attempts to live a meaningful life pose constraints. Aging and dying thus involves continual negotiation with others and continual coming to terms with external, objective social, physical, and physiological reality.

This perspective does not stand in radical contradiction to the theoretical approaches reviewed in the third and fourth sections of this chapter. Instead, it breathes life into them, suggests that greater attention be paid to the ways in which people pass through the changes of later life, and suspends all assumptions about a rigid determination of human behavior either by normative constraints or inner developmental causes. Nor does it negate the clinical position reviewed in the first section nor the value of the attitudinal research described in the second section. Instead, it places the clinical position in perspective as only one way of viewing aging and dying, and it suggests that the attitudes derived from surveys are neither all-encompassing nor stable descriptions of the ways in which people can view death as they pass through the life course.

Theory is good *as a tool* if it helps us organize data and critically and clearly examine them. In this chapter I have attempted, not uncritically, to present some useful tools to help us organize the data to come in subsequent chapters. In Chapter Five I assess data about the following aspects of aging and dying in our kind of society:

1. *The relevance of awareness of finitude:* What are the age-related differences in the amount of time people anticipate living? What importance do people attach to this awareness? What do people think about death in general?

2. *Death and biography:* What is the evidence about the concern with self postulated as preparatory for death in so many theoretical approaches? How is the work of reassessing biography in relation to death accomplished? How does that work prepare the individual for death?

3. *The meaning of death itself:* How do meanings of death change in later life? To what extent can we describe modalities of acceptance, fear, resignation, and so forth that might characterize the ways in which people assign meaning to themselves as dying?

4. *The consequences of different ways of aging and dying:* In particular, is it possible to discover patterned relationships among preparation for death, outcomes of such preparation, and such features as time perspective and morale?

I will examine these questions as they apply to contemporary industrialized society and will be wary of any claims to the universality of the answers. These questions by no means exhaust what is interesting about aging and dying, and I will address other aspects in Chapters Six and Seven. However, these are the questions that arise most directly from the material reviewed in this chapter.

Review Questions
for Chapter 4

1. *Select a scale or index that measures attitudes toward death from among those mentioned in this chapter, and complete it for yourself (you might also have associates complete it). Then consider and discuss the implications of your answers. Do you feel comfortable that the summary score gives a good representation of your own attitudes toward death? How much do your attitudes change from day to day and from situation to situation?*

2. *In a group situation, find out whether someone in the group has ever saved the life of another individual and whether someone believes that his or her own life has been saved (for example, rescued from probable drowning). Encourage the person to try to articulate the sentiments and feelings that arise in such situations and their lasting impact. Do attitudes toward death change when the possibility of death becomes very real? The same considerations apply to those who have lived with the clear*

possibility of death in combat situations or to those who pursue hazardous occupations (such as mining) or sports (such as parachuting or mountain climbing). Why, do you think, do some people tolerate high-risk lives and others actively pursue risk?

3. Question 2 referred to dramatic circumstances. Now consider everyday life styles. What are the implications of your attitudes toward death and various "life-style" features of your life—for example, whether or how much you smoke and drink, whether you fasten your seat belt, and whether you exercise and maintain weight? If most of us fear death, why do our life styles not always reflect this fear?

4. Examine the "mid-life crisis" as depicted in drama, fiction, and films. (Woody Allen's and Ingmar Bergman's films, as well as The Turning Point and Rachel, Rachel, are good examples.) Another way to examine the popularity and popularization of the mid-life-crisis theme is to examine "women's" and pulp magazines and the so-called psychology section of most bookstores, where you are likely to find journalistic treatments of the "male menopause" and related topics. To what extent do you think that popular treatments of crisis in the middle years provide needed relief for those who suffer from it, as opposed to simply creating a new vocabulary that people can use to interpret their lives?

5. Select a "popularized" book dealing with the problems of mid-life and critique its methodology. Pay particular attention to the sample (how many people, what kinds of people, and how well they represent any general population) and to measurement (how systematic, how reliable, and how valid).

5

Awareness of Finitude and Changing Conception of Self

In this chapter I present the evidence for or against the theoretical interpretations reviewed in Chapter Four. In the first section I examine the very small amount of research on the question of awareness of finitude. I then make an analytic distinction concerning the consequences of heightened awareness, treating *concern with self* and *concern with dying* as distinct, although of course related, phenomena. Concern with self in relation to awareness of finitude is the major theoretical issue raised in the previous chapter; here I consider the evidence. Concern with dying is treated in Chapters Six and Seven. This chapter also deals with the question of the timing of self-concern in relation to awareness of finitude. Does self-concern become heightened in mid-life or in late life? Is there a mid-life crisis, or is there basic continuity in the self until later in life or even, typically, into death? Then the evidence concerning the *processes* of self-reflection is discussed. The argument, like the evidence on which it can be constructed, is restricted in applicability to the North American context. Because of space limitations, I cannot address historical and cross-cultural variability as I would like to do.

"Death," Heidegger tells us, "in the widest sense, is a phenomenon of life" (1962, p. 290). However, awareness of one's own impending death can be treated as a variable, for we can be more or less consciously oriented toward our dying or absorbed in our living (Heidegger, 1962, p. 295). Our everyday world is experienced without a great deal of reflection. It is "not an object of our thought but a field of domination. We have an imminently practical interest in it, caused by the necessity of complying with the basic requirements of life" (Schutz, 1967, p. 227). Our interests and plans for action will depend on our biographical, social, and historical situation, but the way in which we order these interests and plans is ultimately affected by our knowledge, at some level, that we will die. Schutz calls this knowledge "the fundamental anxiety" (1967, p. 228).

Death is a certitude that places limits on the time span of our projects and, in essence, throws us into time. Because of death, time is "the ultimate scarcity" (Moore, 1963, p. 6) that necessitates our allocating priorities to those things we want to do or have to do. In Schutz's terminology, the fact that our time is limited by mortality affects the relevance of all our projects. At least in societies with our linear time perspective—as contrasted with societies in which time is viewed cyclically—increasing age lends new significance to the temporal ordering of lives because it increases awareness of impending death as the outer limit or boundary of our projects.

Just how aware are people of their finitude? How much do people think about death? about their own death? In an attempt to answer these questions, let us look first at the frequency of thoughts of death, then at estimates people make of their own life expectancy, and finally at the importance attached to such estimates.

Cameron, Stewart, and Biber (1973) report on a large set of studies of the everyday thoughts of people. The data were gathered from 4420 people, ranging in age from 8 to 99 years. The data-gathering situation was as close to natural as possible. A typical respondent might be approached in a supermarket or at a sports event with the questions: "What were you thinking about over the past five minutes? Did you think about death or dying—even for a moment? Did it perhaps cross your mind?" Respondents were also asked "For the last five minutes, what has been the central focus of your thought?" One of 14 possible ways to code the answers to the last question was "a personal problem-topic concerning death and dying." With these questions it is possible to classify respondents into three categories: (1) no thoughts of death, (2) "in-passing" thought of death, and (3) death as focal thought. The data are presented in Table 5-1.

The trends evident in this table were found in each of the age groups sampled. In almost every age group, a higher percentage of females than

TABLE 5-1. *Percentages Reporting In-Passing and Focal Consciousness about Death and Dying*

Age/Generation	8–11	12–13	14–15	16–17	18–25 Young Adults	26–39	40–55 Middle-aged	56–64	65 + Old	Total
In-passing thought										
Males *n*	108	159	127	86	576	488	398	102	86	2170
% engaged in	19	26	30	17	13	17	21	15	29	17
Females *n*	120	165	136	158	652	443	336	95	80	2250
% engaged in	24	34	28	27	18	21	21	27	38	23
Focal thought										
Males *n*	68	61	88	86	576	488	398	102	86	1953
% engaged in	6	0	3	5	1	3	2	1	6	3
Females *n*	68	73	109	158	652	443	366	95	80	2044
% engaged in	6	5	4	1	3	3	2	3	9	4

From "Consciousness of Death across the Life Span," by P. Cameron, L. Stewart, and H. Biber, *Journal of Gerontology*, 1973, 28(1), 92–95. Reprinted by permission.

males think more often, and more focally, about death. The highest focal thoughts occurred among those over 65. There is nothing to suggest a mid-life crisis of thoughts about death. On the other hand, "Death appears a frequent visitor to consciousness. Sex has been found to cross the mind with only somewhat greater frequency than death and dying for the life-span as a whole, and sex brushes consciousness less frequently than death and dying after middle age" (Cameron, Stewart, & Biber, 1973, p. 95).

Some investigators (Bengtson, Cuellar, & Ragan, 1977; Jeffers & Verwoerdt, 1970; Lowenthal et al., 1975, pp. 138–144) have asked direct retrospective questions about frequency of thoughts of death, and the studies suggest much less thinking about death than was found by Cameron and his colleagues.

In the national survey discussed in Chapter Four, Riley (1970) asked how often people thought about five topics, one of which was "the uncertainty of your own life or the death of someone close to you." Death thoughts were reported as coming "often" by 32% of the respondents, but this was the lowest of the five topical areas. By contrast, three-fourths reported thinking often about family health or financial responsibilities. Both age and education affect answers to this question, as can be seen in Table 5-2. Except for those with little education, increased age is associated with greater self-reported thinking about death. Increased education is associated with less thinking about death, but while this is a strong relationship for the young, it is less strong with increasing age.

TABLE 5-2. *Thinking about the Uncertainty of Life: Percentages, by Age and Education, of Persons Who Think Often about the Uncertainty of Their Own Life or the Death of Someone Close to Them*

Age	Education			
	Junior High School or Less	High School	College	"Effect" of Higher Education
30 and under	47	28	18	− 29
31–40	41	23	18	− 23
41–50	36	37	20	− 16
51–60	41	32	22	− 19
61 +	46	50	40	− 6
"Effect" of Older Age	− 1	+ 22	+ 22	

Note: The smallest base for any percentage is 45.

From *Aging and Society: An Inventory of Research Findings* (Vol. 1), by M. Riley and A. Foner. Copyright 1968 by the Russell Sage Foundation. Reprinted by permission.

Shneidman reports another large survey, which used a similar question and which appeared in *Psychology Today*. More than 30,000 readers returned a questionnaire that included the question "How often do you think about your own death?" Because of the selectivity of those who returned the questionnaire, the respondents approximate the young, well-educated respondents in the Riley study. More than half were under age 25, and only 14% had high school education or less (Shneidman, 1974). In this survey, 22% reported thinking about their own death very frequently or frequently, a figure roughly comparable to the 18%, in Riley's sample, aged 30 or under and college-educated who reported thinking about the uncertainty of life "often."

The same question was asked of more representative samples in two studies—one by Kalish and Reynolds and the other by Bengtson, Cuellar, and Ragan (see Chapter Four). In the Kalish and Reynolds study (1976, pp. 37–38, 203), one out of six respondents reported thinking of his or her own death at least daily, but one-fourth said that they never thought of their own death. One-half said that they thought of it no more than once a year. In line with much other research, Kalish and Reynolds found nonsignificant tendencies for older respondents and females to report more frequent thoughts of death. Blacks and Mexican Americans reported more death thoughts than did Japanese Americans and Anglo-Americans.

Bengtson, Cuellar, and Ragan's study covered a more restrictive age range, beginning at age 45 instead of age 20. Responses to the identical question were found *not* to vary systematically by age, sex, race, or socioeconomic status. In no group did the percentage of those thinking about their own death frequently exceed 20%. In general, both studies support the notion that old age is *not* associated with an inordinate or strongly increasing preoccupation with death.

One more limited survey in this area provides data consistent with these results and brings us closer to understanding them. Lowenthal, Thurnher, and Chiriboga (1975) interviewed people at four "stages" of the life span, ranging from high school seniors to people about to retire and asked "Do you ever find yourself thinking of death and dying?" They also asked "When are such thoughts likely to occur?" With a largely White, middle- and working-class sample, they found no differences by life stage or sex in frequency of thoughts of death. Roughly one-third of the respondents fell into each of the categories *infrequently, sometimes,* and *frequently.* However, the circumstances in which people said they thought of death did vary by life stage and sex. Men and women in the middle life stage (mean age 50) and men in the preretirement stage were most likely to say that they thought about death when they were ill. Women in the preretirement stage, however, were most likely to report thinking about death when others close to them died (pp. 138–142).

In summary, preoccupation with death seems either to be unrelated to age or to rise only somewhat in the later years. However, great differences occur between Cameron's results and those of the retrospective studies that employed a longer time span. Kalish and Reynolds (1976) quote one respondent: "One does think about death, but doesn't remember how often" (p. 38). Cameron, Stewart, and Biber (1973) argue that "people apparently think about death *far* more frequently than they estimate that they think about it" (p. 95). Since, according to the research they cite, this is apparently not the case with the topic of sex, they suggest that death must be more strongly tabooed in our society than sex is (see Gorer, 1965b). This may be called the *taboo hypothesis* and is perhaps consistent with the psychoanalytic interpretations we considered in Chapter Four.

Work is emerging that suggests an alternative explanation based on cohort, or generational, effects. Guptill (1976 and personal communication) reports preliminary findings from a community survey that sought to scale seven items concerning "thoughts of dying." In general, a measure based on a scale score is considered superior to one based on a single indicator. Guptill reports that thoughts of dying are lowest for those who are old and also for those who subjectively define themselves as old. Guptill (1976) raises the possibility of a cohort explanation for his findings: "A number of attitudes characteristic of the young are correlated with high scores . . . while attitudes characteristic of older people are correlated with low scores." Highest thoughts-of-dying scores are correlated with low religiosity, greater cosmopolitanism, and liberalism, all of which are inversely correlated with age. As Guptill (1976) notes, "It may be that chronological age is not as important a variable in determining who is concerned with dying as these other independent variables." Since these correlated attitudes are largely artifacts of cohort differences, although they are partially related to aging in some instances, we can call this a *cohort interpretation.*

Yet another explanation becomes possible by examining additional data from the Riley (1970) national survey. Riley asked this follow-up question: "Under what circumstances are you most likely to think about death?" He reports: "The overwhelming majority report that they are stimulated to think about death under three personal circumstances: an accident or a 'near-miss,' a serious illness, or the death of someone significant to them" (p. 35). This may be called the *situational interpretation.* Although thinking about death is situational, the situations described occur more frequently with advancing age. Illness and the death of others especially occur much more frequently in the later years. Recall the findings by Lowenthal et al. (1975) about the importance of illness and death of associates as situations leading to thoughts of death and their findings that the importance of these situations also differed by life stage.

The importance of situational variables in stimulating thoughts of death in turn suggests that death may come to prominence in consciousness when it is problematical but then it may recede in prominence. That is, certain circumstances may lead an individual to become temporarily troubled about the prospect of dying. The person may then become preoccupied with death as he or she attempts to make sense of death and dying and come to terms with it. Once the prospect of eventual death has been dealt with and made meaningful, attention may return to other aspects of life.

In this view, our thoughts tend to focus on any aspect of our lives that we are not able to take for granted. This may be called the *problematic interpretation*. It suggests that age-related situations lead to cognitive work to make sense of the newly relevant fact of mortality. There should therefore be a certain age-related focusing on death. Although preoccupation with death need not continue once the individual has made sense of it, most research techniques will mask the coming into and receding from consciousness of thoughts of death. We, in fact, know next to nothing of the age-relatedness of thoughts of death (for additional discussion of this topic, see Bengtson et al., 1977; Kalish & Reynolds, 1976, pp. 37–38; Marshall, in press). This may well be because of an undue focus on age as the explanatory variable.

The importance of situations, especially life-threatening ones, in evoking thoughts of death has not been adequately studied (Giambra, 1977b). The problematic interpretation of the concern with impending death is superior to the others discussed, because it allows for the incorporation of the taboo, cohort, and situational interpretations. On theoretical grounds we might wish to examine the relationship between age-related and unrelated life events and thoughts about death. The relevance of such thoughts presumably is influenced by something that is partially correlated with age—the estimates people make about how long they have to live.

Not a great deal of research has been done on the estimates people make of their own life expectancy. As noted in Chapter Two, both the causes and the timing of death are much better understood, and therefore much more predictable, today than they were in former times. In our society some specialists, such as actuaries, make it their business to predict the life expectancy of others, employing the life-table method referred to in Chapter Two. Medical doctors and other health-care personnel make predictions about the timing of death itself and about various career stages in the dying process (Glaser & Strauss, 1968; Sudnow, 1967, Chap. 4). Questions about life expectancy for individuals and groups become relevant in some legal areas. For example, judgments about settlements for lost earnings or lifetime financial support for accident victims can necessitate making estimates of life expectancy (Cain, 1978). These estimates are made more difficult by the lack of direct relationship between the life expectancy of any given individual and the statistical life expectancy for a group. For the same reason, physicians are reluctant to give specific answers to questions about how long a patient might live, since, even if the average life expectancy for patients with similar characteristics is known, there are no guarantees that any individual case will conform to the statistical norm.

One of the few studies in which a representative sample has been asked how long they expected to live is the multi-ethnic research of Kalish and

Reynolds (1976; Reynolds & Kalish, 1974). These investigators also asked how long people desired to live. Two theoretical approaches were used to interpret the findings. Disengagement theory would suggest that highly engaged individuals anticipate living a long life and desire to do so. An alternative interpretation suggests that individuals employ a kind of folk life-table method and that enough people "are aware of their own prognoses that respondent estimates would come reasonably close to actuarial predictions" (Reynolds & Kalish, 1974, p. 225). Other research in this area (Marshall, 1973a) shows that respondents tend to use ages ending in 0 or 5 when projecting how long they will live. The median age to which all respondents anticipated living was 75; the median age to which all desired to live was 80. Increasing age is associated with higher estimates on both of these dimensions. In the present discussion we will focus on the estimated life expectancy; desired life expectancy will be treated in Chapter Seven.

Although women have a higher life expectancy than men, Kalish and Reynolds' male respondents on the average anticipated living slightly longer than women, representing a clear departure from a life-table calculation but supportive of the "engagement" hypothesis, if the assumption that men are more highly engaged than women over most segments of the life cycle is valid (and many will doubtless question its validity).

Black respondents expected to live longer than did those of the other ethnic groups (Japanese Americans, Mexican Americans, and White Americans). With a mean age of 46, the Black American sample anticipated living an additional 33 years on the average, and 31% anticipated living past the age of 90. The White American sample, with a mean age of 48, anticipated living an additional 26 years on the average, and only 17% anticipated living past the age of 90 (Reynolds & Kalish, 1974, p. 227). This highly significant racial difference is additional evidence that people do not employ accurate life-table or actuarial procedures in estimating life expectancy, since Blacks cannot expect to live as long as Whites (see Table 2-1 in Chapter Two for a life table). Bengtson, Cuellar, and Ragan (1977) found the same patterning by race and sex in their Los Angeles study.

Before leaving these data, we should return to the age pattern. Reynolds and Kalish divided their sample into three major age groupings, splitting them at age 40 and age 60. Those who were older expected to live to the oldest age. This is understandable by life-table logic. However, a larger proportion of the youngest than of the middle group anticipated living beyond age 90; or, conversely, those in the middle-age category were least likely to anticipate living beyond age 90. They were also less likely to want to live that long.

Reynolds and Kalish suggest that this departure from life-table logic "must reflect psychosocial processes." They speculate that "although the elderly are willing to die sooner than middle-aged and younger persons, they do not want to die *soon*. Therefore, in moving the time of death sufficiently far away from their present age, many of them move it in to the 90 plus period" (p. 230). By this reasoning, it is not highly threatening for the middle-aged person to anticipate dying before age 90: there are many years before that age. With increasing age, the anticipated age of death is advanced not only by virtue of an actuarial-table kind of logic but also as a defense against the fear of death.

This interpretation does not, however, square with the general finding (see Chapter Four), repeated in the Reynolds and Kalish study, of decreased overt or verbalized fear of death with increasing age or with the findings that Blacks verbalized less fear of death than did members of the other ethnic groups in this study. Reynolds and Kalish, therefore, conclude that fear of death has no effect on expectation of life or, for that matter, on desired life expectancy. In summary, Reynolds and Kalish do not find a satisfactory explanation for the estimation of life expectancy in disengagement theory or in the speculation that individuals use a kind of life-table logic.

Marshall (1975b) suggests that the formation of estimates of life expectancy, or awareness of finitude, can be understood by drawing on social-comparison theory (Festinger, 1954). According to this theory, when objective criteria are not readily available for assessing opinions or abilities, individuals tend to compare themselves with other people similar to themselves. Age is important as a cue to similarity and is therefore important in estimating life expectancy, but cues also operate in important ways within the context of the family.

Marshall's sample had an average age of 80 and an age range of 64 to 96. Using three age groups within this older sample and three life-expectancy categories, he found a significant and strong age correlation. Half the respondents aged 75 or less anticipated living ten years or more, and only 7% anticipated living less than five years. At the other extreme, half of those over 85 anticipated living less than five years, and only 10% thought they would live ten or more years. This middle-class White sample was somewhat less expansive in its estimates than the much larger sample studied by Reynolds and Kalish.

An even stronger predictor of awareness of finitude was a variable constructed by comparing the respondent's own age to the age-at-death of his or her parents. The way in which this crude calculus works is illustrated in the words of a 65-year-old respondent: "Up to now no men in my family have lived past 70. But a brother is going to be 72. But both parents died at 70. They say you die according to when your parents died" (Marshall, 1975b, p. 119). Of Marshall's respondents whose own age had exceeded the age-at-death of both parents, 64% anticipated living less than five years, whereas 46% of those who were still younger than the age-at-death of both parents expected to live ten years or more. The relationship is sustained at least partially independently of age.

Marshall also found that the more sibling deaths experienced by a respondent, the less time he or she anticipated living. Although this relationship is not significantly independent of age, it suggests one of the ways in which age acts to remind an individual that death is drawing near. Moreover, that social-comparison processes are involved is evident from the fact that the deaths of same-sex siblings have a greater effect than cross-sex deaths. That is, a woman is more likely to reduce her estimate of life expectancy if she has a dead sister than if she has a dead brother, and a man is more likely to reduce his estimate if he has a dead brother than a dead sister.

Other factors that affect an individual's awareness of finitude are, as might be expected, self-perceived health and the death of friends. As one respondent said, "When you are up in the sixties and see all your friends around you going, you say 'When am I due?'"

Other life experiences may affect estimates of life expectancy. In an economically insecure group of young men, many of whom were involved in hazardous jobs, Teahan and Kastenbaum (1970; Kastenbaum, 1977, p. 149) found that a large proportion anticipated not only early but also violent deaths for themselves.

In both the Reynolds and Kalish (1974; Kalish & Reynolds, 1976) and the Marshall (1975b) research, large proportions of respondents either could not or would not estimate how long they anticipated living. Chappell (1975) distinguishes the estimate of time left from the meaning of that time. With a sample of long-term hospital patients over the age of 60, she asked respondents direct questions about anticipated and desired life expectancy. She received from 42.5% to 82.5% "don't know" or nonspecific responses to four indicators. Only 17.5% gave specific answers to the direct question "How old do you think you'll live to be?" and only 20% specified how old they would like to live to be.

Chappell argues that these responses do not indicate a lack of knowledge about the imminency of death but, rather, that such knowledge is irrelevant to many of her respondents. Less than 18% of her respondents said they were afraid to die, and only 12.5% said that death would come "too soon" for them (compare with data in Table 4-2). Answers to these questions about life expectancy in Chappell's study and to the ones asked in the Riley survey (1970; see Chapter Four) did not correlate with indicators of expected or desired life expectancy. This finding is consistent with that of Reynolds and Kalish (1974) discussed earlier and also with findings by Bengtson, Cuellar, and Ragan (1977). Chappell, by using several questions, found most of her respondents "ready to die." Since these respondents were institutionalized and almost certain to die in that hospital, they had little to plan for, and therefore it did not really matter very much exactly how long they might live. A similar view that the move to the institution is the last significant change in the lives of the institutionalized aged is found in Tobin and Lieberman (1976, pp. 49–53).

Age, then, is not the only factor to take into account in seeking to understand awareness of finitude. In general, thoughts of death increase with age, and people become more aware that their time is running out. This awareness is highly situational, and, we have seen, the situation is only partially determined by age. "The assessment of one's own life duration is probably a composite, based on at least such factors as one's estimate of normative (actuarial) data, defensiveness against death anxiety, experiences with death in family members or in close friends, the attitudes of family toward death and dying, and relative position in the family" (Tolor & Murphy, 1967, p. 21). Since awareness of finitude is variable and situational, we will do well to focus on these aspects as we consider its consequences.

People may be variously aware of finitude and the mortality of humankind as an abstract issue or as a philosophical problem. We have seen that the level of abstraction of this recognition is under some, partially age-related, circumstances reduced and that the individual comes to a realization of personal mortality and finitude. Erikson and some other scholars believe this comes as a profound realization, an existential crisis of sorts, or an "ego chill" (Erikson, 1958; Leveton, 1966). This is a clinical observation, and we do not know how general it is. The realization of death may be gradual in some cases and virtually nonexistent in other, rare cases.

In any event, in the typical case we may be sure that the realization of finitude intimately binds together self and death. The self becomes the self-as-mortal, or the self-as-dying. The hyphenations that link these terms create a new reality for the individual, and this reality offers the possibility and the challenge of sense making. While our interest is in the self-as-dying, most theoretical approaches in the social psychology of aging and dying focus on the efforts of individuals to make sense of self rather than to make sense of dying. Making sense of self is seen as preparatory for the good death. I will address this position in the remainder of this chapter, postponing consideration of making sense of dying until Chapter Seven. We should remember that separating "self" and "dying" is a useful analytical device, which should not, however, mask their fundamental unity.

Awareness of Finitude
and Legitimation
of Biography

On recognizing that the time left before death is short, the aging individual faces the enormous task of making sense of himself or herself as dying. We may analytically divide this task into the two components of making sense of self and making sense of dying.

Metaphorically, aging individuals come to see themselves in autobiographical perspective. They see the chapters of their life unfolding, and the heightened awareness of finitude that generally accompanies later life brings them into the last chapter. As their autobiography draws to its ending in death, they want their story to be a "good" one, not necessarily a story of success, happiness, fame, and the like, but a story that "makes sense," that is meaningful. I will refer to the process of making sense of the self in this way as *legitimation of biography*. This metaphor of the individual taking an autobiographical view of his or her life can help us understand the heightened concern with the self, or interiority, postulated by theorists discussed in Chapter Four as developing in middle age and the heightened reflection on the self in the life-review process of the disengaging individual (Butler, 1963; Havighurst, Neugarten, & Tobin, 1968; Rosen & Neugarten, 1964).

Autobiography is ideally suited for developing a view of one's life as legitimate, because it is *selective:*

> The person who seeks the connective threads in the history of his life has already, from different points of view, created a coherence in that life. . . . He has created it by experiencing values and realizing purposes in his life, making plans for it, seeing his past in terms of development and his future as the shaping of his life. . . . He has, in his memory, singled out and accentuated the moments which he experienced as significant; others he has allowed to sink into forgetfulness [Dilthey, 1962, p. 86].

Myerhoff emphasizes the value of autobiography in developing and maintaining a sense of identity:

> The search for the sense and meaning which continuity bestows is fundamental to serious autobiographical work, and in this task no audience is necessary but the writer himself, who becomes subject and object at the same time. Self-reflection then becomes self-creation verify, expressive of the powerful human impulse to order [1978, p. 174].

The process by which autobiographical work is done is the process of *reflection,* which, whether done alone or with others, is a fundamentally social process (Mead, 1934b, p. 357; 1964). Reflection occurs throughout life and is the way in which the self is created. Our concern, however, is with the possibility of intensive reflection in response to awareness of finitude. Evidence in this area can be found in studies of the importance given to the self and in studies of reminiscence. Interpreting these studies is made more difficult by the fact that they have almost never been conducted in relation to awareness of finitude. Instead, investigators have commonly assumed that age can substitute directly as an indicator of awareness of finitude.

Another interpretive problem is that both self-focusing and reminiscence—a way of self-focusing—serve numerous functions. However, self-focusing and reminiscence do not necessarily imply any *developmental* relationship in response to heightened awareness of finitude. For example, the selectivity and adaptive characteristics of memory have long been recognized (see, for example, Bartlett, 1967; Hall, 1898; Schactel, 1947). Havighurst and Glasser (1972) maintain that reminiscence occurs at all ages beyond age 10. Thinking about the past may be an escape from an unpleasant present (May,

1967; McMahon & Rhudick, 1964); it may bring amusement and pleasure (Liton & Olstein, 1969); or it may be used as part of a problem-solving process (Mead, 1964), especially in times of stress or crisis (Falk, 1970; Lewis, 1971; Tobin & Etigson, 1968). Social reminiscence may be little more than a vehicle for expressing sociability (Lewis, 1971; Liton & Olstein, 1969; McMahon & Rhudick, 1964); it may allow individuals to make status claims by reminding others of previous accomplishments (McMahon & Rhudick, 1964); or it may perhaps, especially in nonliterate societies, be a vehicle for teaching (Coleman, 1974; McMahon & Rhudick, 1964).

Reminiscence may serve more than one function at a time, whether the functions are recognized or not. Thus, reminiscence may be useful in helping to create a sense of self as continuous in time, in enhancing self-esteem through identifying the present situation with a highly valued past, and in making status claims that invoke positive reactions from others, while at the same time selectively utilizing stored memories and vocabularies to render the past meaningful.

Our own interest, however, is in the adaptive functions of reminiscence in reintegrating the self, in legitimating biography. This is a concern with identity, with maintaining a sense of continuity of the self or selves, over time. As Mischel (1969) argues, "The experience of subjective continuity in ourselves—of basic oneness and durability in the self—is perhaps the most compelling and fundamental feature of personality. This experience of continuity seems to be an intrinsic feature of the mind, and the loss of a sense of felt consistency may be a chief characteristic of personality disorganization" (p. 1012).

Let us now consider the question of timing, about which there is little agreement (Back, 1976; Troll, 1975, pp. 64–65). Turner (1975) analyzed responses from a large community sample in Los Angeles and from college-student samples in Los Angeles, Australia, and England to this question: "These days we sometimes hear people say: 'I don't know who I really am.' Do *you* often, sometimes, or never ask yourself 'Who am I really?'" Responses for 996 persons in the Los Angeles sample are given in Table 5-3, broken down by age and education. The college-student samples provide data consistent with the Los Angeles data for well-educated young people. Turner concludes that "only a minority of students are unconcerned with the question of identity. . . . An overwhelming majority of university students acknowledges a personal quest for identity, in striking contrast to an overwhelming majority of the general adult population who deny any such quest . . . we are mistaken whenever we generalize from the university to the general population" (1975, p. 153).

Specifically addressing the postulate of an increased preoccupation with identity in later life, Turner notes that, with the exception of the grade-school educated, there is an inverse relationship between age and such preoccupation rather than the theoretically predicted upsurge in such concerns in the

TABLE 5-3. *Percentages, by Age and Education, of Persons Who Often or Sometimes Ask "Who Am I Really?"*

Age	Grade School	High School	College	Total
18–29	13.3	30.6	39.2	33.7
30–39	9.1	21.1	20.8	20.3
40–49	0.0	13.6	19.8	14.7
50–59	14.3	4.8	7.8	7.1
60+	3.3	3.8	5.7	4.3
Total	5.8	16.8	22.6	

Note: Total number for table is 121. Marginal frequencies not given.

From "Is There a Quest for Identity?" by R. Turner, *The Sociological Quarterly*, 1975, *16*(2), 148–161. Copyright 1975 by Southern Illinois University. Reprinted by permission.

middle or later years. For those with only grade-school education, a concern for identity increases in the fifties; however, 14.3% is the peak in such concern for those with little education. Turner (1975) speculates that this finding might indicate that aging is a greater crisis for the undereducated, or it might point to "the historical failure of self-definition for the undereducated who came of age in the Depression years" (p. 152). This suggests a cohort effect for those who suffered most during the Depression; but in addition to that effect, educational effects persist independently from and less strongly than the effects of age.

When asked how one discovers the self, most adults endorsed items saying that self-discovery comes through working at difficult and challenging tasks and through helping others, in contrast to responses suggesting less institutionalized methods, such as overcoming inhibitions or revealing deep feelings to others (see also Turner, 1976). There was a slight tendency for this pattern to peak in the fifties, falling off slightly in the sixties. This may indicate declining achievement involvements with age and not necessarily a reluctance to reveal the self to others.

Even if these findings reflect aging rather than cohort effects, they are hardly supportive of the argument for any important mid-life crisis (Gould, 1978; Levinson et al., 1978). The sample size is quite small, with particularly important implications following from the inability to differentiate by age beyond age 60. While Turner's data provide some reason to doubt the existence of a mid-life crisis, they do not allow us to conclude anything about changes that might occur after age 60.

The theoretical approaches reviewed in Chapter Four suggest that the processes I call *legitimation of biography* may begin to intensify as early as the thirties (see, for example, Jacques, 1970; Jung, 1933; Levinson et al., 1978) or sometime vaguely in mid-life (Cumming & Henry, 1961, pp. 224–227), perhaps in the forties (Neugarten, 1966). Butler (1963), on the other hand, suggests that "the life review is more commonly observed in the aged because of the actual nearness of life's termination—and perhaps also because during retirement not only is time available for self-reflection, but also the customary defensive operation provided by work has been removed" (p. 67). When we are busily engaged in the world of work, we may be too wrapped up in activities involving the present to focus on our mortality. However, Butler notes that the process of the life review has been observed in younger persons who anticipate death, such as the fatally ill or the condemned. In fact, it must be stressed that Butler suggests that the life-review process is initiated by the recognition that time is limited because of mortality.

Disengagement theory also postulates awareness of finitude and not age as the initiator of disengagement; and awareness of finitude is also the source of the eighth identity crisis for Erikson (Marshall, 1975b). However, since almost no research has tested these theories directly in relation to awareness of finitude, we shall have to content ourselves, for the most part, with using age as a proxy measure. That is, most investigators assume that older people give themselves less time to live and are therefore more aware of finitude than are younger people.

Whether prompted by age or by awareness of finitude, the weight of the evidence forces the conclusion that the kinds of self-focused legitimation of biography discussed by these theorists occur *primarily in later life and not in mid-life*. Nydegger (1976), commenting on four different research studies on aspects of middle age, concludes that "there is no support in these studies for a crisis interpretation of midlife as *typical*. This is not to deny the existence of such crises in individual lives, but we are cautioned against hasty assumptions about their frequency or typicality" (p. 138). One of these reports (Thurnher, 1976) is from the San Francisco life-transitions study (Lowenthal & Chiriboga, 1972; Chiriboga & Thurnher, 1975); the other three reports are from the Berkeley longitudinal studies (Clausen, 1976; Haan, 1976; Livson, 1976).

In the San Francisco life-transitions study, responses to a checklist of adjectives describing the self indicated a generally more positive self-concept with the four successive life stages studied (the oldest being preretirement). At the same time, the conception of self seemed more restrictive, or "de-energized," and indicative of psychological disengagement (Chiriboga & Thurnher, 1975, p. 64)—a development that others have also found to begin at least as early as the late fifties (Havighurst, Neugarten, & Tobin, 1963/1968; Rosen & Neugarten, 1964).

Differences were found in the developmental patterns of men and women. Men differed more from stage to stage than did women, and the differences were generally in accord with the developmental theories noted in the previous chapter and with disengagement theory (Chiriboga & Thurnher, 1975, p. 67). The data suggest no typical mid-life crisis. Over these four life stages, generally men were found to have self-images that became more crystallized and less diffuse. Women, in contrast, had relatively unchanging self-images over the four stages, but these self-images reflected greater ambiguity and uncertainty than ultimately developed in the men (Chiriboga & Thurnher, 1975, p. 80).

When the research design of a project specifies sampling by "life stages," the likelihood of finding no differences by life stage is quite minimal. The authors are, of course, sensitive to the possibility that any stage differences they find might in fact be cohort differences. In any case, it is very important that, in almost all dimensions studied, sex differences were found to be more important than stage differences. As we noted earlier in this chapter, there were no stage differences in frequency of death thoughts, and this was a rare case in which there were neither sex differences nor stage differences in the frequency of death thoughts (Chiriboga & Gigy, 1975, p. 139).

If a very complex study may be summarized briefly, the data from the transitions study would seem to place the beginnings of legitimation of biography in the sixties and to suggest that the process is marked more by continuity than by crisis. Until the respondents have been studied into their seventies, it is impossible to say whether this rather limited legitimation process will intensify.

The Berkeley studies rely on two longitudinal research projects that began gathering data on people who were children in the late 1920s and early 1930s. These are the Berkeley Guidance Study and the Oakland Growth Study (see Elder, Jr., 1974). Subject attrition and the characteristics of the respondents combined to produce a current subject pool of relatively advantaged respondents who tend to be unusually upwardly mobile (Clausen, 1976). Occupational satisfaction among the men was generally high, and there is evidence that many of them lowered their aspirations between their late thirties and age 50. Women on the whole show few differences in personality, except that women who have worked but are no longer working are less happy on a variety of measures than those who either are still working or have never worked and do not desire to work (Clausen, 1976). For both men and women, family life is important as a source of intimacy. Clausen (1976) summarizes these studies as follows: "The dominant impression derived from our examination of the occupational and family histories of our subjects during the middle years is one of continuity and stability. . . . Few give any indication of a mid-life crisis or crisis of middle-age, though their lives are certainly not free of tension and uncertainty" (p. 106).

Focusing on women from one of the two studies, Livson (1976) found that "middle age can loosen the boundaries of one's life style" (p. 114). This finding allows either continuity or growth, but does not suggest great turmoil or crisis in mid-life.

Haan (1976) assessed cohort differences in self-concept as measured by the Q-sort technique. She found that, for respondents aged 60–75, "importance is given to the preservation of the self's integrity and integration." However, she concludes: "These results do not indicate that the older are passive, disengaged, constricted, or depressed, although they certainly are less striving. The grandparents seem engaged, but in gentle ways that are sensitive to other's needs and conserving of their own integrity" (p. 126).

Findings regarding self-focusing in relation to the eighth identity crisis are similar. Neugarten, Crotty, and Tobin (1964) were able to characterize only a small proportion of their sample as having "integrity," in an operationalization of Erikson's concept, and they found those who were characterized as having integrity to range from ages 56 to 90. This finding led them to suggest greater continuity between middle and old age than is postulated in Erikson's terms.

Commenting on a summary report of the Kansas City research conducted by the University of Chicago researchers (Neugarten, 1973) and on a report of the San Francisco transitions study (Lowenthal & Chiriboga, 1973), as well as on studies of intellectual and cognitive capacities over the life course, Schaie (1973) argues that "the common theme of the chapters . . . is the apparent absence of convincing findings on the nature of developmental processes in adulthood and the observation that directionality of changes is in considerable doubt" (p. 151). We might add that it is something of a tribute to the honesty and rigor of these groups of developmental researchers that they present clear evidence capable of refuting their general theoretical approach. And, yet, not only developmental *change* but also developmental *crisis* is postulated, especially perhaps in versions of developmental psychology directed to lay audiences.

We must distinguish personality change from crisis. As Troll (1975, p. 64) indicates, almost all writers in this area point to significant changes in personality and self-concept in mid-life; but psychoanalytically inclined writers are more likely to see these changes as crises. Whether a change or transition is experienced as a crisis depends partially on whether it is anticipated. "If the expectations associated with an event are clear and the individual possesses sufficient resources to meet the expectations, there usually is no adult life crisis" (Albrecht & Gift, 1975, p. 239). No event is therefore automatically a crisis; whether it is depends on the context and on the meaning given the event by the person experiencing it.

Breytspraak (1974; Breytspraak & George, in press) distinguishes between affective and cognitive dimensions of self-concept. Age-related changes in middle age may lead to a shift away from the ideal self-concept one previously possessed. Breytspraak measured ideal/actual discrepancy in self-concept using the semantic-differential technique and the affective component by a shortened version of the Affect Balance Scale (Bradburn & Caplovitz, 1965). By combining these measures, four self-concept types were produced. However, not only were incongruities frequently found between actual and ideal selves in middle and later life; but incongruities were frequently associated with *positive* affect. Persons with a high discrepancy between ideal and actual self are able to maintain high satisfaction about themselves if they feel that they have resources available for meeting goals. People may be able to tolerate more change or discontinuity than many theories would suggest.

Corroboration for this view, as well as additional insight about the timing of the life-review process, comes from the San Francisco transitions study, which, unfortunately, extends only through the preretirement stage. Thurnher (1974) points out that critical life reviews occur not only in very late life and that they also probably accompany all critical life transitions. "Self-appraisals among women, whether working or not, set in at the period considered normative for the completion of the family cycle; for men they occur at the termination of their occupational careers" (p. 91). These appraisals were found not to affect the morale of empty-nest men, presumably because, Thurnher argues, they could still anticipate correcting past deficits. Women, having invested much of themselves in family, do not have this opportunity.

Leonard Giambra provides a series of research reports on daydreaming that have relevance for both self-focusing and reminiscence. He found that the frequency of daydreaming of any kind declines with age, except for a slight increase in daydreamers in the age range 24–34 (1974). Using factor analysis with data from a questionnaire, he distinguished five different daydreaming-temperament styles but found only one of these to be age related. This was a factor called *neurotic-anxious absorption in daydreaming,* and it was found much less frequently in the later years than in the earlier ones (Giambra, 1977a).

Age differences on two direct questions are of particular importance for understanding reminiscence and the time orientation of everyday thoughts. Respondents were asked "How true is the statement, 'I seldom find myself daydreaming about my younger days'?" There were great age differences in the response categories. Males between the ages of 17 and 34 indicated that they sometimes daydreamed about their younger days much more often than did those between the ages of 35 and 64. The percentage saying that the statement was definitely or usually *not* true rose from 38% for those aged 55–64 to 47% for those aged 65–74 and, dramatically, to 61% for those aged 75–91. These data suggest that active reminiscence in this sample seemed to be most important in the later years, beyond age 75. Also, active reminiscence seemed to be least important in the years of the so-called mid-life crisis (ages 35–44), during which no one described the statement as "definitely not true" and 42% described it as "usually not true."

The other side of this coin is found in responses to the statement "I find myself imagining what I will be doing a year from now." The oldest respondents (ages 75–91) are most likely (29%) to say that the statement is definitely not true. However, the age differences are quite small if the "definitely not true" and "usually not true" categories are combined. There is, therefore, only a slight tendency for those in the later years of old age to retreat from thinking about the future.

In a related study (Giambra, 1977b), women were added to this sample. Sex differences were not appreciable in most instances. Past-oriented daydreams did not increase with age for either sex. Future-oriented daydreams were negatively correlated, although modestly, with age for both sexes; but there was little age-related change beyond age 30. These findings still left open the possibility that the *balance* of thoughts of past, present, and future might change over the range of ages. Therefore, a "difference score" was calculated for each respondent, giving the difference between past/present daydreaming and past/future daydreaming. When the past is compared with the present, middle-aged respondents are least likely to emphasize the past and there is a slight tendency for both sexes to emphasize the past over the present in the 70 + age category.

When the balance of past versus future daydreaming is measured, there is a reasonably strong tendency in both sexes to emphasize the past over the future with increasing age. Females in the 70 + category were found to emphasize the past over the future much more strongly than people of either sex in any age category. Three single items allowing an assessment of thoughts about the *distant* past (which would more directly test Butler's theory), asked about events that happened more than a year ago, about daydreams involving people and places that the person was familiar with when younger, and about events from childhood. Only extremely modest correlations suggested that the early past becomes increasingly important with advancing age, giving only modest support to the life-review theory, if that theory is tested using age as the criterion.

Giambra (1977b) suggests that future work in this area should assess the life-span location of thoughts in relation to life events other than age itself, including the expectation of death. He does not, however, acknowledge that Butler's theory explicitly suggests that reminiscence is heightened in relationship not to age but to the expectation of death. His work, therefore, fails to disconfirm life-review theory and may indeed be thought of as supporting Butler's theory of the importance of expectation of death.

The Process of Legitimation

Like the studies spanning the life cycle, those that focus on older respondents have also tended to obscure the question of timing of legitimation of biography by using age instead of awareness of finitude as the independent variable. For example, Coleman (1974), Gorney (1968), and Linn (1973) failed to find systematic age differences in the timing of life-review or reminiscence processes. With the same general study population as Gorney, Falk claimed that "the findings do not support theories postulating the universal task of life reviewing occurring with the approach of death" (Falk, 1970, p.

124). However, Falk used *actual* distance from death, not self-perceived life expectancy, and she concedes: "It may be that theory and findings are not contradictory. The original perception that the self is mortal may act to heighten reminiscence activity" (1970, p. 108).

Because, as noted in Chapter Four, awareness of finitude is strongly correlated with age but not fully indexed by it, studies of reminiscence or self-focusing in relation to age can never adequately test theories that see awareness of finitude as initiator of legitimation of biography. In addition, it is crucially important to consider legitimation of biography as a process and not simply as a *state*.

Seen in this light, Gorney's findings are consistent with Butler's theorizing that the process is transitory; that is, in response to awareness of finitude, reminiscence is heightened. Once the work of reminiscence has been completed, and past conflicts have been integrated, the intensity of reminiscence decreases (Gorney, 1968).

It is also important that reminiscence in the life-review process is distinguishable from daydreaming or thoughts of the past in general or from other forms of reminiscence that do not focus on making sense of past conflicts (a point clearly made by Coleman, 1974, and Boylin, Gordon, and Nehrke, 1976). The pattern of reminiscence in relation to awareness of finitude may well differ from the pattern of other forms of self-focusing or time perspective in relation to age or to other events such as stress (Tallmer & Kutner, 1969; Tobin & Lieberman, 1976). It is essential to recognize that, as a preparation for death, reminiscence will phase in and out as biography is legitimated. A good example is a rare study using measures of various dimensions of reminiscence in conjunction with measures of the final three of Erikson's identity stages with a sample of 41 elderly (mean age 64) Veterans Administration hospital patients (Boylin, Gordon, & Nehrke, 1976).

Significant correlations were reported between frequency of reminiscence and ego integrity but not, in the earlier stages, resolution; and a negative correlation was found between affect toward the memories and ego integrity. That is, people who could be classified as high in ego integrity were, in fact, actively reminiscing but reported that the remembered events were unpleasant. This finding contrasts with Havighurst and Glasser's (1972) finding of a positive correlation between frequency of reminiscence and positive affect concerning the memories. The authors correctly note that Butler emphasized the life-review process as a calling to consciousness of past *conflicts*, and they add:

> It may be that the elderly men in the present sample were in the process of achieving ego integrity through this evaluative approach. . . . With time, they might achieve higher scores on ego integrity and a less critical attitude toward their past, as unpleasant experiences and conflicts become accepted and perhaps treated more favorably [1976, p. 123].

In research by the present author (Marshall, 1973a, 1975b), data on reminiscence processes were gathered in relation to awareness of finitude, and they are consistent with the interpretation of Boylin, Gordon, and Nehrke (1976). Like other research in the area, this study was based on a limited sample, and the design was cross-sectional rather than longitudinal. The age range was 64 to 96, with a mean age of 80, and the 69 respondents were middle-class retirement-village dwellers. The significance of this research, however, lies in its use of awareness of finitude as a variable influencing legitimation of biography and in its view of reminiscence as both an individual and a social process.

Awareness of finitude was assessed by a direct, fixed-choice question yielding three categories of anticipated years remaining until death. Over the course of three hour-long interviews, a number of questions were asked about time perspective and the importance of memories, and respondents were given a reminiscence task. Following a question concerning their earliest memory, respondents were asked "Looking back, what do you think were the periods of major change—the turning points in your life?" Probing was attempted in an effort to elicit five turning points. For each response, additional questions were asked about the person's age at that time, the perceived importance, and whether the change was for the better or the worse. An additional coding was subsequently made to show whether the event was viewed as self-initiated or as impinging on the person from the outer world—a distinction based on Rotter's (1966) conception of internal versus external control.

In answer to a direct question, the majority of respondents reported attributing high importance to their memories. There was a slight but nonsignificant tendency for memories to be reported as more important for people who anticipated living between five and ten years than for those who anticipated living either longer than or less than five years. Only 5% of respondents who anticipated living between five and ten years said that their memories were not important. The differences are small but lend modest support to Gorney's interpretation (1968) that willingness to introspect on the past is a transitional phase in relation to anticipated life expectancy.

Additional evidence suggests that individualized or personal reminiscence is most intense for people who anticipate living five to ten more years. Those respondents were most likely to disagree with the statement "My memories are the most important thing I own," presumably because during active reminiscence their memories were filled with conflict. The data appear in Table 5-4. During the middle awareness period, the person is also more likely to report disappointments concerning the past life and less likely to express satisfaction with the past life as a whole or a desire to live life over again, if it were to be the same.

Whereas thinking about the past seems most intense and affect-laden during the middle awareness period, talking about the past with others is most frequent when the respondent anticipates living less than five years (see Table

TABLE 5-4.   *Selected Indicators of Reminiscence in Relation to Awareness of Finitude*

| | Awareness of Finitude: Respondent Anticipates Living an Additional | | | |
	Ten or More Years %	Five to Ten Years %	Less than Five Years %	
a. "Right now my memories are the most important thing I own."				
Agree	14	10	36	
Disagree	86	90	64	
Total	100	100	100	
n =	14	20	14	48
Tau C = −.177; sign. = .038				
b. "Do you often *talk* about things that have happened in your past life with anybody else?"				
At least once a week	36	32	62	
Less frequently	64	68	39	
Total	100	100	101	
n =	14	19	13	46
Tau C = −.208; sign. = .020				

Note: Number available for cross-tabulation varies because not all respondents answered all questions.

From "Age and Awareness of Finitude in Developmental Gerontology," by V. W. Marshall, *Omega*, 1975, *6*(2), 113–129. Reprinted by permission.

5-4). It is not possible from these cross-sectional data to discover just why this is the case. Intense personal reminiscence may lead to successful completion of the life review and to a view of one's life that approaches Erikson's concept of "integrity"; this success, in turn, might stimulate the person to reminisce socially more than during the conflict-filled period of the life review. An alternative explanation is that only by reminiscing with others can the life-review process be successfully completed. You may recall that Butler argued that the life-review process is primarily intrapsychic. However, there are theoretical reasons to suggest that social reminiscence is more beneficial than individual or personal reminiscence.

Three *reminiscence styles*—intensity, resolution, and locus-of-control styles—were isolated from the data. Those who reported more turning points (*intensity* style), who said that more of the events turned out "for the better" (*resolution* style), and whose turning points were coded as internal in locus of control (*locus-of-control* style) were significantly more likely to report greater satisfaction with their biography as a whole than were respondents low on these characteristics. They were more likely to say that they were satisfied with their lives, more willing to live them over again, and more likely to think that they had been able to make what they wanted out of their lives.

In turn, people who were characterized by high intensity and favorable resolution and by high internal locus of control were *social* and not *individualized* reminiscers. There were highly significant positive correlations between having a favorable resolution style and internal locus of control on the one hand and reporting talking about the past at least once a week with others. Being often alone was negatively correlated with these styles. Although thinking about the past, emphasizing the past, and reading biographies were associated with giving more turning points on the reminiscence task, they bore no relationship, or a negative one, to resolution and locus-of-control reminiscence styles.

The weight of evidence in this small study supports a theoretical position that reality, including the reality of views of self, is socially constructed. Lowenthal and Haven (1968) have stressed the importance of intimate social relations in preserving positive morale among the aged, and more recently Lowenthal (1977) has suggested that "some kind of broad concept of integrity is a more appropriate measure of the sense of fulfillment in old age than are yardsticks of morale or happiness" (pp. 120–121). These data support the "social reconstruction theory" outlined by Bengtson and Kuypers (Bengtson, 1973; Kuypers & Bengtson, 1973), in which the sense of self is seen as arising in interaction with others. In the same vein, Hochschild (1973) describes the reminiscence activities of the apartment dwellers she observed as follows: "This talk seemed to be a way of collectively reviewing the past in order to 'feel right' about the way it defined them" (p. 75).

Implications

To return to the metaphor introduced earlier in this chapter, there is a time when aging individuals are highly engaged in rewriting their biographies, followed by a time when the autobiographies are largely written. While the evidence from the studies reviewed here is not conclusive, it is plausible that, when people get help from others in rewriting their autobiographies, they are more likely to develop a "good story." A major tradition of sociological research, rooted in the perspective of Cooley and Mead and others of the Chicago School, stresses that the self-concept develops in and through processes of interaction with others. Paradoxically, a great need for interaction appears to come at a period in late life when it is least likely to be available as a resource for validating one's view of self.

Awareness of finitude is not directly related to age but is, however, stimulated by events that are likely to be age related. Until quite late in life, little thought is given to death. It is in life-threatening situations, such as accidents or near-misses, or in response to personal illness or the death of others that one's thoughts turn to death. But these situations tend to occur more frequently in later life.

Even in later life, however, the frequency of thoughts of death may increase little, or even decrease, if viewed in relation to age alone. The relevance of thoughts of death varies according to the anticipated life expectancy, or awareness of finitude. Although evidence for undue concern about the self in mid-life is not as strong as many popularized accounts would suggest and although the mid-life crisis seems to come to relatively few people, the concern with self does, apparently, become intensified when an individual sees death drawing quite near. In mid-life, death is still too abstract to cause great concern for the self.

None of the studies drawn on in this chapter has large sample sizes. None traces these processes over time. All are cross-sectional in design. Measures are usually not directly comparable. Many of the studies are based on specialized samples, such as residents of nursing homes or retirement villages. All the research drawn on, except for Coleman's English study, has been conducted in the United States. Although Eastern religious traditions postulate linkages between self and death that are radically different from those that have been described in this chapter (see, for example, Kapleau, 1971), I am aware of no studies that systematically address these issues in non-Western sociocultural milieus, and I have not attempted such a momentous task.

Finally, some may object to my reluctance to draw on clinical evidence, even when the theoretical arguments have been based on it (for example, Butler, 1963; Gould, 1972, 1978; Levinson et al., 1978). I am not satisfied with this evidence not because I find it wrong but because I am uncertain about its reliability and validity. It is much more difficult to assess the veracity of a clinical judgment than the veracity of data based on more repeatable and standardized measures. This does not mean that clinical reports are not true; it means that they cannot easily be demonstrated to be free of clinical distortion. To push this point just a bit further, I think it fair to say that the evidence from the relatively more-controlled studies reviewed in this chapter fails to provide confirmation for the views of at least one of the clinically based theories (Levinson), while partially supporting those of another (Butler).

As to the relevance of the legitimation of biography in earlier periods in our own historical tradition, we can but speculate. Whether important or not for the adaptive processes of the life review, reminiscence was more important in preliterate societies for its teaching and story-telling functions. Awareness of finitude must have developed in radically different ways when the normal life expectancy for an adolescent was half or less than half of what it is today and when death was so much less predictable and controllable than it is today. Concern with self and legitimation of biography are also undoubtedly influenced by the values of individualism, which, as we saw in Chapter Three, did not emerge until around 1200.

It seems best, therefore, to *claim no universality* for the processes of legitimation of biography in relation to awareness of finitude. These processes may well be historically specific phenomena, and, although I have occasionally hinted at cohort differences within the population structure of our society today, there may be a much greater historical cohort experience differentiating people living in our century from all previous cohorts. There seems little doubt, however, that one of the most important aspects of aging in our own era and in our own kind of society is the growing awareness of finitude and a related concern for making sense of the self-as-dying.

Review Questions for Chapter 5

1. *People of all ages reminisce, but this chapter argues that reminiscence is more important for most people in their later years. Why is this the case?*

2. *The material in this chapter that focuses on the importance of reminiscence suggests a new way of looking at autobiographical writings and novels that assume a biographical framework. What insights can be gained from reading books such as* The Death of Artemio Cruz, Viper's Tangle, The Magic Mountain, Death in Venice *and autobiographies? What are the functions of writing autobiography and of reading it?*

3. *The argument for the importance of making sense of one's own life is restricted in this book to its applicability within societies that emphasize individualism. What are the weaknesses of the argument as applied to other societies, in which the collectivity or the community are presumed to have more importance than the individual?*

4. *Given the important effects of social factors on reminiscence processes, what are the policy implications with regard to the isolation of many older persons, the organization of programs for them, and the differential life expectancies of men and women? What differences in reminiscence would you expect to find on the basis of gender?*

6

Aging
and
Dying
as a Terminal
Status
Passage

One consequence, discussed in Chapter Five, of heightened awareness of finitude is that the individual becomes preoccupied with making sense of his or her biography as one that will have an ending. This chapter examines some other consequences of the recognition of mortality. A theoretical perspective to organize these concerns is given in the first section. The second section deals with changing time perspective in relation to awareness of finitude and with the ways in which anticipated life expectancy can influence decision making. The next section concerns planning for the details of dying and death, including the extent to which older persons plan their funerals and estate management. The ways in which people can die are affected by the environment; so the fourth section examines where people die. The last section discusses some characteristics of the environment in relation to terminal status passage. Of primary interest are the family, community, and bureaucratic contexts of the dying person.

The unifying theme of this chapter is the concept of status-passage control. Much of the evidence discussed can be best understood by postulating that people seek not only to make sense of themselves as dying but also to gain whatever control they can over the dying process, death itself, and, in some cases, the afterlife.

Control of
Terminal Status Passage

The realization of finitude, we have seen, binds together self and death. As the last chapters of an individual's biography are being recorded, he or she is likely to devote at least some attention to making sense of that life and of its drawing to a close. I have argued that individuals continually negotiate with one another to work out some sense and semblance of order, including a provisional but ever-changing agreement as to who they are, were, and will be (for an elaboration of this point, see Chapter Four). At some point in the lives of most people, the sense-making involved in this negotiation will seek to render death itself and the very process of dying meaningful. In addition, people will try to attain control over their final days and their dying—an attempt that is related to making sense of death.

In Chapter Three, we saw that, whereas the major features of the social character of death had been relatively constant until about 100 years ago, since that time death has become both privatized and bureaucratized. Rather than involve the entire community, an individual's death is now likely to involve primarily family members and bureaucrats, such as hospital personnel and funeral directors. As a result, the individual has, in many respects, lost control of his or her own dying, which has become, instead, a managed process. In this social context, individuals will still seek to maintain as much control over their dying as possible and to render it meaningful. As Lofland argues, "The fact that dying is, in the modern world, handled . . . with a bureaucratic form of social organization does not guarantee that either the bureaucratic handling generally or specific bureaucratic arrangements will be perceived as satisfactory" (1978, p. 36). Moreover, in a secular age where the meaning of death has become dislodged from religious certainties, where the meaningfulness of death and dying can no longer be taken for granted, it may be argued that "if we know anything about humans, we know that they do not confront meaningless situations for very long. In the face of meaninglessness, they construct for themselves new sets of beliefs, new orientations, new ways of looking and feeling which fill the void" (Lofland, 1978, p. 36).

It can also be argued that the pursuit of meaning and control—for these are related pursuits—is particularly important in the last chapters of life. Aging can be viewed as a career or status passage (Becker & Strauss, 1956; Hughes, 1937, 1971; Glaser & Strauss, 1971; Marshall, 1978–1979; Spence & Lonner, 1978–1979). To speak of aging as a career is to point to a person repeatedly negotiating his or her way from one age-related status or position to

---

another, finally coming to the end of life. The concept of *career* (I will use the term *status passage* as equivalent) is useful because it has both an objective and a subjective reality as used in sociological analysis and because it provides a way of looking at the experiences of people over time. Objectively, a career is "a progression of statuses and functions which unfold in a more or less orderly though not predetermined sequence in the pursuit of values which themselves emerge in the course of experience" (Foote, 1956, cited in Spence & Lonner, 1978–1979, p. 52). Subjectively, a career is the individual's changing and developing perspective of movement through the sequence over time (Hughes, 1971). To speak of aging as a career is to emphasize not just movement but also participation and purpose (Simić & Myerhoff, 1978, p. 240).

A number of dimensions of careers, or status passages, have been described by Becker, Glaser and Strauss, Hughes, and Marshall. Any career can be described in terms of movement in physical space and time. Different stages of a career may be long or short, and they may be associated with geographical mobility. Movement in social space, such as proximity and social status, can also be properties of a career or status passage. A career may be traversed alone, aggregatively, or collectively. The passage may be guided or controlled by others, or it may be self-guided. There might be formal or informal teachers. Careers may vary in moral legitimacy; they may be honorable or dishonorable, respectable or deviant. The ways in which objective properties of careers are viewed by those persons experiencing them constitute the subjective aspects of the career. Suggestions for analysis based on the concept of career or status passage can be found elsewhere (Glaser & Strauss, 1971; Hewitt, 1976; Marshall, 1978–1979; Spence & Lonner, 1978–1979); here we will focus on selected properties that are salient in the career of aging and dying.

The most important property of the aging and dying career is probably its *inevitability and irreversibility* (Glaser & Strauss, 1971, p. 15; Lofland, 1978, p. 14; Marshall, 1978–1979). It is possible to suspend or terminate many careers and shift to others. One can skip school or withdraw from it; leave home, spouse, and children; have an abortion; resign an office; or quit a job. While such career moves often occur under considerable constraint and at cost (Becker, 1960), they do entail at least some exercise of choice in most instances. The other side of this coin is that one can be expelled from school; be thrown out of the home or deserted by one's spouse; experience a spontaneous abortion; be impeached; or get fired. Career stages or phases then can vary greatly, depending on whether or not they occur volitionally; but aging and dying happens to people whether they like it or not. The inevitability and the irreversibility of the aging and dying career have important implications for the degree to which it is likely to be taken seriously by those experiencing it. Its properties, but not its existence, can be partially controlled. While one does not automatically have to "make do" with a boring job or a bad marriage, one has no choice but to make the best of aging and dying. We will return to this issue after considering some other important properties of the career of aging and dying.

Lyn Lofland (1978, Chap. 2) describes some important features of the "dying role" that readily translate into our concern with aging and dying as a status passage. She argues that an important characteristic of the dying role is that it is *transitional,* according to its sociological definition and experience. Except for a minority who are born into a situation in which they are immediately defined as dying, one's career as dying is always something *entered into.* One moves from nondying to dying. Also, one is not expected, once in the dying role, to stay there; one cannot be "dying" indefinitely. In this sense, the dying role is like the "sick role" (Parsons, 1951, p. 437), in which the individual is felt to be under the obligation to try to get well, even though it is recognized that he or she is not responsible for the illness. Just as one is not expected to be dying indefinitely, one is not expected to be sick indefinitely. Of course the two roles differ in their anticipated outcome.

Since the outcome of the dying career is death, one of its important properties is that *there are no graduates.* "Dying," Lofland notes, "like old age, lacks an alumni group" (1978, p. 46). This implies that there is no one who has undergone the passage and completed the career transition to teach incumbents or "passagees" (Rosow, 1973). A related property is that, unlike most other careers, dying is *nonrepeatable.* We die once, so we cannot benefit from the experience or "practice" the passage.

While the transitions of aging may be more or less formally defined (compare the official transition of retirement with more gradual processes of loss of energy), the career of dying is marked, Lofland argues, *by official definitions.* Dying, like marrying, being a student, or working, is marked by the fact that "entry is guarded by gate-keepers who monitor prospective entrants and make decisions about whether or not they qualify for admission" (Lofland, 1978, p. 46). This has a number of implications and consequences. Seldom can a person in our society accomplish self-definition as dying, without enlisting the aid of an official arbitrator, specifically a physician. On the other hand, as the work of Glaser and Strauss (1965), in particular, has shown, official definitions can be made without the assent, and indeed without the knowledge, of the individual. Although an individual has a certain range of choices in attempting to negotiate or bargain over the application of official definitions and knowledge about their application, the importance of official labeling agents is a factor reducing the amount of control an individual can have over entry into the dying role.

Official gatekeepers may also participate in role exits (discussed in the third section of this chapter). That is, the decision whether or not to prolong life—and thereby the dying career—as through "heroic measures," is largely in the hands of parties other than the dying person, such as doctors and the courts with participation by family members. This is another arena for bargaining and negotiation but is seldom an area in which the person "in the career" has a great deal of freedom of action.

Another important feature of the dying career is that it is undergone, ultimately, as *a solo passage*. In the literature, much is made of this property, and it is indeed true that no one can do our dying for us. Too much should not be made of this feature, however, because in many respects it is trivial in that it accurately applies only to the very last phase of expiration. There is great variability in the extent to which an individual is in physical proximity and social interaction with others who may share similar experiences as dying persons themselves or who may simply join the individual in the dying career as relevant and significant others. Since the self is social, then the self-as-dying is also social. Some people spend significant periods of time in their aging and dying career alone; however, most people are at least co-present with others much of their dying career; and genuine social collaboration is a possibility.

It is important not to fall into the trap of considering "dying" only as the period following official pronouncement that a person is "terminally ill." People can be in many careers at a given time (Spence & Lonner, 1978–1979); and the aging and dying career is entered with heightened awareness of finitude when the individual becomes highly aware that life will indeed end in the not-too-distant future (see Chapter Five). The self-focusing and legitimation of biography described in the previous chapter are, therefore, one phase in the aging and dying career. The phase of legitimation of biography follows a rough pattern of heightened reminiscence and preoccupation with self and past, followed by a lessening of reminiscence, self-preoccupation, and concern with the past. Concomitantly, the individual experiences other changes in relation to death and becomes concerned with the meaning of death itself and with setting his or her house in order in preparation for it. Subsequent sections of this chapter deal with those other concerns. We begin, however, by paying somewhat closer attention to the changing time perspective of the person in the aging and dying career.

Changing Time Perspective in Relation to Awareness of Finitude

It is important to emphasize that people near death are not solely preoccupied with the past, even during periods when the reminiscence, or life-review process, might be at its peak. People must orient their actions toward the future, as we are goal-seeking creatures who make plans, anticipate the results of possible actions, and rehearse them in our imagination.

Some scholars, more on intuition than on evidence, argue that awareness of finitude produces an altered conception of the future, making it more vivid. Peter Koestenbaum, who believes that the heightened awareness of mortality leads to anxiety and a feeling of separation from the taken-for-granted world, also argues that this heightened awareness of finitude "leads to a complete reevaluation and transformation of the meaning of our individual human existence. We become aware of the urgency to find meaning in life" (1964, p. 254). Noting that the disengagement theorists propose that awareness of finitude leads to withdrawal from the mainstream of life and a feeling that present gratification should take precedence over future planning, Robert Kastenbaum argues that, "on the contrary, many people intensify their participation in life in order to obtain the greatest possible yield from the time remaining to them" (1969, p. 131).

Many people, including William James, have argued that time appears to pass more swiftly with increasing age (Fraisse, 1963, p. 246). Some argue that this phenomenon is caused by the scarcity of time left to the individual and its consequent higher evaluation (Wallach & Green, 1961), while others suggest that, with increasing age, a given unit of time becomes proportionately smaller, in comparison to the amount of time that has passed.

Kuhlen and Monge (1968) review these and other theories of the correlates of estimated time passage and conclude that greater activity is associated with a perceived faster rate-of-time passage. For example, institutionalized aged appear to experience time as passing more slowly than noninstitutionalized aged. Kuhlen and Monge found no evidence that older people experience a faster rate-of-time passage than younger people; rather, they found that estimates of rate-of-time passage depended on the extent to which time was filled with activity. In turn, this led to a slightly negative relationship between age and estimated rates-of-time passage.

The ability to fill time varies with degree and type of engagement with others. In one study, the data suggest that "getting rid of unwanted duties and obligations and settling for ease and contentment (but not necessarily inactivity) as a way of life may represent one of the major adaptive tasks for older people" (Chiriboga, 1975, p. 98). Beyond facilitating ease and contentment, withdrawal from intense activity with others facilitates self-focusing and life review and allows time for reflecting on the meaning of impending death (Kalish, 1972; also, see Chapter Seven).

Attitude toward use of time changes in the direction of ease and contentment following completion of the adaptive tasks of legitimating biography and death (Marshall, 1973a, 1975b). When these tasks have been completed, the individual is free to return to other investments. However, the renewed focus on other activities occurs within a different framework once the individual is prepared to die. Successful preparation for death leads to a new kind of freedom for the aging person, who is free to anticipate the future with no anxiety about impending death and with a sense of gratitude or appreciation for the time remaining. The person who is accepting of impending death is also accepting in general.

Spence (1968) distinguished between planning for change and planning for the future and found that planning for the future was positively related to satisfaction or morale whereas planning for change was negatively related to it. Those who plan but do not desire change—composed planners—show the highest levels of life satisfaction. With my own respondents (Marshall, 1973a, 1975b), people who had successfully legitimated death and biography fell into the same category, planning further ahead into the future, although not intensively, while not desiring major changes in their lives. It appears that successful preparation for death acts through changes in the conception of the future to increase satisfaction with the present situation in life. Preoccupation with self and the past declines, and a renewed interest in the future becomes manifest. This leisurely attitude toward the future is well described in the words of one of my respondents: "I spend all day doing nothing, and when I go to bed at night it's only half done."

It is truly unfortunate that so little gerontological research has gathered specific data on anticipated life expectancy, because existing research offers tantalizing hints that it is important in many ways for the plans and behavior of aging individuals. Any rational allocation of resources by an individual ought to take into account the factor of anticipated life expectancy. This is most obvious, perhaps, when making financial investments, such as purchasing annuities or life insurance, but the problem exists for many other resource-allocation situations as well (Katona, 1965; Morgan, 1963; Thurow, 1969).

I would like to review one situation from my own research (Marshall, 1973b), because in many ways it exemplifies the way in which estimates of life expectancy influence future planning. In the retirement community I refer to as Glen Brae, just under 400 residents had paid entrance fees guaranteeing lifetime care. In addition to these fees, which in the late 1960s ranged from $14,000 to $45,000 depending on type of apartment obtained, individuals signed contracts agreeing to pay monthly maintenance fees of $330 and up to cover meals, housekeeping, and medical expenses. The contract allowed the administration to alter the monthly rate as necessary. The initial entrance fee is lost on a 2% monthly calculation, so that any resident who wants to leave the community after 50 months—or who dies at any time—will lose his or her entire investment. This "lifetime care" provision is not uncommon in retirement villages.

A fully rational person contemplating entry to Glen Brae would face a difficult choice. Because of the high initial payment, the move would not be a good investment if the individual did not live long. With only a few years to live, a person might well find some better use for this large amount of money. On the other hand, because monthly payments are to go on until death, the move to the retirement community might turn out to be a mistake should the person live too long and not have enough money to continue making monthly payments. In short, a rational decision to move to a retirement village involves an accurate prediction of life expectancy; but we have seen in Chapter Five that such estimates are not very accurate. A rational decision also depends on an accurate estimate of the raises in rents that might accrue over that estimated life expectancy as a result of inflation or other factors. There are other considerations in a fully rational decision, such as the costs and benefits of alternative living arrangements, but, at the very least, estimated life expectancy is inextricably bound up with this decision.

As it happened in this particular case, the monthly rental fees were raised considerably higher than had been anticipated by residents; increases averaged 18.6% a year over a five-year period (Marshall, 1973b). Many residents were caught in a situation in which they had underestimated both their longevity and the inflation in their rent. One resident described the situation as follows: "I think that, with the rapid increase in rates here, there are people in great anguish that they will not die until they've spent everything they've got. You see, if you could just make it come out even, it would be very nice." Another formulates the more general implications of the problem that affects any older person who is not very wealthy: "I just got my bank statement, and it isn't too high. I'll have to be careful from now on. If you knew how long you had [to live], you could figure it out to the cent. But you can't." Glaser and Strauss (1968, p. 85) discuss a similar case of a hospital patient whose insurance ran out.

Leonard Cain has stated the general implications for policy if it were possible to use actual distance from death instead of age:

> The farther an individual moves from the year of his birth, the less significant is that fact for the purposes of gauging functional capacity. . . . If age could be counted backwards from death, rather than forward from birth, more equitable opportunity to receive return on pension investments could be accomplished, housing and health service planning could be improved, and a larger percentage of the elderly could have the option of a few years of leisure at the end of their lives" [Cain, 1976, p. 366].

As Cain points out elsewhere (1978), Ryder (1965) had earlier articulated an identical concept but argued that it could be applied only in the aggregate and not in the individual case, relying on actuarial or demographic considerations. Cain, however, cites legal examples in which "counting backward from the estimated time of death" is being used in the individual case. These include cases in which the courts take into account not only general or population actuarial data but also personal medical history, genetic factors, and personal health-related habits.

Cain (1978) also discusses a procedure whereby elderly plaintiffs and defendants could request being moved up in the queue for access to the courts as a response to a tactic employed by some attorneys to take advantage of court delays in the case of elderly plaintiffs—a tactic based on the knowledge that pressure for settlement intensifies in relation to the plaintiff's age and health, both of which affect the opportunity to benefit from a financial award. In Canada it is now possible to grant early parole to prisoners who are terminally ill (*Toronto Globe & Mail,* February 22, 1979). These examples show that actual distance from death is increasingly recognized by society as relevant for the planning and the allocation of time. It is, therefore, only reasonable to expect that individuals, especially as they become highly aware of finitude, will adjust their planning and activities to their understanding of that limit.

In later life not only estimates of personal life expectancy but also estimates of the life expectancy of others become relevant. These estimates of life expectancy to some extent influence the young, but they attain a particular poignancy in family situations in the later years. Among the young, as we saw in Chapter Three, career opportunities are sometimes created by the death of the incumbent of an office, the owner of property, and so on. Among the old, the issue of interest to us is "living for another." Older spouses become concerned about the life expectancy of each other, and sometimes, although accepting of their own impending death, they hope it will be postponed until after the death of the other. One of my respondents at Glen Brae, an 87-year-old man, when asked how long he would like to live, replied "As long as my wife does—longer, 'cause I want to look after her. Outside of that, I think I'm old enough. I mean you lose your outlook on life to some extent, realize your time is limited" (Marshall, 1974a, p. 29).

A female resident said "If I were to die tomorrow, I would suffer mentally, knowing I leave a husband who loved and needed me in several ways." This kind of response was not infrequent in my own research setting, and I suspect it is quite common among married couples and in other close kinship and friendship relations. It lends a particular accent to the views that older people take of their futures, and it constitutes a special kind of engagement that is certainly not described by the rather gross and empty social life-space measures commonly used to measure engagement and disengagement.

This consideration of time perspective in relation to awareness of finitude has been brief and limited, but we can draw together a few generalizations that can at least be considered suggestive of further research in this area. The most important alterations of time perspective probably occur in relation to the legitimation of biography through reminiscence or life-review processes. Although from mid-life on both the present and the past are seen in the light of "intimations of mortality," the way in which individuals view the future and plan their activities is more directly affected when awareness of finitude becomes highly salient. This awareness does not usually occur until the late sixties or later and not, I have argued, directly in relation to age. At this time the person withdraws interest and investment in the future and becomes preoccupied with the meaning of his or her biography as it has unfolded over the years. The future is not absent from consciousness during this period, and indeed the constriction of the estimated future prompts the process of actively rewriting the biography.

Moreover, as will be seen in Chapter Seven, the future is relevant at this time because the end of that biography is also the object of sense-making, or legitimation endeavors. Together, these activities, *if successful,* constitute the development of a more fully meaningful and highly integrated view of the self as a creature in and over time.

> Biographical time is the way in which a person organizes his experiences into his lifetime. It has an organization at any given moment which relates his past to the present in as meaningful a way as he is able. A person uses his past both as a guide to the future and as a way of establishing an identity [Loeb, Pincus, & Mueller, 1966, p. 185].

However, "perspective" on one's life requires at least two points from which to view it (Kastenbaum, 1965), and I have suggested that, under conditions of high awareness of finitude, the ultimate future becomes an organizer of the present and the near future. As the person completes the autobiography and renders life meaningful, his or her view of the future changes as well. There is a return to a focus on the future, and the outer limit of planning ahead becomes extended. However, the density of planning—the way in which future time is filled with specific plans—is not as fine-grained. The future is viewed in a relaxed way, often with a special appreciation engendered by the knowledge that the remaining days are few.

It is probably fair to say that, while age is of less importance than awareness of finitude, the social circumstances in which people find themselves in their later years are of great importance in affecting time perspective. The degree of engagement with others, the extent to which financial and other affairs are contingent on the timing of death or the length of life, and whether one anticipates a future shared with others or alone—all probably contribute in little-researched ways to the stance the aging and dying person takes toward the future.

If people at any age have foreknowledge of the timing of their death, it is likely that they will try to wrap up loose ends, settle unfinished business, and take steps to ensure that death does not disrupt the ongoing flow of affairs any more than necessary. They are also likely to plan at least some degree of active use of the future.

Two studies have asked people what they would do if they *could* predict that they would die at a specific time. Despite the extremely hypothetical nature of these questions, the results show interesting age differences. Back (in Kastenbaum, 1966) asked rural men "If you knew you were going to die within 30 days, what would you do?" Kalish and Reynolds (1976, pp. 68–70) asked their Los Angeles respondents "If you were told you had a terminal disease and six months to live, how would you want to spend your time until you died?" The age differences were similar in the two studies. As Kalish and Reynolds summarized, "The modal response for the young was to express their concern for others; . . . for the elderly was withdrawal into prayer or contemplation or other inner-life involvement" (1976, p. 68). There were no sex differences of note. Preoccupation with self among the elderly might indicate that they have fewer ties to others—that they are more highly disengaged—and that their deaths are anticipated to have fewer consequences than the death of one younger (Kalish & Reynolds, 1976, p. 70). It is also possible that this age pattern is really a cohort or generational one and not primarily caused by transitions of aging per se. For example, younger generations may be less religious or given to turning to prayer and contemplation.

Planning for Death and Dying

Given that death is one of the few certainties we experience, what plans do people make concerning it? At the societal level, meanings are constructed and social institutions are created and sustained in order to incorporate the occurrence of death. Inheritance and retirement systems, for example, smooth the transitions and replacement processes necessitated by death; religions provide beliefs to symbolically restore social integration and often to provide a place for the dead to remain in association with the living. Religions also provide the rituals to reaffirm those beliefs and to provide the social regulation to restore social harmony. These societal concerns, reviewed in detail in Chapter Three, provide the context for addressing these same issues at the individual level. The contemporary historical context in which the aging individual must accomplish his or her own dying is markedly different from that of the past, because the typical age of death, cause of death, and meanings of death have changed. Together these changes constitute what, in Chapter Three, I have called the *changing social character of death*.

The contemporary social character of death diminishes the general community concern for death and places the locus of its "problems" within the family and between families and bureaucrats, such as medical personnel and funeral directors. I argued in Chapter Three that people have largely lost control over the conditions surrounding their own death and dying. Within that framework, however, it must be remembered that the institutional and organizational features of death and dying are social creations not entirely resistant to manipulation and change. At the very least, people can vary in the extent to which they follow common patterns of managing their dying or develop innovative ones.

We will now consider different types of planning for death: the purchase of life insurance and making of wills, both of which reflect a concern for others; the making of funeral plans, which may reflect concern for oneself or for others, and desires and wishes concerning the timing and style of the terminal stages of dying, which again may show concern for self or for others.

Zelizer (1978) describes the development of life insurance early in the 19th century as an aspect of the general rationalization and formalization of death. Just as the funeral moved from a family to a neighborhood affair and later to a business, so the care and protection of widows and surviving children moved from the family and community to the business world. To become a successful business, life insurance had to overcome a tendency on the part of many people to associate, in a magical way, insurance with death. That is, many people felt that life insurance was a bet on the life of the insured and that to make such a bet was a sacrilegious courting of disfavor. Life insurance could, then, be tainted because it turned something sacred—human life—into a monetary commodity.

Zelizer (1978) describes how, until late in the last century, life insurance officials downplayed the rational and economic aspects of life insurance while promoting its benefits in altruistic, even religious, terms. Life insurance was promoted as a gift instead of a rational investment and as an obligation to one's spouse and children—an obligation that became increasingly important with the development of a large propertyless urban class who were dependent solely on wages and could not leave land or property to survivors.

As the meaning of life insurance—as marketed by its proponents and advocated by others—changed, so too did the meaning of death (see Chapter Three). Zelizer (1978) takes the position that the ambivalence concerning the meaning of death allowed for a resolution of the problem of the sacrilegiousness of life insurance by making it part of the ritual of a good death. "More and more a good death meant the wise and generous economic provision of dependents. A man was judged posthumously by his financial insight as much as by his spiritual qualities" (Zelizer, 1978, p. 603). This theme was reinforced by another advocated by the life insurance companies: providing life insurance was a form of immortality—an economic immortality in which even the dead could continue to provide for the economic well-being of their families (Zelizer, 1978).

Americans purchase more life insurance than people in any other country in the world. Other high-ranking nations are Japan, France, and Canada, in that order. United States residents owned, on the average, life insurance policies valued at $11,870 in 1977. Overall, life insurance values in the United States for that year came to $2.8 trillion. The amount of coverage for each insured individual is in the range of $25,000, and for each family, over $40,000 (*Toronto Globe & Mail*, October 31, 1978).

Older people are somewhat less likely to own life insurance than younger people; yet Kalish and Reynolds (1976, pp. 61–62) found that 60% of their Los Angeles sample aged 60 years and older owned life insurance and that somewhat more men than women owned insurance. John W. Riley, Jr. (reported in Riley & Foner, 1968, p. 337) found 69% of those over 61 years of age to have insurance. The reasons why older people have less insurance may be complex. Older people are, on the whole, less financially able to own insurance and may, in fact, be beneficiaries rather than owners, or they may have no children or others whom they might wish to protect through insurance (see Kalish & Reynolds, 1976, p. 62).

Making a will is another way to plan for death. Bengtson and Kuypers (1971) have noted that the young are often viewed by their elders as "social helpers" and that attempts are often made to control and influence them even after the death of the parental generation. Back and Baade (1966; also Rosenfeld, 1979, pp. 16–17) argue that the state has intervened in order to place some controls over the desires, and often whims, of testators (people making wills) through laws governing succession, trusts, and property. These same laws may serve to protect the old from the young. Wilbert Moore (1966) notes that the prolongation of later life may lead to substantial depletion of any inheritance, in turn causing impatience and perhaps ambivalence among their potential heirs. The universality of this dilemma is shown by the fact that it is the stuff of so much literature and drama.

Our concern in this chapter is less with the broader societal implications of testation (but see Back & Baade, 1966; Goody, Thirsk, & Thompson, 1978; Moore, 1966; Rheinstein, 1965; Rosenfeld, 1979; Sussman, Cates, & Smith, 1970) than with the individual implications. The most representative recent data on will making and on other aspects of planning for death, along with the national survey results of John W. Riley, Jr., are those gathered by Kalish and Reynolds from their Los Angeles study (see Table 6-1). In contrast to the relationship between age and the purchase of life insurance, increasing age is strongly related to will making and other kinds of planning for death such as buying a cemetery plot, making funeral arrangements, and arranging for someone to be responsible for one's affairs.

Over 80% of the respondents in the Riley, Jr. (1970) national survey on attitudes toward death thought that it was better to make some plans about death than not to do so. One out of four adults in the survey had made a will,

TABLE 6-1. Plans for Death, by Age

Survey Item		Age			
		20–39	40–59	60 +	
Have you made out a will?	Yes	10	22	39	(.001)
Have you taken out life insurance?	Yes	61	76	66	(.05)
Have you paid for or are you now paying for a cemetery plot?	Yes	7	17	44	(.001)
Have you made funeral arrangements?	Yes	3	11	24	(.001)
Have you made arrangements for someone to handle your affairs?	Yes	13	27	44	(.001)

Note: Significance levels are for chi-square calculations. The sample included 434 respondents of various ethnical backgrounds from Los Angeles County.

Adapted from *Death and Ethnicity: A Psychocultural Study,* by R. A. Kalish and D. K. Reynolds. Copyright 1976 by the University of Southern California Press. Reprinted by permission.

and about the same proportion had made funeral or cemetery arrangements. Age was an important factor, but education had an even stronger effect on people's attitudes toward death. For persons over 61, 83% of those with less than high school education felt it best to make plans. This percentage rose to 87% for those with high school education and to 92% for the college educated. People age 30 and under were least likely to think it important to make plans, but even here the lowest percentage (76%) was among those with less than high school education (Riley & Foner, 1968, p. 336). The percentage having made funeral arrangements rose regularly by age from 11% of those under age 30 to 50% of those over 61 (Riley & Foner, 1968, p. 337). Kalish and Reynolds (1976, pp. 46–47) report similar findings from their study (see Table 6-1).

Finally, it is important to note that the effects of age and education are strongly interactive; that is, being highly educated makes more of a difference in planning for death among older people than among younger people. While, among those of any educational level, increasing age is associated with making more plans for death, age makes twice as much difference among those with less than high school education (Riley & Foner, 1968, p. 337). Neither education nor age is a "pure" variable, in the sense that each indexes many other characteristics. Thus, higher education is associated with higher income, White racial characteristics, and membership in a younger age cohort; and age differences can, of course, reflect various historical experiences and generational effects.

The interpretation of these data is, therefore, somewhat hazardous. The association of planning for death with higher education gives some support to the general argument that the scientific and technological aspects of our culture are conducive to an individual orientation of control over death. Note our earlier discussion of Parsons' (1963; Parsons, Fox, & Lidz, 1973) argument in Chapter Three. Higher education exposes people to the scientific ethos and indeed contributes to enmeshing them in highly scientific areas of the socioculture. As Riley, Jr., has observed, the various changes in the characteristics of the aged population may have profound effects on the planning for and orientation to death. He asks whether "increasing education in the future will mark an increasingly active adaptation to death, a decrease in anxiety, and a more positive definition?" (1968, p. 32).

Some insight into the desire people might have for control over their dying process comes from reviewing the small amount of research on whether people would wish to know of their own terminal status. Kalish and Reynolds (1976, p. 55) asked respondents in their Los Angeles survey to imagine that a friend of the same sex was dying. Nearly 60% of persons between the ages of 20 and 59 thought that their friend should be told of his or her death; fewer people over the age of 60 thought so. However, when the respondents were asked if they would like to be told of their own death, the age differences disappeared; in all age groups, at least 79% of the respondents said that they would like to be told if they were dying. There were no sex differences on these variables.

Are these age differences or cohort differences? It is very possible that these attitudes reflect differences other than age between the age cohorts. One significant difference is education. The modal educational level for the youngest cohort (ages 20–39) was some college; for the middle-age groups (ages 40–59), high school graduation; and for the elderly (60 +), grade school (Kalish & Reynolds, 1976, pp. 51–52). Also, half of the older respondents were born outside the United States, as compared to less than one-fourth of the younger respondents. About 40% of the older group were widowed. Most of the decline with age in the proportion thinking that their friend should be told is accounted for by the Japanese-American respondents in this multi-ethnic sample. The overall picture, as summarized by Kalish and Reynolds, is that people seem to be saying "I know I can handle this, but I don't know about those people" (1976, p. 55).

The attitude "I can take it; others may not be able to" has been found to be prevalent among physicians. Feifel (1965) surveyed a number of studies that showed that, while about 80% of physicians thought their patients should not be told that they were dying, about the same percentage indicated that they would themselves prefer to be told. The problem of gaining knowledge about one's terminal condition must be one of the most severe constraints on people as they try to control their dying process (Duff & Hollingshead, 1968, pp. 306–320; Glaser & Strauss, 1965; Millman, 1977, Chap. 6). Considerable clinical opinion states that dying patients know they are dying anyway and do not need to be told, but the empirical basis for that assertion is weak (Cartwright, Hockey, & Anderson, 1973, pp. 163–165; McIntosh, 1977; Rosenthal, Marshall, Macpherson, & French, 1980, Chap. 5; Waitzkin & Stoeckle, 1972). Hinton (1967, pp. 95–99) argues that there are plenty of signs available by which patients can come to know that they are dying but that such a realization comes gradually.

The great majority of respondents in the Kalish and Reynolds (1976) study said that, if they had been told that they had a terminal illness, they would try very hard to control the way in which they showed their emotions in public (p. 206). Whereas 80% of the males, as opposed to 70% of the females, agreed with this statement, there were no age differences. Older persons were more likely than younger ones to say that they would accept death peacefully rather than fight it actively (Kalish & Reynolds, 1976, p. 68). These are aspects of what Lofland (1978) calls *stance*—that is, "the character of emotional tone or orientation or personal philosophy that is expressed in the role [of dying]" (p. 55).

In addition to stance, Lofland describes other dimensions of the dying role that involve varying degrees of choice and control. One such dimension she calls *space,* which refers to how much of himself or herself an individual wishes to devote to the role of dying (1978, p. 50). Goffman's (1961b) concept of *role distance* is also relevant here. Role-distancing behavior is behavior that a person displays to show others and self that he or she is not completely engrossed in a particular role. The person who is dying is also other persons as well; seldom is anyone completely engrossed in any role. If role distance is seen as a sociological analog to what psychologists refer to as *denial*, then it is apparent that inattention to one's own dying does not have to be seen as defensively motivated. A person's failure to be completely engrossed in his or her dying need not reflect a fear of dying; instead, it may simply be customary role-enactment behavior.

Another dimension mentioned by Lofland (1978) is *population*, which refers to whether a person "chooses to play out the dying role alone or with others who are also playing it out" (p. 51). Population, Lofland notes, is a dimension severely constrained by bureaucratic exigencies such as the tendency for people to die in hospitals.

Knowledge, which we have already considered, is another property outlined by Lofland (1978, pp. 52–55), and it intersects with population and stance. For example, Kalish and Reynolds (1976, p. 68) found that people of all ages express a wish to spend some time with family, including children, before they died; they also express a wish to have the services of a clergyman. If knowledge of terminal illness is kept from a person, it may be difficult to fulfill these wishes; and, if collusion surrounds the dying patient in a closed or pretense awareness context—that is, a context in which the family members are aware of a terminal diagnosis but the patient either is not or is constrained to pretend ignorance of the diagnosis—the quality of interaction with family or clergy will be false and strained.

Hochschild (1973, p. 83) notes that the residents of Merrill Court tried to guess how long people had to live as a means of trying to reduce the unpredictability of death, which they found upsetting. Matthews (1975; 1979, pp. 141–143) notes that the unpredictability of death is a problem for older women. A nursing-home resident in my own research (Marshall, 1973a) maintained a record book of the death of each of his fellow residents, behavior that can be seen as a search for predictability. On the Templer Death Anxiety Scale, uncertainty about what the future might bring has been found to be associated with high death anxiety among older women (Bascue & Lawrence, 1977). It is the uncertainty and not the death itself that seems to be the fearful stimulus, however. More generally, uncertainty is noxious because of its implications for control, as we saw in respect to financial uncertainty.

Within medical sociology in general, and not simply with respect to dying patients, considerable agreement exists that people wish to know about their situation so that they can have a sense of, and opportunity to exercise, some control over it (for the classic study, see Roth, 1963). Control can imply either active or passive euthanasia, and the desire for control may be expressed through a "living will" that asks that unusual or heroic measures not be taken to preserve biological life in the absence of psychological or social vitality (see Lofland, 1978, p. 86; Marshall, 1975a).

Congressional hearings have been held on the subject of death with dignity; death with dignity is incorporated into patients' bills of rights; and support is growing for at least voluntary euthanasia or a policy of "no heroic measures." Support is, not surprisingly, particularly strong among the aged (Collette, 1973). It is also strong on the part of the medical profession (Crane, 1975; Degner, 1974; Rea, Greenspoon, & Spilka, 1975; Travis, Noyes, Jr., & Brightwell, 1974; Williams, 1969) and perhaps even stronger among nurses (Hoggatt & Spilka, 1978–1979).

Preston and Williams (1971) asked nursing-home and veterans' home residents the question "If you were fatally ill, in great distress, and under heavy medical expense, would you want the doctors to do *nothing* to keep you alive?" They also asked whether, under the same circumstances, the respondents would want the doctors to do *something* to shorten their lives. The first question measures attitude toward passive euthanasia, the second toward active or positive euthanasia; and the two can be viewed as representing varying degrees of control orientation toward death. Almost half of the men, who ranged in age between 60 and 95 (mean age 72), rejected positive euthanasia; one-fourth favored negative but rejected positive euthanasia; and one-third favored both negative and positive euthanasia. Within that age range, age made no difference in responses, but those who claimed that religious faith was important to them were more likely to reject both kinds of euthanasia (Preston & Williams, 1971, p. 302).

The fact that all these subjects were institutionalized may lead to a less active control orientation toward death and dying or a greater passivity or indifference toward the manner of dying. Chappell (1975) studied an institutionalized older sample and characterized half of her respondents as simply "waiting for death." I have contrasted a retirement village and a home for the aged/nursing home as settings varying in the degree of passivity they might encourage in their residents and the control residents might take over all aspects of their lives, including their dying (Marshall, 1975c). This issue is the theme of the last section of this chapter.

A preference for control or predictability, even over extended life expectancy, was found in an ingenious study of 14 hospital patients with operable bronchogenic carcinoma, or lung cancer (McNeil, Weichselbaum, & Pauker, 1978). The median age of these patients was 69 years, and the age range was 48–80. Surgery or radiation therapy are two principal treatment modalities for such patients. Because of its preliminary nature, this study was conducted after choice of treatment rather than as a guide to selection of treatment.

The patients were given hypothetical choices and asked which they would prefer. The choices were between a fixed period of certain survival and a chance or gamble on longer survival. For example, a patient, given a hypothetical situation in which there was a fifty-fifty chance of living 25 years or dying, was then asked how many years of certain life he or she would consider equivalent in value to taking that gamble. Then the same patient was presented with a fifty-fifty choice between the value established in the first choice and immediate death. Repetition of this procedure allowed construction of a utility curve that described the utility or value to each person of survival for various periods. Of the 14 patients, 12 were averse to risks throughout the entire period, and the other two were risk taking only in the first few years. That is, all patients preferred certain life for a brief period, followed by early death, to taking greater chances with the possibility of living longer. Certainty was preferred to extended life (for a similar study with consistent results see Sackett & Torrance, 1978).

It is not easy to interpret these data. Lung-cancer patients were selected because the treatments—radiation therapy versus operation—differ primarily in their effect on survival rates and not on quality of life; however, the situations were fully hypothetical and presented to the patients after choice of treatment. The authors speculate that this high reluctance to take risks was caused by the advanced age and serious illness of the patients. The data, they note, "suggests that older patients with life-threatening diseases often prefer a treatment with a lower five-year survival but a smaller chance of immediate death from the treatment" (McNeil, Weichselbaum, & Pauker, 1978, p. 1401). Someone who wanted to assume high levels of death fear might argue that certain survival is chosen because of high death fear. But this choice suggests earlier death and can be interpreted as an acceptance of the inevitable. I believe that the latter interpretation is more consistent with both the overall tendency for death fear to decrease with age and the general preference most people have for predictability in their lives, as well as a general phenomenon of increased cautiousness with advancing age (see research reviewed in Botwinick, 1978, Chap. 8).

A related indication of the struggle for control is described in a study of 51 terminal-cancer patients. The investigators observed that "when problems seemed too overwhelming and strength was small, patients tried to gain control of situations. The patient is well aware by this time that he has no control over his disease or life span; therefore, he tries to gain control in the only ways he can" (Simmons & Given, 1972, p. 224). This attempt often leads, the authors claim, to patients refusing baths, medication, ambulation, linen changes, or other treatments.

In summary, the changing character of death makes it more important to plan for it and to try to control it, because it is likely to take a long time for a person, once launched on a dying career, to complete the passage through it to death. Most people do, in fact, make plans for death, including legal and bureaucratic arrangements. In the later stages of the dying career, control becomes increasingly salient as time becomes more highly constrained by bureaucratic exigencies. Much of the variability in the amount of control an aging and dying individual can exercise has to do with the environment in which the last stages of dying occur. The next section describes where people die and the final section examines the ways in which variability in the environment is relevant; important aspects to be considered are family, community, and bureaucracy.

Where the Old Die

Because dying is a process rather than a state, it takes time and can occur for any individual over a variety of settings. Glaser and Strauss (1968), for example, report on many dying trajectories involving moves between hospitals, nursing homes, and residences and depending not only on health but also on social conditions, such as relations with other family members and economic status.

In the past, most people died at home rather than in hospitals. Lerner (1970) presents data showing that "the proportion of all deaths in the United States occurring in institutions has been rising steadily, at least for the last two decades and probably for much longer than that. It may now be as high as, or higher than, two-thirds of all deaths" (p. 7). Other countries vary. In England and Wales, for example, about half of all deaths occur in the home (Hinton, 1967, p. 147). At least in the United States, the proportion of persons dying in institutions has increased greatly, from less than 50% in 1949 to over 60% in 1958, and this trend is continuing (Lerner, 1970, p. 20).

Although most institutional deaths occur in general hospitals, when we consider the aged, we find a complicated picture in which homes for the aged and nursing homes become more important than is sometimes thought. We might not expect many of the aged to die in homes for the aged or nursing homes, because we know that only about 5% of people over age 65 and 19% of those over age 85 are institutionalized in the United States. Of these, about 60% are in institutions for the aged and dependent and 8% in mental institutions (Enos & Sultan, 1977, p. 124). Even in countries with the highest rate of institutionalization of the aged—the Netherlands and Canada—not more than 10% of those over age 65 are institutionalized (Schwenger & Gross, 1979).

While in the United States only about 5% of people over 65 *reside* in nursing homes at any given point in time, a much larger proportion of the aged *die* in such homes. Kastenbaum and Candy (1973), examining obituary data, found that 23% of aged deaths in metropolitan Detroit occurred in nursing homes and other extended-care facilities and that most of these deaths (85%) took place in nursing homes. Wershow (1976) analyzed 200 White and 260 Black deaths in Alabama nursing homes, and his evidence lends support to Kastenbaum and Candy's finding. A similar pattern was reported for a somewhat privileged sample in North Carolina (Palmore, 1976), and the same general patterns, although with some exceptions, have been reported for Springfield, Illinois, a city of about 100,000 (Lesnoff-Caravaglia, 1978–1979).

Nursing-home policies regarding admission of patients from hospitals and discharge of patients to hospitals vary greatly. Wershow points out that, since Medicare and Medicaid are reluctant to continue paying a nursing home after a patient has been moved to a hospital, the patient is frequently discharged from the nursing home, and the death will appear in hospital rather than in nursing-home statistics. On the other hand, when Medicare and Medicaid are reluctant to continue paying hospital bills, the patient might be forced to leave the hospital, perhaps to go to a nursing home. This transfer might happen in the case of a critically or terminally ill patient, as is evident in Wershow's data from the fact that 3% of the nursing-home deaths occurred within one day of admission. However, the larger movement between these sites is from nursing home to hospital, and it involves patients suffering acute health crises or simply nearing death.

— A study employing national data (Ingram & Barry, 1977) provides additional support for the interpretation that many more old people die in institutions than customarily live there, and it also shows that this trend is increasing. Using data furnished by the U.S. Bureau of the Census, Ingram and Barry show that, over the period from 1963 to 1974, there was a great increase in the number of nursing homes in the United States, in their size in terms of numbers of beds, and in their rates for admissions, discharges, and deaths. While there was a 23% increase in the number of nursing homes over that period (to 15,700), there was a 130% increase in the average number of beds (from 40 to 75). More than a million persons now reside in such institutions (Ingram & Barry, 1977, p. 304).

Not everyone has the same chance of being institutionalized, however. Blacks are less likely than Whites to be institutionalized in later life (Manard, Kart, & vanGils, 1975; Palmore, 1976). Palmore, examining participants in the Duke longitudinal survey of aging who were followed prior to their deaths in 1976, found that 26% of them had been institutionalized at some time before their deaths, although not all died in institutions. People had a greater chance of being institutionalized if they lived alone, were single or separated, and had no living children. Women were more likely to have been institutionalized than men (33% versus 20%), but this difference was almost wholly accounted for by the above factors. Those who reported that they could not make ends meet had less chance of being institutionalized than people who could better afford institutions (Palmore, 1976).

✱ The proportions of those dying in institutions are not likely to decline in the foreseeable future. While most people with a concern for the aged tend to look with disfavor on institutional care, it is also estimated that perhaps two million aged Americans living in the community have health and demographic characteristics that are comparable to those of the aged who are institutionalized (Brody, 1973). Thus, in one study of a Visiting Nurse service in New York City (Mitchell & Goldfarb, 1966, discussed in Bennett, 1973), 13% of old persons visited in the home were deemed to be in need of old-age home or nursing care. The possibility for the aged who need health services to remain at home would be enhanced if there existed a larger, more comprehensive system of community health services (Brody, 1973; Bennett, 1973), but there is little reason for optimism that this will develop soon.

✤ The conclusion of these considerations is that many older people who do not expire in nursing homes actually do some of their dying there, and many who do not usually live in nursing homes do die in them. The nursing home, therefore, assumes a much greater role as a context in which older people die than would be expected from the well-known statistic that only 4% or 5% of those over age 65 live in nursing homes.

In the United States and Canada, most older people are more likely to actually expire in a hospital than in a nursing home. The difference is consequential, since hospitals epitomize the bureaucratic and technological handling of death and dying (Illich, 1976, especially pp. 201–208; Lofland, 1978). Hospitals tend to be organized for the purposes of "cure" rather than "care" (Rosenthal, Marshall, Macpherson, & French, 1980), making it possible for death to be considered a failure. Most hospitals are oriented toward acute rather than chronic patients, giving differential care on the basis of patient age (Crane, 1975, p. 177; Sudnow, 1967, pp. 103–105). Also, hospitals are more likely to be places where teaching activity occurs, sometimes resulting in artificial prolongation of life for purposes of instruction (Crane, 1975, p. 81; Duff & Hollingshead, 1968, pp. 318–320; Kastenbaum, 1977, p. 201; Sudnow, 1967, pp. 105–106).

While the hospital may be well designed to prolong life and fight off death, it is not usually designed to ensure a good death. Recognition of this fact has led to the development of hospices—special hospital wards devoted to giving total labor-intensive, but low-technology, care (with the notable exception of a commitment to giving high pain relief) to the dying (Kastenbaum, 1977, pp. 224–231; Lofland, 1978, pp. 83–85). That hospices are growing rapidly is indicative of more widespread changes in attitude toward care of the dying that have been part of the thanatology movement (see Lofland, 1978, Chap. 3); still not many people currently die in hospices or hospice-like settings.

Little wonder, then, that studies of dying hospitalized patients, as well as those of people dying at home, indicate that most people prefer to die at home (Aitken–Swan, 1959; Hinton, 1967, p. 148; Rossman & Kissick, 1961). Glaser and Strauss, although noting that in some cases patients cannot be sent home because they need specific hospital facilities and that sometimes patients who are sent home may pose great strains on the families, argue nonetheless that

> sending the patient home is sometimes of course the most satisfactory solution for patient, staff, and family. The patient dies in a familiar environment, surrounded by his kinsmen, and the staff is spared a period of strain, if not an

ordeal. The ideal conditions for dying at home are difficult to achieve, though when all or most of them are present the family is usually relatively eager to have the patient at home [1965, pp. 183–184].

In a large British study of deaths, Cartwright, Hockey, and Anderson found a marked trend away from home deaths (from 49% in 1954 to 35% in 1969); the proportion of deaths away from home is still higher in the United Staes. They attribute the trend to broad social changes:

> Greater mobility, smaller families and an increase in the proportion of women who work outside the home have made it less likely that people who are ill will be living with or near close relatives who are able to devote much time to their care. At the same time improved housing amenities and community services give some aid and support to people who are ill at home [1973, p. 2].

Among improved amenities and services must be counted noninstitutional congregate residential facilities, such as high-rise apartment buildings and retirement communities, which place large numbers of like-situated older people in close proximity to one another. A number of investigators have remarked on the particular advantages of such communities in helping people to cope with impending death. In addition, "natural" age-segregation processes of the population, such as the aggregation of large numbers of older people in resort and retirement communities and in apartment buildings (Rosow, 1967), might approximate the conditions of more planned age-dense congregate residential facilities.

Because more older people live alone instead of with family members, and because more *very* old people, especially women, do so, it is possible that, of those who do die in their own homes, more will die alone. This is suggested by one small English study (Bradshaw, Clifton, & Kennedy, 1978). A study of 181 people who were found dead in their homes in the English city of York during the years 1966 and 1977 found that the number of such deaths was increasing. Of the 181 people found dead, 143 were over retirement age and two-thirds were over age 70. The concentration of such home deaths in later life does not, the authors state, imply neglect of the aged. On the average, a body would be found within about two and a half days of death, usually by a neighbor or, to a somewhat lesser extent, by a family member. This implies that the deceased were not unduly isolated from contact with others. Moreover, three-fourths of the deaths were sudden and probably could not have been prevented even if medical assistance had been made available. Some 7% of the deceased had declined to make formal arrangements for the contingency of dying; about a third were described as "recluses" and another fourth as "independent."

These, then, are the settings in which people die. They vary widely in degree of bureaucratization and in the way they allow for social regulation or personal control over the status passage of dying. The next section examines some implications of these objective properties of the contexts through which people enact the last status passage of life's career.

Environmental and Community Contexts and the Aging and Dying Passage

In the last section I hinted at some of the implications of the physical or geographical context of aging and dying—whether the person dies at home, in a hospital or another institutional setting, or in an age-dense social environment. However, the physical setting is only part of the context of the aging and dying person, being in a sense the stage on which the dramas of aging and dying are enacted. This section focuses on the family and community as human contexts that more directly enmesh the aging and dying and help to shape their careers.

Most old people live at home, and, although most eventually die in a hospital or other institutional setting, the early stages of dying occur within a family context. Kathy Calkins Charmaz (Calkins, 1972) has provided a useful analytical framework for examining these early preinstitutional or noninstitutional phases of the dying career. Two major patterns of aging and dying in family context were discovered: a *chronic-illness pattern* and a *gradual-aging pattern*. In the latter, the individual—a spouse or parent—is viewed as gradually growing older and less able to maintain self-care; age is the focus of familial concern. In the former case, illness is the focus of concern, and a chronically ill family member is viewed as a patient: "The illness had become merged with his identity. In addition to becoming a focal point of family interaction, the illness becomes a basis of the life style of the family members" (Calkins, 1972, pp. 24–25) as they assume the burden of care. People may of course move from the gradual-aging pattern to the chronic-illness pattern following an acute-illness episode, such as a heart attack or a stroke. Calkins found that physicians and other professionals are important definers of entry into the movement through these patterns for middle-class, but not for working-class, people.

Although caring for aging and dying family members is often defined as burdensome, Calkins found a "sense of obligation to provide a dying kinsman with care for as long as possible." Moreover, this sense of obligation is *unquestioned:* "Shouldering the burden is the only viable alternative, and often is taken for granted as the only way of managing the situation" (Calkins, 1972, p. 25).

The familial burden of caring for an aging and dying relative may take many forms and may vary in intensity. It might involve increasing commitments of time in visiting aging or chronically ill parents and grandparents, giving financial support, or making provisions for living space (see also Townsend, 1963, Chap. 5). Cartwright, Hockey, and Anderson (1973, pp. 29–34) found in their interviews with British people close to the deceased that only 18% of the noninstitutionalized were reported not to have needed any kind of help before they died. Nearly one-third had needed help in caring for themselves for at least a year before their deaths; many had needed overnight care.

Calkins notes that, when other family members live in close proximity to the aging person, they are likely to assume the burdens of care directly. In other circumstances, they may assign them to specific family members, such as an unmarried or widowed daughter, or delegate them to outside agencies. In the British study, Cartwright, Hockey, and Anderson (1973, p. 32) found that wives, husbands, and then daughters were most likely to be involved in giving help to the dying person (see Kalish, 1972).

The extent to which the obligation of care is defined as burdensome is affected by the degree of predictability of the course of dying. When the prognosis and timing of death are relatively certain, feelings of obligation to give care are increased without increasing the sense of burden. In cases of uncertain timing, feelings of being burdened are more likely to be experienced by caring family members (Calkins, 1972; see also Glaser & Strauss, 1968). The living arrangements of those in either the gradual-aging or the chronic-illness pattern are tenuous, since aging individuals and their families seem to avoid institutionalization and hospitalization in the face of deteriorating health.

Calkins observes that the most tenuous living arrangements of all are those of aging spouses, for the amount of care necessarily depends on the health status of both. In my own observations in a retirement community (Marshall, 1974a), I found numerous married couples and other cohabiting kin pairs in which both people living together expressed a great willingness to die, or an acceptance of death, as long as they could live longer than their spouses or cohabiting relatives. The burden of caring for a spouse or other relative may then be experienced as an important way in which life itself is given meaning and a sense of worth. There is evidence, however, that in cases of prolonged dying careers, the burden on spouses or other family members becomes excessive (Ball, 1976–1977).

Calkins further observes that aging persons themselves, if they are cognitively competent, try to control what happens to them as they grow weaker and their health deteriorates. They may, in some cases, struggle to delay institutionalization—a superb literary example of this struggle is found in Margaret Laurence's novel *The Stone Angel* (1968)—in others, they may seek to accelerate institutionalization in order to relieve their families of the burden of care (Kalish, 1969a). It is in decisions regarding institutionalization that physicians play important roles—roles that involve making the decision itself, legitimizing the decision made, and assuaging the guilt of family members. Institutionalization does not, of course, remove all family burdens, but it changes them by forcing the family to conform to routines of the hospital, nursing home, or other institutional facility (Calkins, 1972; Rosenthal, Marshall, Macpherson, & French, 1980; Townsend, 1962, pp. 336–337) and by placing a greater emphasis on visiting rather than on direct health care.

Calkins' framework shows great promise in pointing to the important conditions influencing the ways in which giving care to the aging and dying will be experienced or defined by family members:

> The closer the kinship relatedness, attachment, and proximity, the more likely the burden of care will be assumed by the family. If these conditions exist and the supporting relative is aware of the ill person's deterioration, then the family may maintain a definition of unquestioned obligation for the burden of care [1972, p. 36].

One critical difference between men's and women's contexts of dying is that women are much more likely to die alone, or at least without a spouse present, because they are more likely to be widowed. There are about four widows for every widower in North America and a ratio of three to one for those above age 65 (for the United States, see Lopata, 1973; for Canada, A. M. Matthews, 1979). This means that women are much more likely than men to experience bereavement over the loss of a spouse and to be without the possible support of a spouse when they themselves are nearing death (Shanas, 1979). A typical woman can expect to survive her husband by several years. If widowed, she will on the average face over 19 years in that state (Carter & Glick, 1970). It has been argued that attitudes toward death are more strongly influenced by intimate interpersonal relationships than by other factors such as subculture or cultural values (Marshall, 1975a; Pandey & Templer, 1972); and widowhood is clearly a major factor affecting the nature of interpersonal relationships.

As noted earlier, it is wives, husbands, and daughters, in that order, who are most likely to give assistance to the dying person (Cartwright, Hockey, & Anderson, 1973, p. 32; Shanas, 1979), and this suggests that males are more likely to get help than females. Although the area of interpersonal relationships is little understood, it seems probable that giving such care must influence the way an individual views his or her own impending death, through direct learning or role-modeling processes and also as an outcome of the bereavement process. Moreover, as we will see in Chapter Seven, much of the vocabulary of motives on which people draw to make sense of their own death is related to factors of economic security and to the avoidance of becoming a burden; and these factors are strongly associated with widowhood, since many more widows than old people in general are poor.

The ways in which the bereavement experience might affect a widow are influenced by the kind of death experienced by the husband, by the husband's age at death, and by the number of years spent in widowhood. Older widows are generally reported to be less emotionally affected by the loss of the spouse than are younger widows and to suffer less psychological disturbance (Ball, 1976–1977; Calvert, Northeast, & Dax, 1977; Parkes, 1964a, 1964b; Vachon, 1979). However, some studies report a higher incidence of somatic complaints (physical illnesses) and even death among bereaved persons in general (Parkes, 1964b, 1972; Parkes, Benjamin, & Fitzgerald, 1969; Rees & Lutkins, 1967; Young, Benjamin, & Wallis, 1963). Parkes (Parkes, Benjamin, & Fitzgerald, 1969), noting that about three-fourths of the increased death rate among the bereaved was attributable to coronary thrombosis, arteriosclerotic heart disease, and other types of heart disease, has utilized the term *the broken-heart syndrome* to describe a process that, although little understood in its dynamics, has been referred to in common parlance for centuries. The first year of bereavement is generally thought to be the period when the widow or widower is most vulnerable to deterioration in health (Ball, 1976–1977; Clayton, Desmarais, & Winokur, 1968; Clayton, Halikes, & Maurice, 1971; Maddison & Walker, 1967; Parkes, 1970), but some evidence indicates continuing or even greater deterioration in health after the first year (Bunch, 1972; Cox & Ford, 1964; Vachon, 1979). In one investigation of younger widows, the investigators argue that "most widows continue the psychological work of mourning for their dead husbands for the rest of their lives" (Glick, Weiss, & Parkes, 1974, vii).

The type of death and the way in which it is perceived have an effect on health. In one well-designed interview study (Vachon, Formo, Freedman, Lyall, Rogers, & Freeman, 1976), widows of cancer patients were suffering more in their health one to two months after the death than widows of men who died for other reasons. When the illness was defined as "lingering" rather than as "terminal," the time perspective of the woman was extended and, when death came, it was less "expected" and therefore more of a shock to her. It was noted that the prolonged stress of a lingering illness led to deterioration of physical and emotional health in the person who would become bereaved. Post-bereavement mortality or ill health may then be partly a function of pre-bereavement stress (see also Gerber, Rusalem, Hannon, Battin, & Arkin, 1975); comparison to Calkins' framework is relevant here.

Ball (1976–1977), in a questionnaire study of 200 widows bereaved from six to nine months, found that an interaction between the age of the widow and the length of the illness affected the widow's grief reaction. While, in general, the younger widows (aged 18–46 in this study) experienced a stronger grief reaction than middle-aged and older widows (the latter being over age 60), sudden death led to more intense grief at all ages. This finding suggests that what has been called *anticipatory grief* is operative in situations of prolonged or expected dying. However, middle-aged and older widows were found to be more "irritable" after a prolonged death than after a sudden death experience, whereas younger widows were more irritable after a sudden death experience (see also Glick, Weiss, & Parkes, 1974, p. 14). After age 45, anticipatory grief did not play an important part in mitigating the post-bereavement grief experience.

This finding is consistent with the notion put forth by Bernice Neugarten of the "normal expectable life cycle." Noting the finding by Parkes (1964b) described above that older widows suffered less in their health than younger ones, Neugarten suggests that "it is more often the timing of the life event, not its occurrence, that constitutes the salient or problematic issue. . . . Major stresses are caused by events that upset the sequence and rhythm of the life cycle" (Neugarten, 1970a, p. 86).

I have noted that the typical woman can expect to survive her husband and that the experience of having grieved for a spouse tends to make a woman view death differently from the way in which her husband viewed it. Most women will survive their husbands long enough to get through or beyond the experience of intense grief. Kalish and Reynolds (1974) present some interesting data on 37 widows, many of whom had been widowed for a long time. These women were compared with matched controls, and, on a large number of dimensions, there were no significant differences between the two groups. Considering the small sample size and the lumping together of people who had been widowed for greatly varying periods of time, it is nonetheless worth considering some of the nonstatistically significant trends. Many of these "seem to arise from having attended to the dying process of a loved one. Widows were, therefore, more capable of telling someone he was dying . . . they were more likely to believe that dying patients should be made aware of their condition . . . and they [were] somewhat more inclined to feel that people should be permitted to die if they wish" (1974, p. 191). Kalish and Reynolds also found that widows took a more peaceful approach to death, being less willing to fight in order to live. These researchers suggest that this attitude might develop because widows' own lives have less meaning and death, for some, implies reunion with the spouse in the afterlife.

A number of these factors may well act together to provide the older woman with many reasons to feel that death is at least as desirable, if not more desirable, than continued living. Women are more likely than men not only to survive to later old age but also to be alone (Chevan & Korson, 1972), often lonely (Atchley, 1975; Lopata, 1973b; Tunstall, 1966), economically insecure or dependent (Atchley, 1975; Harvey & Bahr, 1974), suffering from ill-health, and at times stricken with grief.

An as yet relatively unexplored implication of the age differential in life expectancy is the different kind of relationship a dying woman is likely to have with her children than a man is with his. As Neugarten has observed (1977), a woman has a fairly good chance of being predeceased by at least one of her sons. As well, children will typically be several years older at the time they might be called upon to care for a dying mother than when they might care for their dying father. The children, who are the most crucial members of the widow's support system (Lopata, 1978, 1979; Shanas, 1979), will therefore often themselves be in old age or retired when their mother dies, while they will be actively engaged in the activities of the middle years at the time of their father's death. This observation raises the question of the importance of grandchildren and other relatives in the care of very old dying persons. Unfortunately, we do not have a large research base with which to address such a question, but indications are that siblings and the extended family are not an important support system for the widow (Lopata, 1973a, Chap. 4; 1979, Chap. 7), whereas friends are important for widows without children (Adams, 1968; Arling, 1976; Vachon, 1979).

The effect of bereavement on the orientation of widows toward life and toward death has often been viewed through stage theories. Caution is in order, however. It must first be remembered that there is little research on widows, and most of it (Glick, Weiss, & Parkes, 1974; Marris, 1958; Vachon, 1979; Vachon et al., 1976) is restricted to younger widows. All the criticisms leveled earlier in this book (see Chapter Four) at Kübler-Ross' stage theory of dying, which she views as a kind of proactive grieving process from the perspective of the dying person, can be leveled at any of the stage theories of grief, which generally take the form of a "two-weeks, two-months, two-years" formula (two weeks of intense grief and shock, two months of strong grieving, two years of lessened grief, recovery, and restoration of the self). Bugen (1977) has criticized stage theories of grief as follows: (1) the stages are not separate entities but blend together and overlap; (2) the stages are not necessarily successive; (3) it is not necessary for everyone to experience each stage; (4) the intensity and/or duration of any stage might vary considerably; and (5) there is little empirical evidence to support the concept of stages. Bugen argues that we can benefit from the description of the various emotional states suggested by stage theorists without having to order them sequentially. Bugen argues that the quality and intensity of the social relationship, as well as the extent to which the death was viewed as preventable, are important dimensions to take into account when seeking to understand grief, and he presents clinical data within that framework.

Most people, given enough time, appear to adjust to the death of a spouse and build a new life. There is some suggestion that men might find widowhood a more difficult experience than women (Barrett, 1978; Berardo, 1970; A. M. Matthews, 1979) and for reasons readily understandable in terms of the general dimensions of predictability and control that run through so much of this research literature. In order to make sense of the fact that older widows appeared less severely affected by bereavement than younger widows, I drew on Neugarten's argument (1970a) that the timing of an event is more important than its occurrence. The same argument applies to sex differences. It may be that women now anticipate being widowed as a normal part of the course of family life and that men and women, not entirely unrealistically, have different conceptions of what they might expect over the life course (Neugarten & Hagestadt, 1976). If the order of death is anticipated, it may well be less traumatic. The same interpretation emerges from Calkins' finding that an uncertain prognosis and timing of the course of dying increased the feeling of burden among care givers. Finally, without wishing to extend this interpretation too far beyond the limited data available, the reason Kalish and Reynolds found widows less willing than matched controls to fight against death might be not that life has no meaning without the spouse but rather—or, perhaps, in addition—that death itself now seems appropriately timed.

I would now like to turn from the family context to that of the community without, however, entirely leaving the question of timing. Although *community* is a central concept in sociology and has been given a plethora of meanings and formal definitions (Wirth, 1964), for our purposes a general definition is acceptable, one that uses the term *community* to refer to "the organization of social activities to afford people daily local access to those broad areas of activity which are necessary in day-to-day living" (Warren, 1972, p. 9). These areas of activity would include the spheres of production-distribution-consumption, socialization, social control, social participation, and mutual support. While such domains of activity are not restricted to one geographical locale, they have relevance for community insofar as they are organized so as to intersect in one locale (Warren, 1972, p. 10). As Wirth (1964) observes, "A territorial base, distribution in space of men, institutions, and activities, close living together on the basis of kinship and organic inter-dependence, and a common life based upon the mutual correspondence of interests tend to characterize a community" (p. 166). Community can be found locally within geographical areas, but the focus may well be on a clustering of the organization of such activities along ethnic, religious, or age-based lines. Indeed, a central analytical dimension for understanding communities is their variability in inclusiveness, such as the extent to which all activities of everyday life can be provided for within one's own ethnic community.

In Chapter Three, while addressing cross-cultural research on aging and dying, I characterized a good death as one in which the ties that linked an individual with others in the community were severed at exactly the point of demise (see, for example, Counts, 1976–1977). Such a death is rare, and ritual preceding and following death is often used to approximate this state of affairs. An example that epitomizes the ritual handling of dying in the community context is given by Myerhoff:

> Jacob Kovitz died in the middle of the public celebration of his ninety-fifth birthday, amid friends and family gathered to honor him at the Aliyah Senior Citizen's Community Center, which had become the focus of life for a small, stable, socially and culturally homogeneous group of elderly Jews, immigrants to America from Eastern Europe. The event was remarkable in many ways: It dramatized the ubiquitous human passion for continuity. It called attention to several kinds of continuity and the manner in which they overlap. And it

pointed up the ways in which ritual provides and presents continuity [1978, pp. 163–164].*

Jacob Kovitz was an important person. At the community center parties were held every month to celebrate the birthdays of everyone born within that month; however, Mr. Kovitz was president of the center, both a formal and informal leader, and his birthday was celebrated individually. He had been very sick for the three months preceding his final party but was determined to celebrate his birthday among his family and to deliver his annual birthday speech to the community. Myerhoff says "Jacob had always controlled himself and shaped his life, and he was not about to give that up. Evidently, he hoped he might die the same way" (1978, p. 186). To do so, he and his family drew on the ritual resources available in his community, and Myerhoff describes how his life and his death were given meaning in terms of shared symbols within his community, while, at the same time, the ritual treatment of his death contributed to his community's collective sense of continuity: "Jacob's death revived the idea, or at least the hope, that sometimes people die meaningfully, properly and purposively. Death is often felt as the final manifestation of helplessness, accident, and disorder, but here death seemed apt and fulfilling" (1978, p. 198).

As Myerhoff notes, in this community setting, Jacob's death fulfilled all the defining characteristics of Tamed Death, noted by Ariès and discussed in Chapter Three. These were "his foreknowledge of death, its occurrence in a public ceremony which he directed, his attitude of calm acceptance, his use of the occasion to express the meaning of his life, and the presence and participation of those with whom he was intimate" (Myerhoff, 1978, p. 166). Jacob Kovitz was unusually favored in being closely tied to a community that gave active support, for it has been argued (for example, Lopata, 1973a) that the processes of urbanization and industrialization have mitigated the possibility for community support to be provided in circumstances surrounding death. However, when facing death becomes a matter of common interest, it is possible for people in communities to organize themselves in order to render death more meaningful and to maximize the extent to which an aging individual can maintain control over it.

In congregate facilities for the aged, residents are frequently reminded of the presence of death (Bengtson, Cuellar, & Ragan, 1977; Hochschild, 1973; Marshall, 1975a, 1975c; Townsend, 1962). Townsend (1962, p. 95) found that, in nursing homes and homes for the aged in England, 17% of the residents died each year. Gubrium (1975a; also Ross, 1977, p. 100) has described death as a "main event" in such places, and I have pointed out that death is the most newsworthy event in such a place (Marshall, 1975b).

*From "A Symbol Perfected in Death: Continuity and Ritual in the Life and Death of an Elderly Jew," by Barbara G. Myerhoff, reprinted from Barbara G. Myerhoff and Andrei Simić (Eds.), *Life Career—Aging: Cultural Variations on Growing Old.* Copyright 1978, pp. 163–205 by permission of the publisher, Sage Publications, Inc. (Beverly Hills/London).

Jennie Keith-Ross (1977, pp. 98–100) describes how the first death to occur in a new retirement community generated confusion and uncertainty among the residents. The residents expressed concern not about death itself but about the undignified funeral service that resulted from the fact that typical ways of handling a community death had not been constructed. Through a committee, the residents had the director establish a set procedure for announcing deaths and funeral services. Ross argues: "In a new community, response to one event can become the basis for definition of a new rule for approved behavior. Given their sense of shared fate (if her death is handled in this way, mine will be too) and the confrontation with a common problem (the close possibility of death), one death was a sufficient stimulus for demanding a norm of ritual response" (Ross, 1977, p. 100).

In the retirement community I studied, the administration left the residents free to develop their own response to death as a community event (Marshall, 1975a, 1975c), and the residents began to do so within a year of the founding of the community. Their existence as a "community of the dying" was openly recognized in the resident-run newspaper, and a procedure for discreetly announcing death on a bulletin board was initiated. The residents developed a low-key but matter-of-fact way of managing death and dying and provided mutual support to the bereaved, while assuring themselves that their own deaths would be handled with similar compassion, dignity, and care (Marshall, 1975a).

Another example of the community context facilitating a good death is the Hutterite Brethren. Eaton (1964) notes doctors' reports that the Hutterites fear death less than most Americans, partly because of their strong religious beliefs and partly because the community guarantees that survivors will suffer no economic losses from the death. Beyond that, however, Eaton describes a matter-of-fact attitude toward death and a ritual recognition that, although very simple, contains the properties of the Tamed Death.

Hochschild, describing a low-income apartment project for the aged, reports that death

> was a fact of life . . . and there was no taboo against talk about it. . . . Although each individual faced death essentially alone, there was a collective concern with, as they put it, "being ready" and facing up, a concern the young could not share with them in quite the same way. The deaths of fellow residents meant a great deal to the community and they reveal a great deal about it [1973, p. 79].

It appears, then, that regardless of social class, when large proportions of the population face the same community concerns with death because of common age, they will likely develop ways of dealing with death, making sense of it, and in a sense routinizing it.

The possibilities for gaining community support in the last stages of aging and dying may well be higher in rural areas (Chasin, 1971). Lozier and Althouse (1975) describe the life of the aged in a small West Virginia community. Retired persons there customarily spend a great deal of time on the front porch. This allows them to interact with passers-by and to have a great deal of control over how much interaction they will have with others. With increasing age, and perhaps health decrements, the aging individual will be more tied to the porch and less free to leave it. As this happens, others in the community are more likely to come to visit, offering minor services and conversation. As strength diminishes even more, so does interaction, which comes to be more restricted to kin and close friends. Periodic health crises will remove the person into the house. Reappearance on the porch brings a renewed flurry of interaction from passers-by. Lozier and Althouse identify a community-regulated pattern of interaction that varies according to health and the visibility afforded by customary use of the porch. This pattern continues to involve the aging person, and it functions until the very end in the highly supportive manner:

> At some point, the old man never recovers sufficiently to resume a routine of appearance on the porch. The community networks provide a running assessment of his condition, and the prognosis becomes negative. He is now socially defined as being in a terminal state. Now, with the expectation that he will die before long, it is likely that an opportunity will be sought, on a warm day when he is feeling better, and he will be brought out again to the porch. Now, instead of being in "recuperation," he is described as "sick on the porch." Notice of appearance on the porch in a terminal condition is rapidly broadcast, and for a couple of hours, perhaps, he will be receiving his final public attention. Withdrawn again to the house, he will be cared for by the more restricted society of kin and close friends until his death [1975, p. 10].

The community and related ritual supports will be of little aid to the dying unless they are able to be active participants. Ritual does not always mitigate death fear and render death and dying appropriate; it can also evoke fear of death (Bengtson, Cuellar, & Ragan, 1977; Marshall, 1975c) or accentuate the "otherness" and uncontrolled nature of death. I have described one setting, a Catholic nursing home, where death is treated with considerable formal funeral ritual but where death has the character of something outside of and other than the individual (Marshall, 1975c). In that setting everything about the lives of the residents, including their dying, is organized *for* them instead of *by* them.

The vivid presence of death, or its frequent occurrence, does not automatically ensure that it will be well handled as a community event. More generally, living in age-segregated housing does not automatically guarantee that one will receive assistance or support from neighbors, either about death and dying or about anything else (Sherman, 1975). However, age-dense environments probably offer greater opportunities for the development of supportive networks of social relations (Rosow, 1967).

The large proportion of older people, especially those very near to death, who reside in institutional settings often find these settings highly impersonal and bureaucratic, and their course of dying becomes subject to the exigencies of organizational routines of the setting (Carpenter & Wylie, 1974; Glaser & Strauss, 1965, 1968; Gubrium, 1975a, 1975b; Gustafson, 1972; Marshall, 1975c; Stannard, 1973; Townsend, 1962). A number of observers have put forth the thesis that the extent to which the lives of residents of such institutions can be satisfactory is greatly influenced by the degree of independence and resident-initiated organization that is possible in them (Aldridge, 1956; Kalson, 1972; Marshall, 1975c; Messer, 1967; Seguin, 1973).

The end point of failing to encourage resident participation in an initiation of activity is "social death," which "occurs when an individual is thought of as dead and treated as dead, although he remains medically and legally alive" (Kalish, 1966, p. 73). The institutional resident who accepts such a definition will consider himself or herself, for all practical purposes, dead. In such situations, resignation is probably a common attitude toward impending death (Chappell, 1975; Marshall, 1975c). However, before giving up, an institutional resident or a hospital patient may engage in a protracted struggle to assert maximal control over his or her final days.

Speaking of hospital patients, Kastenbaum says that "the person with a life-threatening illness surrenders options and controls over much of his existence in an effort either to receive the direct benefits of medical advances or to contribute to the eventual development of successful treatments" (1977, p. 207). Gubrium (1975a) found nursing-home patients less fearful of being dead than of the process of dying. They were usually very anxious to gain more information about their prognosis, a common finding among hospital patients (Roth, 1963; Rosenthal, Marshall, Macpherson, & French, 1980; Waitzkin & Stoeckle, 1972), but were often unable to obtain it. Administrative staff did not wish to give information to patients, because they believed it would frighten them, while floor staff controlled information in deference to authority and because they believed that informed patients might react negatively to unhappy news, thereby disrupting the staff's own work.

Kastenbaum, studying 200 nurses and attendants in a geriatric hospital, found that they responded in five general ways to the patients' expressed death thoughts: through giving reassurance, expressing denial, changing the subject, expressing fatalism, and engaging in general discussion—for example, asking "What makes you feel that way?" The most frequent response was some form of avoidance of full discussion through denial, change of subject, or expressions of fatalistic belief. Over four-fifths of the floor staff evaded any discussion of the patients' thoughts or feelings. Some staff felt that avoidance was best for the patient, while some admitted that it was largely in protection of themselves (Kastenbaum, 1967a, 1967b).

Interviews with 68 nursing-home workers from a variety of institutional settings showed that nurses who were most experienced with dying patients were most likely to respond to them by avoiding them (Pearlman, Stotsky, & Dominick, 1969). With a small sample, Howard found the same response

(1974). In his British survey, Townsend found that "most of the staff . . . did not care to face up to the unpleasant truths about death and took refuge in euphemisms in their relationships with residents. In over half the institutions it was policy to withhold information" (1962, p. 96). Reviewing the general literature in this area, Schulz and Aderman (1976) note the common myth that, even though staff do not discuss death and dying with patients or residents and frequently withhold prognoses from them, most people nonetheless know when they are dying. They argue that a large proportion of terminal patients are unaware of their prognoses or at best might be classified as in a state of "uncertain certainty" or "middle knowledge."

Weisman and Kastenbaum, using a psychological-autopsy method by which geriatric-care staff come together to reconstruct the final months and days of patients who have died, found that explicit references to impending death were reported as being made by only about half the patients. They argue, however, that many patients wish to express their thoughts but find no one willing to listen; others do speak of death, but staff are not seriously listening to them and may, in fact, avoid them and other patients near them (1968, p. 21). Staff hear few negative views concerning impending death, perhaps because they are not ready to hear such views (Kastenbaum, 1967a).

The way death is treated becomes a test of the quality of the relationship between staff and patients or residents. Prompt removal of a body from a nursing home or a hospital ward, for example, can symbolize a lack of dignity to another resident or patient who has only the same fate to anticipate (Townsend, 1962, pp. 95–96).

There exists, however, considerable evidence that hospital staff find the deaths of older patients less troublesome or disturbing than those of younger ones. Sudnow (1967) and Coombs and Goldman (1973) argue that this is because death in the aged is more likely to be anticipated, lacking the shock value of sudden death. Glaser and Strauss (1964, 1968; Glaser, 1966) argue that older patients have little social value and that, therefore, their death constitutes low social loss to health-care personnel. It may also be argued (Rosenthal, Marshall, Macpherson, & French, 1980) that the death of an older patient creates a feeling of relief among health-care personnel who may be frustrated by their inability to "do anything" dramatic or definitive on behalf of older patients. In any event, work with older patients is apparently viewed by many as a kind of "dirty work" (Hughes, 1964), with low prestige and few of the rewards of working in more dramatic "curing," rather than "caring," areas. Television drama seldom focuses on chronic care; it usually deals instead with dramatic cases of cure.

The health-care staff on a hospital ward or in a nursing home can create an environment that fosters fear or denial of death. Most professionals caring for the terminally ill report feeling inadequately prepared to deal with the dying. Their own anxieties about death may well be higher than those of their patients. For instance, in research on an extended-care unit, Moore and Newton present the following information:

While only seven per cent of the patients admitted to fearing death, 35 per cent of the staff and 25 per cent of family members did so. Fully two-thirds of the staff and family members feared dying alone while 28 per cent of the patients indicated such apprehension. Only 17 per cent of the patients admitted fearing the events associated with dying, 62 per cent of the staff and 38 per cent of the family members so indicated. While staff and family members pointed to concerns such as bodily suffering, pain, changes in mental state, effects on friends and family, patients mostly failed to list any such concern [1977, p. 135].

The investigators in this case found massive and consistent evidence of claims on the part of these patients (average age, 68; age-range, 37–92) that they do not fear death. The investigators' faith that these people *should* fear death is perhaps attested by the fact that they go on to say that these findings "suggest the use of denial on the part of these life threatened elderly patients" (1977, p. 135; for examples of the same faith, see Kimsey, Roberts, & Logan, 1972; Roberts, Kimsey, Logan, & Shaw, 1970). For present purposes, however, the major point is that an *environment* of death fear surrounds these patients.

The last phase of the terminal status passage is enacted for most people in institutional environments such as a nursing home or hospital. Institutional staff may wish to permit no stance on the part of residents or patients other than compliance to institutional regimes (Lofland, 1978, p. 72), but I have suggested that the course of dying can be understood as a struggle for control over the passage. One possible outcome for the patient is capitulation. In an admittedly surprising finding, Felton and Kahana (1974) found that of 124 residents of three homes for the aged, those who were classified as higher on *external* control on a situational measure were better adjusted and had higher life satisfaction and morale.

The customary measure of locus of control (Rotter, 1966) often used in such studies (for example, Kuypers, 1972) measures, as a personality trait, the extent to which people view their life experiences as originating in the external world and happening to them or as outcomes of their personal, internal endeavors. Felton and Kahana (1974), however, designed indicators that "reflect the potential for real control over the environment in the institutional setting" (p. 295). They argue that, since most residents have little control over their environment, a stance of external control is more congruent with their situation.

On the other hand, using the Rotter measure, Goldstein (1976) found that chronic hemodialysis patients who were high on external locus of control tended to deny their illness and were less personally adjusted than those with high internal control. In another study (Nehrke, Bellucci, & Gabriel, 1977–1978), nursing-home patients were found to be higher on external control than respondents in public housing or in the wider community. The nursing-home residents were also, however, least fearful of death (as measured by Boyar's and also by Templer's death-anxiety scales). The community residents were younger, better educated, and more satisfied with their lives, and they scored lower in external control. These data, the authors suggest, show that "the community residents who have the most to look forward to and who feel they are effective in shaping their future are most fearful of death since they cannot control death. The nursing home residents, in contrast, are basically at the end of their lives and have few alternatives, aside from death, available to look forward to. Rather than despair, however, it may be that the nursing home respondents, as in Swenson's study, were looking forward to death as a release from disability and dependency" (1977–1978, p. 364). This is a plausible interpretation but must be treated as speculative, since the death-anxiety scales employed are not unidimensional (Marshall, in press; Thorson & Perkins, 1978). The interpretation does, however, suggest the importance of health and the ability to remain independent.

These factors also emerge as important from a study of 40 lung-cancer patients who were studied over a four-year period. For these patients, dying itself was relatively devoid of threat, and the emotional problems encountered by the patients emanated largely from family, friends, and hospital staff:

> The interaction of the patient with the environment in which dying occurred often produced extreme feelings of discomfort in both the patient and the staff. The patient's discomfort did not appear to be related to the dying behavior, although that was the interpretation of those observing the patient. It was related to the inability of those surrounding the patient to come to terms with his death and to painful medical procedures [Dudley, Verhey, Masuda, Martin, & Holmes, 1969, p. 321].

The authors point out that many patients recognized that the changes they were undergoing were hazardous to their emotional well-being, and they sought to avoid change at all costs. This was difficult because these patients had few behavioral alternatives. Lieberman has also reported a concern with feelings of losing control of oneself in relation to the environment: "During the last few months of life, there is a sharp rise in the focus on one's body and the feeling that it is a less adequate instrument" (1966, p. 71). Felt inadequacy is also experienced with respect to social relations, which Lieberman found became of heightened importance during the very last stages of dying.

In a very sophisticated study that compared critically ill patients, noncritically ill patients, and well controls (mean age, about 50; age range, 21–82), the critically ill patients were found to be more desirous of being free from external control than were people in the other groups (Thomas & Weiner, 1974). They were also higher on expressed need for affection and expressed affection; in addition, this need increased as a function of severity of their disease. The expression of affection, the authors note, may be a way of soliciting affection in return, and the changes in desire for internal rather than external control "may be an indication of a reaction against the control already placed on them in the form of hospitalization or physical restrictions" (p. 278). This conclusion is consistent with the previously reviewed study (Dudley et al., 1969), where emotional anxieties of the lung-cancer patients were "sometimes related to fear of what would happen to them in terms of resuscitative procedures and to power struggles between the patient who insists on dying and the hospital staff who refuses to grant the patient the right to die or even to talk of death" (p. 324).

In summary, it seems fair to conclude that the institutional setting—be it a hospital, nursing home, or home for the aged—militates against the exercise of maximum personal control over the status passage of aging and dying, a passage that may last for days, weeks, months, or even years. Moreover, when the institution is not simply fulfilling the functions that might otherwise be fulfilled by the family or community of the older dying person, it structures the ways in which the resident or patient can relate to family and community.

In this chapter I have reviewed several facets of the terminal status passage of aging and dying. Human beings are viewed as creatures who attempt to give direction to their own lives, who attempt to negotiate with others, or struggle with them, in pursuit of a life after their own fashion. That pursuit extends to the final chapters of the autobiography, and, indeed, I have suggested that in the final stages of life control becomes more important than in earlier stages.

Control over one's death and dying is probably more important in today's world than it was formerly; at the same time, control is more difficult to sustain because the course of dying now takes longer than in earlier eras, because the dying person is likely to be old and older people are relatively powerless and control few resources, and because aging and dying is a status passage that usually brings the individual into contact with bureaucratic institutions that have a force of their own.

Factors affecting the character of this final status passage include one's family and community situation; and these factors, in turn, have a great deal to do with where one dies. Family and community can help the individual who is seeking to control the aging and dying status passage (although this is not inexorably the case), whereas the general failure of the institutions to ensure death with dignity is signified by the urgency with which reforms are being advocated.

Maintaining control over the status passage of aging is one of three analytical dimensions of aging and dying that I am using to organize an understanding of the available data. It is quite possible that I have overworked the theme somewhat, and I am not distant enough from the material to realize the extent to which my category has led to a kind of selective screening or filtering of the data. However, I believe that the concept of status-passage control is important; this importance may be more apparent by concluding with a translation of that concept into the overriding metaphor of this book.

My metaphorical understanding of aging and dying is that we come to a point in life where we realize that time before death is short. As meaningful and meaning-seeking creatures, with a sense of autobiography, we can now locate the self in the last chapters of life. The concept of control of the status passage of life in these last chapters is represented metaphorically by *authorship*. We saw in Chapter Five that people wish to develop a view of their entire biography as one that makes sense, that is meaningful, that is "a good story." In this chapter I have argued that we want it to be *our own story*. We want to be, and be known as, the author—to leave a *personal* mark. This desire perhaps has something to do with the quest for some kind, or any kind, of symbolic immortality, which Lifton (1969, 1971) has suggested characterized humankind (see the fifth section of Chapter Four). I see this quest as particularly important in our society, because I think it is related to the individualism that characterizes our era and the threats to individualism that we have constructed.

Review Questions for Chapter 6

1. *Physicians are major "gate keepers" regulating entry into the role of dying. Discuss the relative power of physician and patient in the doctor/ patient relationship and how it affects communication between patient and physician and other factors in the dying trajectory. How do age-related factors such as cohort differences in education and attitudes toward authority further affect the doctor/patient relationship?*

2. *What has been and might be the impact of the women's movement on the support systems available to older women and to widows? How do the bases of support available to women and to men in bereavement differ? How do women and men differ in the way they anticipate their own impending deaths?*

3. *What mechanisms or strategies could prospective applicants to the Glen Brae retirement community adopt in order to minimize the problems posed by uncertainty over life expectancy discussed in this chapter?*

4. *Do you think that different life insurance rates should be established for men and women? Should the contributions to social security and other retirement benefits plans be different for men and women? What are the practical and political considerations involved?*

5. *Have you discussed with your parents what arrangements they prefer for their own funeral and for that of the surviving spouse (if applicable)? How typical are such discussions? What makes them difficult or uncomfortable?*

6. *Using hypothetical illnesses and social circumstances, construct your own utility curve along the lines of McNeil, Weichselbaum, and Pauker, as discussed in this chapter.*

7. *This chapter has stressed some of the positive effects of congregate community life on aging and dying. What are some of the negative effects—that is, in what ways can congregate living make acceptance of death and the assumption of personal control over it more difficult?*

7

Making Sense of Death and Dying

Recognizing that the time left before death is short, the aging person faces the problem of making sense of the self-as-dying. I have taken the position that, analytically, this problem can be differentiated into three related tasks: *legitimating biography* as life draws to a close (Chapter Five), *maintaining control of terminal status passage* (Chapter Six), and *legitimating the death* that draws ever closer, which is the focus of this chapter.

In reality, these processes are interrelated in the meaningful and meaning-seeking life of the aging and dying person. Thus, while the previous chapter focused on efforts to maintain control over the status passage of aging and dying, this chapter focuses on the effort to render that status passage meaningful. Trying to make sense of the passage and trying to control it are cognitive and behavioral aspects of the same problem; the cognitive problem of making sense of death is interwoven with making sense of biography.

In the first section the interrelationship between the meaningfulness of life and that of death is described. In the second section some evidence that many older people develop good "reasons for dying" is reviewed. The next section returns to the very important area of the relationship between religion and the meaningfulness of death (first discussed in Chapter Three). The fourth section draws some threads of the argument together, and the last section provides some speculation about the future.

The Integration of Life and Death

The ways in which people make sense of their impending death are no different from the ways in which they make sense of the death of others and are, in fact, no different from the ways people make sense of anything. Again I draw on the theoretical view of human beings as engaged in the *social construction of reality*, a view outlined in Chapters Three and Four. I find it useful to assume that people will seek to render their lives, including the end of their lives, meaningful; that this process is inherently social; that it is symbolic, involving the use of language; and that it concerns the social negotiation of identity—the sense of who we were, are, and will be.

Any symbolic universe may be employed in legitimating death, but legitimation may be seen as having two aspects. McHugh maintains that anomie (meaninglessness) stems from the inapplicability of two types of rules that actors use in creating the definition of their situation:

> First, whatever the content of an interaction, the actor invokes the rule that it has intelligible purposes; second, whatever the content of intelligibility of purpose, the actor invokes the rule that there may be some means by which purposes can be attained. The disorder of an interaction, then, hinges on the decision by the actor that one or the other of these rules is inoperative—that purpose is unintelligible or means unavailable [1968, pp. 50–51].

We need only emphasize the unity between life and death to see the applicability of this description to the situation of the aging and dying person. Either continued life or an acceptable, accountable death, together with the means for attaining it, must be formulated. Drawing on Wittgenstein's (1953) concept of language game, Simko adapted this approach to the legitimation of death in a non-Western culture:

> The language-game that will be described is member's knowledgeability of death and the here-after, that is to say, that prior to the time of physical death a person already "knows" about death and about the after-death state, can talk about it, and acts in particular ways based upon this "knowledge" [1970, p. 121].

Actor's "knowledge" of death may be viewed as accounts that place death within a taken-for-granted symbolic framework. Formulating such accounts can be seen as a process of defining the situation (McHugh, 1968;

Simko, 1970). Accounts may provide "good reasons" or legitimations for continued living or dying. I will argue that legitimations for dying are unavoidably interwoven with and contingent on legitimations for continued living. It should be stressed that people, in seeking to render continued living and/or dying meaningful, are not completely unconstrained by either physical or social factors. For example, since reality is constructed through conversation, a major social factor is whether or not an individual has the opportunity to talk with someone else; and a physical constraint may be that continued living is much harder to legitimate for persons undergoing severe pain.

Evidence of legitimation of death among the elderly comes from a variety of sources. First, people who use formal measures of death fear or death anxiety find that increasing age is associated with less fear and anxiety. Second, the evidence shows that high death-fear or anxiety scores among the aged are related not to age but to other factors such as generalized depression. We can thus make inferences about the legitimation of death from correlates of death-fear scores. Third, a number of clinicians have given reasons why death is considered appropriate by the elderly themselves, and, although their data bases are often unsystematic or undescribed in their reports, we can view them as highly informed observers. Fourth, there exist a number of self-reports by dying persons or their intimates describing the ways in which they came to terms with their own death. Here the problem is one of generalizability and unknown representativeness. Fifth, there are some community-based studies, using participant observation data, that show high levels of acceptance of impending death among the aged. Sixth, there is a very small amount of direct survey evidence on the legitimation of death. Drawing on all these sources of information, it is possible, despite the limitations of each, to conclude that large proportions of the aged do make sense of, or legitimate, their impending death and become, on the whole, accepting of it. It is also possible to draw a few conclusions about the conditions favoring successful legitimation of death.

I have already considered, in the second section of Chapter Four, the literature on attitudes toward death and dying, and it is only necessary here to consider its implications for legitimation. In Chapter Four, I noted the general finding, from several studies, that fear of death declines with advancing age. This finding, from large survey studies using single indicators and batteries of questions about death (Bengtson, Cuellar, & Ragan, 1977; Kalish & Reynolds, 1976; Riley, Jr., 1970; Riley, Foner, Hess, & Toby, 1969), has also been demonstrated from a number of smaller studies in diverse settings, many of which used scales (Chappell, 1975; Jeffers, Nichols, & Eisdorfer, 1961; Kalish & Johnson, 1972; Marshall, 1975a; Sharma & Jain, 1969; Swenson, 1961; Templer & Ruff, 1971).

Confusion in the interpretation of this research literature can be reduced—I would not be so bold as to say eliminated—if lack of evidence for fear of death is considered roughly equivalent to *acceptance* of death, *resigna-*

tion to it, or *indifference*. Neither acceptance nor resignation nor indifference implies *desire for death*. A person can be willing to die without wanting to die *ever* or wanting to die *now*. Successful legitimation of death seems, as argued in Chapter Five, to lead people to a renewed enjoyment of life at the same time they are ready to leave it. Legitimation of death involves a vital balance between being ready and willing to live or to die (Marshall, 1974a).

This vital balance between maintaining reasons for living and developing good reasons for dying is illustrated by the "living for each other" theme explored in the third section of Chapter Six. Living for each other represents a continued state of engagement that provides a legitimation for the desire to live longer. This type of legitimation was touchingly illustrated by a woman, age 96, who lived with her sister, age 90, in the retirement community I studied, Glen Brae. She told me about a dream, although I had not asked about dreams, and mentioned it during two interviews spaced more than a month apart: "I dreamed that I knocked at the door—St. Peter's—and I said, 'St. Peter, let me in.' And he said, 'No. Go back—you're needed.' And I did." When I asked this woman how old she would like to live to be, she replied "I'd like to live as old as I am useful. And after that I'm perfectly willing to go. I told you St. Peter wouldn't let me in." Was death a blessing? "Oh! Well, if I were dependent upon anybody, then I would say it was a blessing. But no, I don't think it's a blessing. I agree with St. Peter—that I'm needed" (Marshall, 1974a, pp. 28–29).

This woman simultaneously expressed legitimations for living and dying. At the end of the series of three interviews, she commented again on her dream:

> My dream—it bothered me to think that I was doing so little. I decided I could be spared and asked St. Peter to let me in. He said, "No—you're needed. Go back to where you came from." A silly dream. I'm glad that I'm physically able and mentally able to do things. . . . I don't know how my sister could get along without me and how I could get along without her [Marshall, 1974a, p. 29].

When I asked the younger sister how old she would like to live to be, she answered by saying she would be willing to die when she was no longer of use to her sister. Presumably both sisters viewed death as being "spared" from the indignities of physical decline and, in particular, the inability to continue to make a useful contribution. When that time comes, the good reasons for dying lie ready at hand. Life and death are bound together in people's sense making.

Keith (1979) has emphasized the relationship between life and death. Drawing on Diggory and Rothman's (1961) finding that people who feel they have realized their life goals are less likely to fear death, on Erikson's (1963, p. 269) thesis that those unable to arrive at a positive conception of their past life will be unhappy and die in despair, on Lynn Nelson's (1977) argument, based on social-learning or reinforcement theory, that people who have found their past life rewarding should anticipate greater rewards through continued life and, therefore, find the thought of impending death a noxious stimulus, and on the common-sensical notion that death will be positively viewed as a respite by people who view their past life as unhappy, Keith arrived at a typology of joint attitudes toward life and death.

  People with generally positive attitudes toward their past life would be either *positivists* who would have a positive attitude toward death or *activists* who would have a negative attitude toward death. People negatively disposed toward their past life were classed either as *negativists* who would have a negative attitude toward death or *passivists* who would have a positive attitude toward death. Attitude toward death was measured by a 12-item Likert-type index that reflected whether death was evaluated positively or negatively. Attitude toward life was measured by a 10-item life-satisfaction index. Both measures were dichotomized, and cross-classification sorted respondents into the four cells. Data were gathered by interview from 568 small-town Missouri residents ranging in age from 72 to 99.

  The respondents fell about equally into the four cells of this typology, with the smallest percentage (19%) being activists and the largest percentage (33%) being positivists. Across this age range there were no age differences; however, there were sex and income differences. Women were more likely to be positivists and passivists, whereas men were more likely to be negativists and activists. Looking at attitudes toward death in isolation would, therefore, show that the women in this sample view death more positively than the men do. People with higher incomes were more likely to evaluate both life and death positively.

  Four life areas were investigated to see if change or discontinuity affected attitudes toward life and death. These areas were marital status, health, church involvement, and informal contacts with family and friends. Men and women differed in the extent to which changes in these four areas affected their attitudes toward life and death. Women were more likely to have experienced changes in all these areas. Discontinuity in role relationships was associated with higher frequency of negativists or passivists, affecting the evaluations of life more than the evaluations of death. Among men, however, continuity was more likely to be associated with positive attitudes toward life and lower acceptance of death.

  Keith's study is interesting because it links attitudes toward life with those toward death and because it assesses these attitudes in relation to continuity or change in social role relationships. A more finely differentiated view of the many ways in which attitudes toward life and death are related is suggested:

  The dominant hypothesis offered in the literature, and the one receiving the most support in this research posits that persons who have attained their goals and view life positively will have more accepting attitudes toward death. This hypothesis, however, is perhaps over-simplified in that a substantial proportion of the respondents exhibited different orientations toward life and death [Keith, 1979].

The ties that hold a person to life can be varied, but in later life they are likely to be few and slender (Marshall, 1974a) as social relationships gradually narrow or cease to exist and as age-related decrements in energy, independence, and activity accumulate. The reasons for living may seem less important; the aging individual may simply be "tired of living," and the reasons for dying may make more sense.

 *Reasons for Dying*

One of the most important and least understood aspects of later life is the fact that virtually no older person wants to live forever. Munnichs calls our attention to *Gulliver's Travels,* in which the adventurer found, to his delight, a society of immortals, only to learn that they were "disillusioned, lonely people, worn with age, who have lost life with death. Life without end seems meaningless" (Munnichs, 1977; the example is also discussed by Walton, 1976). Life in the shadow of death can also lose its meaningfulness, while death itself can be imbued with meaning. What is the evidence on how long people desire to live?

To begin with a quite hypothetical case, Back and Gergen (1966b) report one survey of over 1400 respondents, of whom 61% of those under age 40, 61% of those aged 40–59, and 68% of those over age 60 said they would *not* want to live to age 150. Of 106 retirement-community respondents (average age, 80; age range, 64–96), most of whom were in quite good health and reasonably economically secure, who were asked "Would you like to be 100?" none gave an unconditionally affirmative answer. Conditional affirmative answers were given by 19 residents. Conditional replies indicate that the individual can see why continued life to that age *could* be appropriate but has no certainty that these reasons will obtain. For example, a respondent might say "Only if I had my health" or "Only if I could continue to be active" (Marshall, 1973a, 1975a). For most respondents like mine and those reported by Back and Gergen, death at the age of 100 or 150 would be "too late" in terms of their personal desires; and we saw in Chapter Four that, in general, most people of any age do not feel that death *always* comes too soon; rather, it may come "just on time" or "too late."

In Chapter Four we looked at awareness of finitude, defined as the amount of time an individual anticipated living. Awareness of finitude was found to vary not only by age but also by a number of factors affecting the calculus of life expectancy in individuals and in subgroups of the population. After asking people "At what age do you expect to die?" Reynolds and Kalish (1974; see Chapter Five) asked "Now, if you could choose, to what age would you like to live?" The median age to which all their respondents, who varied by ethnicity as well as by age, social class, and other factors, *expected* to live was 75; the median age to which they *hoped* to live was 80. Both men and women selected ages leading to the same median figure of 80. There were no sex differences in median age for the desired future, except for Japanese Americans; the men of that group wished to live longer than women. However, there was a slight tendency for more males in all ethnic groups to want to live to a very old age, beyond age 90. Black respondents both expected and wanted to live longer than respondents from other ethnic groups.

Among the three age groups (20–39, 40–59, and 60 +), the oldest were likely to want to live to a later age than people in the younger groups. However, they indicated a desire for fewer additional years than younger people. As we saw in Chapter Five, Reynolds and Kalish (1974) interpret these data as follows: "Although the elderly are willing to die sooner than middle-aged and younger persons, they do not want to die *soon*. Therefore, in moving the time of death sufficiently far away from their present age, many of them move it into the 90 plus period" (p. 230). Reynolds and Kalish also asked a direct question about fear of death: "Some people say they are afraid to die and others say they are not. How do you feel?" Fear-of-death responses had no relationship to either the expectation of death or the desired life expectancy. Blacks, who had indicated a desire to live longer than other groups, actually indicated slightly less fear of death than other ethnic groups. The authors confess to be lacking an explanation for these findings. The oldest subjects indicated much less fear of death than either of the other two age groups.

Bengtson, Cuellar, and Ragan (1977), with a large multi-ethnic sample of over 1200 people in Los Angeles, found a slightly negative association between perceived *proximity* of death and frequency of thinking about death, while expressed fear of death was slightly associated with the latter. In general, there was almost no association between perceived proximity to death (awareness of finitude) and other attitudes toward death. Even health status predicts attitudes toward death less well than age itself, and there is no relationship between health status and expressed fear of death.

It is not so much through events alone but through the meaning given to such events that reasons for dying can be developed. Through the manipulation of symbols, we arrive at a view of the appropriateness of events in the world, including death. Symbols can be manipulated individually—for example through reading and reflection; but the most powerful mode of using symbols to bring about a definition of reality is talking with others. Much talk in later life has the function of giving meaning to death. Funeral orations, which are heard with increasing frequency by older people, are examples; the death of another is placed in a meaningful context—a context of spiritual values but usually also the context of the life of the deceased.

When the death of another is conversationally rendered sensible, the language becomes available for self-application. Thus, a woman says of her husband's death that he died well: "I mean he had never done anything to regret. Nothing to complete. Nothing to make right." The same language can then be applied to herself: "It is appropriate that I die. I have accomplished what I wanted to accomplish; I have no wrongs to right and no regrets" (Marshall, 1975a, p. 1128).

I will now briefly outline five major nonreligious types of legitimation for death found in my own research (discussed at length in Marshall, 1973a). The extent to which any individual would use such language in application to his or her own impending death would vary according to the cultural or subcultural milieu, as a pool of symbols available for use; by the presence or absence of significant others with whom to interactively and conversationally construct this aspect of reality; and by health and other factors that can serve as reference points for these symbols. Respondents were not given this typology and asked to select a suitable response. The typology was formulated inductively from inspection of answers to questions put to respondents.

You may recall that no respondents gave unqualified affirmative answers to the question "Would you like to live to be 100?" Most simply said they would not. They were, in all cases, asked "Why not?" Almost all respondents said that death did not "always come too soon," implying that it sometimes comes "too late" or "on time." In all cases they were asked "Under what circumstances does death *not* come too soon?" Respondents who could give answers to these questions were deemed to have facility in the "language game" of legitimating death. A small minority were unable to answer one or both of these questions. While the first question posits a quite abstract situation, since most would not live to be 100 in any case, the latter is not so abstract; and most respondents had little difficulty with either question. The analysis is of first-listed response, since many gave several reasons why death is appropriate. In what follows I do not distinguish between answers to the stimulus questions (but see Marshall, 1973a, 1975a).

Type One: Death is preferable to inactivity.

This legitimation explicitly links an evaluation of death with one of life. In McHugh's conception of the causes of anomie, actors offering this legitimation can formulate a conception of life—the good life is the active life—but cannot formulate the means to attain this goal. For example, one respondent who did not desire to live to age 100 said "Few people that do so can get around and know what's going on. If you live beyond the point where you can know what's going on around you and participate . . . " (Marshall, 1973a, p. 180).

This legitimation bears an interesting relationship to disengagement theory. A highly disengaged individual, having no desire to be active, should not offer loss of activity as a reason for dying. This is, on the other hand, the type of legitimation that an activity theorist might predict would be offered by many.

Additional information on this legitimation comes from a consideration of the research and theory of Diggory and Rothman (Diggory, 1966;
Diggory & Rothman, 1961). They assumed that death is feared. Rothman
(1963; see discussion in Diggory, 1966, pp. 245–249) had found that college
and high-school-age subjects who failed in an experimental task showed both
a decrease in self-evaluation esteem and an increase in death imagery as
scored from the TAT method. Diggory and Rothman (1961) sought to explore
the kinds of values that are related to death. Among five values that are
threatened by death, two "purposive activity" items rank high. These are that
people fear death because they can no longer have any experiences and because all their plans and projects would come to an end. Diggory and Rothman's interpretation is that the fear of death may be associated with loss of
utility of the self (1961) or that "people fear death because it eliminates
opportunities to pursue goals which are important for self-esteem" (Diggory,
1966, p. 405). These values tended to be ranked higher in importance by
middle-class subjects than by upper- or lower-class subjects. People who did
not claim a religious preference ranked the values higher than those who did.
Of the latter, Jews ranked the values most highly, followed by Protestants and
Catholics. By age, those aged 25–39 and 15–19 ranked the values higher than
those up to age 55 + . Thus there is a decline after age 40 in the extent to which
activity values are brought into relationship with death. Regrettably, the age
cut-off point is so low as to preclude making generalizations about differences
in later life.

Type Two: Death is preferable to the loss of the ability to be useful.

As with the previous type, this legitimation explicitly links an evaluation of death with one of life; it rests on a formulated conception of life—the
good life is the useful life. This conception is more explicitly social than the
activity legitimation. The goal of the good, or appropriate, life is known, but
the means of attaining this goal are seen as decreasingly available with aging.
When asked if death is something to be feared, one respondent said "I think
more and more, no." Asked why, she said "Well, you know it's inevitable,
and when you get to the point where you're no longer useful, you begin to
wonder whether you're wise to stay on this earth and not be as useful"
(Marshall, 1973a, p. 183).

Usefulness as a reason for not dying is closely tied to activity. Findings
from a study of trapped coal miners are instructive in this regard. Interviewed
after their rescue, these men were asked to describe their concerns while
trapped in the mine (Lucas, 1968; more fully discussed in Lucas, 1969).
Lucas describes their great concern for the vacant roles they would leave. He
explains:

> Premature death creates a number of vacant roles; this phenomenon has also
> been called social loss. Social characteristics such as age, education, occupa-
> tion, family status, social class, and accomplishments influence the total value

which the dying individual embodies; they indicate the social loss to family, occupation, and society at death. Aged people, for instance, have made their major contributions to family, occupation, and society. Their loss, while felt by the bereaved, is considered less than if they were younger. The aged often have a far greater sense of completeness of roles than younger people, for social loss or vacant roles derive much of their meaning from the length of the anticipated future [1968, p. 9].

Glaser and Strauss (1964; Glaser, 1966) make the same point in discussing the low "social loss" of aged and dying patients.

Type Three: Death is preferable to becoming a burden.

Vernon has observed that "for most people the fear of living under certain conditions is stronger than the fear of death. Generally, older individuals are more fearful of living in an incapacitated dependent condition than they are fearful of dying" (1972, p. 134). Although with a small sample and very low response rate of just 30%, Templer (1971b) found a negative correlation between physical health measured by the Cornell Medical Index and death anxiety, as measured by his Death Anxiety Scale. That is, the worse the physical health, the less the death anxiety.

A different light is shed on the relationship between death anxiety and health, however, by research reported from a sample of 472 males (age range, 25–82), in which anxiety, measured by the Cattell test, was compared to self-perceived physical health measured by the Cornell Medical Index, and physicians' ratings of health. The health scores were unrelated to anxiety scores among older subjects. In younger and middle-age groups—that is, up to age 55—anxiety was related to self-reported physical health. In other words, anxious people were more likely than nonanxious people to report ill health. The authors note:

> In old age, the imminence of death transforms the individual's perception of his health. Among young and middle-aged persons, regardless of anxiety level, illness is presumably seen in terms of pain and inconvenience, not in terms of threats to life. For these groups, health problems can be attended to, since they do not arouse intolerable anxiety. With age, a change in the significance of health symptoms occurs, and ill health becomes an ominous threat to one's continued existence [McCrae, Bartone, & Costa, 1976, p. 56].

Low self-reporting of physical symptoms is, therefore, attributed to defensive denial and, as the authors note, this interpretation is consistent with Templer's (1971b) view that retired subjects are denying physical health symptoms because of death anxiety.

What can be made of this interpretation? It is not tested directly, because McCrae, Bartone, and Costa do not have measures of death anxiety —only of general anxiety—and Templer does not have data on physical health except self-reported data. As McCrae, Bartone, and Costa argue, "Future research should explore the relation between manifest death anxiety and health concerns over time and across age groups" (1976, p. 57). I hope that such research takes a somewhat more *social* slant, because, rather than an individual being highly anxious about *personal* death, he or she might be anxious, if health is deteriorating or likely to fail, about social relationships and a move from independency to dependency.

Richard Kalish (1969a) emphasizes that Americans have been highly rewarded through most of their lives for being independent, since independence is a predominant value shared by most Americans. Increasing age threatens the ability to continue to be independent. The person who is independent can be thought of as maintaining self-control.

> The elderly person must not only face the imminence of death, but also of the loss of ability to perform tasks for which he had been so thoroughly rewarded, such as walking, writing, reading, and of course that art of such concern to contemporary *and* turn-of-the-century Americans—control of the elimination processes. With each degree of loss of physical and intellectual alertness, and equally tragically, with each degree of assumption that this loss will occur, dependency becomes more immediate and very likely more frightening [Kalish, 1969a, p. 79].

In relatively nonmodernized societies, the aged might go off to death houses, wander off alone to die, or obtain assistance in dying so as not to be a burden to the *community* (Kalish, 1969a; see also Guemple, 1969). Now, however, the expressed desire is not to be a burden to the *family*. As Kalish notes:

> If allowed to choose between living with their children or entering an institution, many elderly Americans select the latter. This choice not only enables them to avoid being a physical and emotional burden upon their children, but enables the older person to be dependent upon individuals whose affirmed role is to offer support in such circumstances, rather than upon their children for whom the dominant role would reverse a lifelong pattern [1969a, p. 81].

My own data suggest that not only would many people prefer institutional living to being a burden to their families; they would rather be dead than either of those alternatives. For example, these are reasons why some of my respondents did not wish to live to be 100:

> I might not be useful then. I might not be able to make other people happy. I don't want to be a burden, I think is what I mean to say.

> So few people who live that long are much comfort to themselves. Very few of them are spry enough to dress themselves, possibly to feed themselves.

> I'd rather be dead than be in the infirmary—it would be repulsive—a burden to friends.

> I don't think (I'd like to live to 100). I'd assume I'd have to be propped up too much and have to depend on other people [Marshall, 1973a, pp. 184–185].

These are relatively privileged retirement villagers, but the *burden* legitimation was also found in the lower-class home for the aged I studied. One respondent said "No, thank you! Oh glory! When my birthday came around they said, 'You'll live to be 100.' I said, 'Glory be to God, no.' I'd be a burden. I'm afraid to be a burden" [Marshall, 1973a, p. 185].

Living in a community where others do sometimes become a burden surely reinforces the use of this legitimation. As one man at Glen Brae said, "I'd much rather conk out than be a load to somebody—or to myself. I feel so sorry for some of the people you see here in the infirmary" (p. 185).

Like the previously discussed legitimation, this one too rests on a conception of life: the good life is the independent life. The means to this end lie primarily in the continuance of reasonably good health. Good health is also the means to the end of remaining active or useful; however, these legitimations represent a different case from that in which good health is itself the end, as it is in the next two legitimations. In McHugh's formulation (1968, pp. 50–51), the sensibility of continued living or intelligibility of purpose is clear; but continued living is not legitimated, because the actor does not view the means for attaining that purpose as existing. In the two types of health legitimations that will now be discussed, the intelligibility of purpose itself is in question.

Type Four: Death is preferable to loss of mental faculties.

Here the very intelligibility of continued life is threatened by the anticipation of mental deterioration. This legitimation is found in the statement of one woman:

> Mother lived to be 96; grandmother 98. I mean I'm afraid that I will.

> A retired minister said to my husband, "I don't mind death, but I do mind dying." That hits a lot of us. You don't want to live too long. Though you see people here in their 90's at dinner who are very alert. The mind—if only the mind is alert and normal. And that's why people dread the idea of strokes, because it changes the mind and personality. A grim prospect [Marshall, 1973a, pp. 186–187].

For those who have "lost their faculties," as residents customarily put it, death constitutes a blessing—that is, it is legitimated. Living with progressive mental deterioration, either in the family or in the community, provides the documentary proof that death can be appropriate. Asked whether she grieved at the death of her husband, one woman said: "No. He was sick three and a half years. He didn't want to live. He wasn't afraid to die. No sense in being a vegetable." Asked whether death was a blessing, she said "Yes, for the person who is sick, like my husband. There is a woman over in the infirmary. No mind. Just like a vegetable" (Marshall, 1973a, pp. 186–187).

Loss of faculties, of course, makes the individual a burden to others and is, therefore, sometimes related to the *burden* legitimation. Asked how old he would like to live to be, one man responded "It's a question of mentality. Unless my mind clears up I wouldn't want to live much longer —it's a burden and responsibility to my wife. It bothers me. I'm not accustomed to being dependent" (p. 188). This man's wife would like to live as long as her mind is good. The man recognized that his mental capacities were failing. Death was legitimated for himself almost immediately—unless his mind cleared up. The same legitimation was available to his wife for application to her husband's death and also for eventual application to her own death. The social character of legitimation is evident in this sharing.

Type Five: Death is preferable to living with progressively deteriorating physical health and concomitant physical discomfort.

This legitimation was the most frequently endorsed by my respondents. Continuing health can, of course, be viewed as a prerequisite to maintaining activity, usefulness, and independence. Many viewed health as an end in itself or focused on the pain and physical discomfort of poor health. These difficulties, like the previous legitimations concerning mental deterioration, can be viewed as threats to the very intelligibility of life, making death more clearly intelligible than continued life. Thus, one man, who did die within three months, described the major frustration of becoming old: "Well now, I'm getting old. The old bones are rusty, and I'm tired. I really am. I'm tired" (Marshall, 1973a, p. 189).

Swenson (1959) found with his institutionalized and noninstitutionalized respondents that "the poorer the individuals' physical condition, the more positive will be his attitude towards death." Munnichs, whose research in the Netherlands pioneered the study of what I refer to as *legitimation of death,* emphasizes the way in which health conditions affect an individual's view of death:

> In spite of his reconciliation of the idea of the finitude of existence the old person remarks: "But I shall be quite pleased to live some more years." He adds a restriction to this, if he only does not fall a victim to some illness or other. That's what he would regard as terrible [1966, p. 49].

One Glen Brae respondent argued that the advantages that accrue with old age balance out the disadvantages: "As long as you are well. I think the thing everybody fears when you reach this age is you see your friends—not dying, because you don't fear that—but becoming incapacitated" (Marshall, 1973a, p. 190).

Widespread acceptance of this legitimation for impending death is evidenced in the growing death-with-dignity movement. One of my respondents said that death does not come too soon:

> If a person has been ill a long time and suffered. After all, nature is just, and sometimes we have upset nature. It's sometimes meant to be. . . . There are residents here, and I am one of them, who have statements in our medical

records—not to be kept alive—"Keep us comfortable; let us go" [Marshall, 1973a, p. 190].

A resident at St. Joseph's poignantly said "We old—no good no more. Before, I no use no medicine. When you be old you see you no good no more. Best thing to go away [to die]. . . . I don't want to live no more I say. I can't eat anything. I can't drink anything. I got to watch myself" (p. 190). This resident agreed with the statement "To die is to suffer." When I probed "But you want to die?" he replied "Well, what I going to do?" This resident is dying everyday and would just as soon have it over with. For many, then, death can be, as Feifel has noted, "a friend who brings an end to pain through peaceful sleep" (1959, p. 126). As the poet Hanz Zinsser (1950) has artfully said:

Now is death merciful. He calls me hence
Gently, with friendly soothing of my fears
Of ugly age and feeble impotence
And cruel disintegration of slow years.

Other Legitimations

These legitimations are only a few of many possible. The following quotations from my retirement-village respondents convey some of the additional nonreligious meanings that people can use to render their impending death meaningful.

I just think it's too messy a world, and I can do nothing about it.

I don't see myself as contributing. I see myself as using resources that others could have. I believe that we go from plane to plane. I'm very excited to see what's on the next plane.

I'm not very keen about living too much longer. To tell you the truth, the problems of the world—violent age—sick of wars. At one time I thought it would be interesting to live to see how things came out. But they are not.

You outgrow everybody. You become a monument rather than a person.

I'd outlive all my friends and contemporaries. And I suppose I don't think I'd relate enough to the younger people to make it interesting to live [Marshall, 1973a, pp. 191–192].

Since many people possess and can quite easily recount several different legitimations for dying, it is apparent that many people can find one or more reasons why their death should be appropriate. Nonetheless, some people do not appear to be able to give any such reasons in an abstract discussion or to apply the reasons to themselves. There is some evidence that this inability is related to the availability of a conversational other.

People who are married and living with a spouse were more likely to give legitimations for death than were single or widowed people who lived alone (Marshall, 1973a). Since one might expect the former to be more involved with the activities of life and less "ready to die," this contraintuitive finding suggests the importance of conversation in the *social* construction of reality (Marshall, 1973a, 1975a). Other evidence for the social nature of the legitimation of death comes from the correlation of legitimation types with sociodemographic variables such as age, sex, perceived health status, friendship ties, and, importantly, the length of time a resident has lived in a retirement community (Marshall, 1975a).

These reasons for dying are in many respects relatively new phenomena and a result of the changing character of death; they are a complement and often a substitute for religious legitimations. Religious interpretations of the appropriateness of death, however, are still important; and they are discussed in the next section.

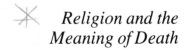

Religion and the Meaning of Death

The effect of religious adherence, belief, or devotion on the meanings people hold about death, or the reverse effects of meanings of death on religious phenomena, have been no better understood than the relationship between age, aging, and religious phenomena. In both cases, religious phenomena that are patterned by age may be a function of generational or cohort effects. That is, some studies find greater religiosity in later life, but it is possible to attribute the religiosity to any one of a number of factors, including aging and partially age-related factors, such as awareness of finitude, the persistence of cohort differences from earlier life, or generational experiences throughout life that are differentially arrayed by cohort. People might be religious in later life because they were always religious, because they became religious with the wisdom of aging, because they saw military service and war (no atheists in the fox-holes), or because in later life they began to worry about what happens after death.

Another difficulty with assessing the relationship between religiosity and the meaning of death held by individuals is the problem of conceptualizing and measuring religion. Different studies, often portraying conflicting results, measure religious or denominational adherence, church attendance, participation in informal religious activity, private devotional practices, specific beliefs about the deity or the afterlife, or the depth of religious commitment or religiosity. These dimensions do not always relate to one another in simple ways. A good review of this problem is found in Mindel and Vaughan (1978; see also Heenan, 1972), who found that a majority of elderly respondents living in central Missouri, while not attending religious services regularly, were often involved in nonorganized religious activities. Religiosity, as a set of behaviors or as a set of feelings about the sacred, must clearly be distinguished from church attendance (Feifel, 1974).

When the meaning of death is of interest, it becomes important to assess the degree of belief in the afterlife; however, not all religious people believe in an afterlife or have much certainty about it. A larger percentage of Catholics than of Protestants believe in life after death; Jews are even less likely than Protestants to believe in it. For each sect, those religiously active are more likely to believe in an afterlife (Berman, 1974; Kalish, 1963; Osarchuk & Tatz, 1973; Reid, Gilmore, Andrews, & Caird, 1978; Shneidman, 1974, pp. 208–209).

Interestingly, not all people wish for an afterlife. Shneidman (1974, pp. 208–209) reports that 34% of his predominately young and well-educated respondents to the *Psychology Today* questionnaire on attitudes toward death are indifferent about whether or not there is an afterlife, while 11% "definitely prefer that there not be a life after death." While religiosity for Catholics, Protestants, and Jews is associated with larger proportions wishing for an afterlife, not all highly religious persons hold this view.

Belief in afterlife does not have a clearly understood relationship to anxiety or fear about death either. Some studies find little relation (Berman, 1974; Berman & Hays, 1973), while, in two studies, the percentage of persons who report an increased belief in the afterlife following a life-threatening experience is less than 7% (Kalish, 1969b; Berman, 1974).

Diggory and Rothman (1961; see also Chapter Four), with their opportunistic sample of whom few were very old, found less expressed fear of loss of experience or the ability to complete plans and projects among Catholics than among other groups. The fear that death would mean the end of "purposive activity" increased in this order: Catholics, Protestants, Jews, other/none. Diggory and Rothman suggest that this rank order corresponds to declining certainty of belief in the afterlife. For those who believe in the afterlife, they argue, death does not imply the end to purposive activity. This may account for the finding by Kalish and Reynolds—that loss of "purposive activity" is feared more by the young than the old—in their Los Angeles study that used the same indicators (Kalish & Reynolds, 1976, p. 209).

In support of this interpretation, Chappell (1975) found with an institutionalized, and largely female, sample that active church involvement led to feelings of continuity between the past life and the future. On the other hand, Keith (1979) found that women, but not men, derived comfort concerning the future from religious involvement.

Some evidence that degree of religious involvement is more important than religious affiliation comes from research by Templer and Dotson (1970). Among college students for whom religion was considered to be of little importance, no significant relationship was found between death-anxiety scores (on the Templer DAS) and several variables of religious affiliation, belief, and activity. However, among subjects preselected as being highly involved with religion, lower DAS scales were obtained. Templer's summary might possibly be applied to older subjects as well:

> Those Ss [subjects] who have a strong attachment to their religious belief system, attend religious functions more frequently, are certain of a life after death, believe the Bible should be interpreted literally, and judge the strength of their convictions to be strong . . . apparently have lower death anxiety [Templer, 1972, p. 362].

Care should be exercised in assessing reports of relationship or lack of relationship between death anxiety and belief in the afterlife, because the death-anxiety scales employed may include items that themselves tap belief in afterlife, making it possible to confound the results. This problem is evident, for example, in the well-known Fear of Death Scale (Lester, 1966, 1967b) which includes, at the low-fear end of the scale, items such as "What we call death is only the birth of the soul into a new and delightful life" and "We should not grieve over the dead, because they are eternally happy in heaven." With this scale, Lester (1967c) found that highly religious individuals might have either a very high or a very low fear of death.

More generally, as Feifel (1974) and Nelson (1977) observe and as I have noted elsewhere in this book, such studies too often employ unidimensional, or presumably unidimensional, indices; and, since different indicators have been used in most studies, it is difficult to compare results.

Another problem is the diversity of subjects with whom such studies have been conducted; the subjects include the mentally ill and, most usually, college students (Marshall, 1978, in press). Few studies have been done with "normal" older subjects along a dying trajectory, and few have assessed changing attitudes toward religion (Feifel, 1974).

Additional problems with assessing the relationships between religiosity and attitudes toward death are enumerated by Nelson (1977). A major problem is what Nelson refers to as "an untested linearity assumption." This is the assumption that additional increments of religiosity or any religious variable are associated with additional increments of some death-related variable. More of X is postulated to be associated with more of Y. However, instead of a direct and uniform, or straight-line relationship, two variables might be associated in other ways, such as curvilineally (as in Lester, 1967c). Persons either very high or very low on X might be high on Y. Many often-quoted studies, such as those of Alexander and Adlerstein (1959), Faunce and Fulton (1958), Feifel (1959), Jeffers, Nichols, and Eisdorfer (1961), Swenson (1961), and others noted by Nelson, do not allow for discovering a curvilineal relationship, because religion or religiosity is dichotomized.

Given all these problems, I am tempted to avoid the area entirely. However, it is important to confront the problems in this area, given that so many scholars have postulated an important link between death and religion, even to the point of suggesting that fear of death is the basis for the development of religion (see Leming, 1977; see also Chapter Three). Fortunately, there is research that allows us to draw some tentative conclusions.

In Nelson's own research (1977), over 1200 males living in Virginia were surveyed by mail. Their age distribution approximated that of males over the age of 21 in that state, but non-Whites and lower-class persons were underrepresented. A scale was developed to measure "death avoidance" and "unwillingness to be near or touch the dead and . . . reluctance to experience situations reminiscent of death." Although this is but one of many dimensions of attitudes toward death, a virtue of this measure is that it was developed as part of a larger attempt (Nelson & Nelson, 1975) to develop multidimensional measures of death attitudes using factor analysis. This measure is thus more carefully and sensibly developed than many. A large number of religiosity variables were measured.

As Kalish also found in his early factor-analytic study (1963), Nelson and Nelson found religious participation to have a *curvilinear* relationship to death attitudes—in this case to death avoidance. Religious meanings (belief in an afterlife, belief in hell, and "a sense of being saved in Christ") interacted to produce variable scores on death avoidance. The greatest death avoidance was evidenced by people who believed in hell but were not confident of personal salvation. On the other hand, a nonreligious meaning for death—that is, agreement with the statement "Death is the end of everything good"—was associated with lowest levels of death avoidance.

Leming (1977) also found a curvilinear relationship between fear-of-death scores on a scale of his own construction and measures of religious belief, experience, and ritual participation. Nelson goes so far as to argue that Parson's claim (1951, pp. 371–373) that religious interpretations for death are more satisfactory than secular ones is empirically unsupported. It can be said with some certainty that religiosity and death attitudes are not related in any simple, direct, or linear manner.

In another study that did use multidimensional measures of both religiosity and death attitudes, Feifel (1974) compared 95 healthy and 92 terminally ill subjects. On a variety of measures of conscious death fear, death imagery, and "below-the-level-of-awareness reactions to death" measured by a word-association test, no significant differences were found between religious and nonreligious healthy or terminally ill subjects, most of whom indicated little conscious fear of death but ambivalence and an increasingly negative stance at deeper or nonphenomenological levels. Feifel concludes: "A major finding of the study is that religious predisposition *per se* does not appear to be associated significantly with the strength of fear of death. Moreover, this state of affairs does not change much in the context of personal nearness to death" (1974, p. 360).

This finding contrasts with that of an earlier study using multidimensional measures of both death and religious variables. Swenson (1961), who had not found much fear of death among institutionalized or community-living older persons, using an adjective checklist (see Chapter Four) found that "persons with more fundamental religious convictions and habits look forward to death more than do those with less fundamental convictions and less activity" (p. 51).

In a British study, John Hinton (1963) found that terminally ill patients who were interviewed several times over the course of their dying were less anxious, but more depressed, if they had strong religious beliefs. It appears then that the effects of religion in relation to death are quite multidimensional and that this may relate in part to variability in religious meanings, especially meanings about life and death.

Peter Berger argues that, seen historically, religion has been the most effective and widespread instrumentality of legitimation. Religion has been used to give meaning to both life and death. The experiences of life "however painful they may be, at least make sense now in terms that are both socially and subjectively convincing" (1969, p. 32). This does not, however, mean that life or death will be viewed positively, for as Berger argues, "It is not happiness that theodicy primarily provides, but meaning" (Berger, 1969, p. 58).

A number of theorists have made this argument in terms of suffering, which can itself be interpreted very broadly to encompass disappointments with the past life, physical pain accompanying serious illness, and other unpleasant aspects of dying such as loneliness, anxiety about the unknown, and the like. Berger (1969) argues:

> To be sure, the individual suffering . . . desires relief from these misfortunes. But he equally desires to know *why* these misfortunes have come to him in the first place. . . . Theodicy . . . serves a most important purpose for the suffering individual, even if it does not involve a promise that the eventual outcome of his suffering is happiness in this world or the next [p. 58].

Religious meanings can themselves create anxiety about an afterlife, as Weber's classic analysis of the Protestant ethic demonstrates (Weber, 1958). They can also lead people to accept unhappy aspects of their lives, for, as Geertz (1966) has argued, "Where the more intellective aspects of what Weber called the Problem of Meaning are a matter affirming the ultimate explicability of experience, the more affective aspects are a matter of affirming its ultimate sufferableness" (p. 19). A well-known example of this acceptance in the Judeo-Christian tradition is the case of the suffering of Job (see Bakan, 1968, especially Chap. 3). Perhaps for that reason, I found residents of Glen Brae who claim religion is important and who frequently reaffirm these meanings through religious activity or through contemplation such as reading the Bible are less likely than those who are not religious to have legitimated their biography (Marshall, 1973a, Chap. 6).

Whereas I found few religious legitimations for death among residents of the nondenominational, middle-class retirement village I studied, a larger proportion of lower-class residents of the Catholic home for the aged used religious meanings in discussing the appropriateness of death.These meanings were expressed in simple language and represented basic beliefs—for example, that death meant reunification with a loved one or that death was "God's will." In this setting, the residents on the whole seemed *resigned* to death, but not positively accepting of it, as was more often the case in the retirement village (Marshall, 1975a, 1975c).

It may be that religious ideas alone are not adequate to provide a positive acceptance of death. Rather, the *ability to actively use ideas* and adapt them to one's own situation might be more important. In the San Francisco transitions study, a measurement of the complexity of thoughts about death was derived. Catholic and Protestant women had more simple responses than Jewish women, although there were no significant differences by religious affiliation among males. Among men at all life stages and among women in the later stages in this research (mean age, about 60), people more involved in religion, either through feelings or through participation, thought more about the prospect of their death and were better able to deal with it. While complexity of death thoughts was found to be higher among those who anticipated shorter lives and those who were more highly disengaged, the authors are unclear as to whether, or how, complexity of thoughts about death might lead to better dealing with it than a simple ritualistic or relatively unthinking utilization of a religious verbal formula like "Death is God's will" (Chiriboga & Gigy, 1975).

In our society, religiosity is highly associated with personality characteristics of "external control," and fate tends to be placed "in God's hands" (see Berman & Hays, 1973), whereas internal rather than external locus of control appears to be related to adjustment in later life, as indexed, at any rate, by life satisfaction (Palmore & Luikart, 1972), coping abilities, and avoidance of feelings of failure (Kuypers, 1972; see also Chapter Six). As noted in Chapter Three, religious meanings in North American society are not congruent with other important aspects of the culture that stress the ability of human beings to take control over their own destiny, to be captains of their own fate.

Before leaving the area of religion and religiosity, a word should be said about the future. Persuasive evidence exists that at least one relatively young cohort is much less religious than had been the case until just recently. Wuthnow (1976) has amassed a great deal of evidence that shows that the cohort of people who reached adulthood after 1960 is much less religious on a variety of measures than people from older cohorts. These measures include belief in God or that God created the world, the value of following God's will, church attendance and activity, and private prayer. Wuthnow suggests that a countercultural generational unit influenced by several historical factors in the 1960s is largely responsible for this difference. It would be extremely speculative to attempt to assess the impact of this secularization on death-related attitudes and behavior. However, as Wuthnow argues, if this change indeed reflects an important discontinuity, any attempts to assess the importance of religion and its effects over a long time span that rely on an evolutionary conception of gradual accumulative change are likely to be highly misleading.

In summary, religious meanings are today probably no more efficacious in helping people to make sense of their experiences in the terminal status passage and to make sense of dying and death itself than many other vocabularies. Even among older cohorts, who are and always have been more religious than are today's young people, religion is of benefit only to some, and that benefit depends on the context of the religious beliefs they hold, the strength with which they hold them, and their ability to actively use religious meanings in sense-making endeavors.

This does not imply that people no longer seek to relate their dying to something larger than themselves, nor does it imply an absence of ritual surrounding death and dying. Glen Davidson (1971) makes this case persuasively. In Chapter Three we saw that Davidson, like Ariès, views death as demanding a linking of the life of an individual with the life of society. Davidson, it will be recalled, sees individuals as seeking *telos,* a sense of purpose that transcends individual death. He discusses this idea in terms of colonial New England and New France; in both societies the orientation toward dying and toward death and burial became occasions for reaffirming the sense of societal mission or destiny. Dying for one's country would be an example of this unity between individual and societal destiny.

Davidson argues that efforts to seek *telos* are still common in our society. Based on interviews with nearly 100 terminally ill people, he concluded that their dying was highly normatively governed, which suggests a unity between individual and society. In addition, "almost all of the interviewed patients acted out rituals which used myth and symbols identifiable with a culture . . . acted ritually in an effort to maintain or recover a sense of order" (Davidson, 1971, p. 427). With the erosion of any single all-encompassing symbolic structure, Davidson notes that a variety of ritual orientations to dying were available for use, and he himself presents a list of seven "dramas" through which dying is enacted. He notes that denial or avoidance can be ritually enacted by dying patients and by others around them (see especially Glaser & Strauss, 1965, Chap. 5). However, other rituals reaffirm values of hope, fulfillment, and acceptance. Each, Davidson argues, draws on culturally available resources: "When the patient begins to sense that he is dying, he pulls from his repertory of possibilities a script for action which his culture has prepared him to expect to bring resolution to the situation's conflict" (1971, p. 429).

Religious meanings are then just one class of meanings available for reaching a sense of placement and appropriateness of an individual in the world. Rollo May has written of the effects of death on the human community as follows:

The awareness of death . . . is the ultimate source of human humility. The fact that you and I at some time will die puts us, in the last analysis, in the same boat with every other man, free or enslaved, male or female, child or adult. The facing of death is the strongest motive, and indeed requirement, for learning to be fellow men . . . in the long run, we are all in the same boat. This is what Theseus meant in Sophocles' play *Oedipus at Colonus* when he said: "I know that I am only a man, and I have no more to hope for in the end than you have" [1967, p. 58].

In one sense, then, death is a humanizing factor. May continues: [Death] places us all in need of mercy and forgiveness by the others, and makes us all participate in the human drama in which no man can stand above another (1967, p. 59).

Some Paradigmatic Considerations

In this book I have drawn on both comparative and historical material from time to time to give some context to the analysis. In this section, and before taking a brief look at the future of aging and dying, I attempt to systematically draw things together. No theory of the sociology of aging and dying will be proposed. It would be impossible to induce one from the rather limited knowledge base that now exists, and in any case a general, and therefore highly abstract, theory would probably not do justice to the phenomenon (Bengtson, 1973, pp. 41–42; Lowenthal, 1971). I have been developing the arguments of this book within a paradigm, however, and will attempt to systematize that paradigm now.

Some limitations should be acknowledged. First, my concern is with the impact of mortality on the social organization of society and on the lives of persons undergoing terminal status passage and not with any other specific or general aspects of aging. Second, while I have tried to attend to comparative and historical material, I use it for perspective on North American society and not to produce a comparative sociology of aging and dying that would have claims to universality. However, if the analysis facilitated such a task, I would be very happy.

In Chapter One I mentioned that the organization of the chapters in this book is a guide to a rudimentary sociological theory of aging and dying. That is, it is a sketchy paradigm that suggests phenomena to look at and gives hints about the relationship among various phenomena. The prospect and the occurrence of death pose problems for individuals. These are cognitive problems of trying to understand finitude and organizational or institutional problems of devising ways to deal with it. But humans organize in societies, and death poses cognitive and organizational problems at the societal level as well—as a focal point for the development of shared beliefs concerning the intelligibility of death and as a phenomenon that must be controlled if the disruptiveness of death, or even its threat to societal survival, is not contained.

Neither individual nor societal responses to the fact of human mortality are inexorable or preprogrammed. At least, I have not found it useful to make assumptions about, for example, universal fear of death or all societies "disengaging" people so as to minimize the disruptiveness of death. Rather, humans come together to create the social and personal responses they make to death and dying. In many cases these humanly created patterns of action and of meaning concerned with death and dying—in other words, the institutionalization of death and dying—take on a reality of their own, thereby forming the context in which individuals must fashion their own dying. In Chapter Two, the social problematics of death were examined, and responses to death at the social level were reviewed in Chapter Three. From that point in the book, the focus shifted to the individual in the social milieu; that is, the focus became social psychological. In Chapter Four I examined a number of assumptions about the psychological importance of death and dying for individuals, especially as this importance might become heightened with increasing age, and I elaborated on the cognitive assumptions I had made. These assumptions stress the human need to render experience sensible or meaningful and to maintain some degree of control over life.

Here the metaphor that gives this book its title should have become clear: when people see themselves in the final chapters of their autobiographies, they wish to produce a "good story"—one that, right up to the end, in death, makes sense—and they wish to have personal authorship, or control, over it. Analytically, this metaphor gives three dimensions of concern to the person who is highly aware of finitude, and to each dimension I have devoted a chapter. Chapter Five shows how people try to arrive at a view of their past life as meaningful. Chapter Six focuses on the attempt to exercise control over the final chapters, the terminal status passage, and Chapter Seven shows attempts to make death meaningful.

The historical and comparative material reviewed in earlier chapters suggests the *sociohistorical specificity* of the patterns of aging and dying that are manifest at the social psychological level in our own society. Indeed, I have been at pains to criticize theories that suggest *universal* processes by which people become oriented to their finitude. No one would be unhappy were we to discover processes of aging and dying that were experienced by everyone in all societies in all historical periods; but the prospect of doing so is rather remote. This can be said without denying the relevance of sociohistorical features in affecting the contemporary way of aging and dying.

Within our own sociohistorical context, then, the material reviewed in this and earlier chapters can be restated in a limited number of generalizations:

1. With aging comes a growing awareness that one's own death draws near. This awareness is not a simple function of age but develops through a

complex process involving a comparison of one's own age to the age-at-death of significant others, as well as an estimate of health status.

2. The realization that death is drawing closer poses a cognitive problem for the individual, encompassing two related dimensions. The individual will seek a sense of the appropriateness of life as a whole. To develop this sense of appropriateness, the individual will begin to reminisce intensively. While personal reminiscence is important in this process, reminiscing socially with others is crucially important in attaining success.

3. When people recognize that time is limited, they also seek to make sense of death itself and their own impending death. Reasons that legitimate the deaths of others can be applied reflexively in making sense of one's own death. Those who have the opportunity to discuss the deaths of others with intimates are aided in the process of making sense of their own death.

4. In addition to the cognitive dilemmas leading to legitimation of the self as dying, people want to exercise some degree of status-passage control over their terminal status passage. The importance of doing so is heightened by the inexorability of this passage.

5. Given the contemporary sociocultural milieu, with its bureaucratization and technological treatment of death and dying, some degree of conflict between the individual and others who have control or jurisdiction over aspects of the terminal status passage is to be expected. The outcome of this struggle has relevance for the legitimation processes described above.

6. Those successful in legitimating their own death and those successful in legitimating biography adopt a time perspective suggestive of an enhanced mode of living the time remaining to them.

7. Not only impending death but also life itself must be legitimated for the aging. Reasons for living can and do frequently coincide with reasons for dying. Indeed, once the problem of impending death is successfully faced, life may be grasped with a new enjoyment.

This view of the consequences of heightened awareness of finitude stems from the presuppositions of phenomenological sociology and symbolic interactionist social psychology that humans are basically motivated to endow experiences with meaning, that the meaning of biographical experience has temporal dimensions, and that the process of endowing experience with meaning is best viewed as a *social* construction of reality in response to problems or disturbances in taken-for-granted reality.

Neugarten has remarked that, while the individual develops a sense of self very early in life, "it is perhaps not until adulthood that the individual creates a sense of the life cycle, that is, an anticipation and acceptance of the inevitable sequence of events that will occur as men grow up, grow older, and die" (1970, p. 79). My suggestion is that this sense of the life cycle attains a new significance when the old come to view their life in relief against the knowledge that their time is running out. More than just anticipation and acceptance of the future, we find retrospection and acceptance of the past as well.

The paradox of identity is the recognition that, with changes in self-concept and relations with others, the individual is still the same person:

> Each person's account of his life, as he writes or thinks about it, is a symbolic ordering of events. The sense that you make of your own life rests upon what concepts, what interpretations, you bring to bear upon the multitudinous and disorderly crowd of past acts. If your interpretations are convincing to yourself, if you trust your terminology, then there is some kind of continuous meaning assigned to your life as-a-whole. Different motives may be seen to have driven you at different periods, but the overriding purpose of your life may yet seem to retain a certain unity and coherence [Strauss, 1969, p. 145].

Attainment or, we may say, symbolic construction of this sense of continuity is undoubtedly a life-long process. Thurnher and Chiriboga (1972; see also Thurnher, 1974), for instance, report evidence for "a systematic trend toward improved self-concept with age" up to the immediate preretirement years. At the same time, "While there is a trend toward greater stability with age, the self-concept of the elderly is not static, but appears open to the influence of life experiences be they positive or negative" (pp. 1, 5). Moriwaki (1973) found that retired individuals participated in selective "self-disclosure" with others; an important factor—"search for continuity"—involved discussing feelings about growing old and past accomplishments. In particular, self-disclosure of feelings about dying was associated with higher scores on a measure of psychological well-being.

While reconstruction of biography at earlier ages is a largely unexamined aspect of the aging process, my contention is that the recognition of impending death makes such a task more crucial for the individual. Noyes (1972) presents evidence that the life-review process occurs instantly among the great majority of persons who experience sudden death (his data came from accounts of survivors of falls and drowning). With "normal" aging and dying, the process, triggered by the heightened realization that death is drawing near, can proceed at a more leisurely pace. Moriwaki's suggestion that selective self-disclosure, including feelings about impending death, enhances the successful development of the sense of continuity thus corroborates my argument.

Lyman and Scott (1970) develop a notion of the experience of time that lends some sense to the characterization of living while dying. They develop concepts for two types of experience of time. The *humanistic* dimension encompasses "the complex subjective experience that activities are governed by personal decision, are entered into with a sense of mastery or control, and are exhibited through self expression." Alternatively, by *fatalistic time tracks* they "refer to the subjective experience that these activities are matters of obligation or compulsion, are outside the active domination of the social actor, and are vehicles of coercive or conformist rather than individual expression" (pp. 191–194).

We have seen that those who are successful in legitimating their life as a whole also are likely to accept personal responsibility for the events of their life. They view their past as of their own making. According to Lyman and Scott, people experiencing time fatalistically see themselves as compelled by time factors outside their control. But to legitimate death is to gain mastery over it as the ultimate limit, by accepting the limit as appropriate at any time. Fate, by being accepted, can be overcome.

The related processes of legitimating self and legitimating death thus free the individual from the constraints of both past and future. This makes possible a way of experiencing that Simmel refers to as "the adventure":

> An adventure is certainly a part of our existence, directly contiguous with other parts which precede and follow it; at the same time, however, in its deeper meaning, it occurs outside the usual continuity of life. . . . The adventure . . . is independent of "before" and "after"; its boundaries are defined regardless of them [1959, p. 244].*

That Simmel regards the adventure as an experience of transcendence is clear from the following passage:

> In contrast to those aspects of life which are related only peripherally—by mere fate—the adventure is defined by its capacity, in spite of its being isolated and accidental, to have necessity and meaning. Something becomes an adventure only by virtue of two conditions: that it itself is a specific organization of some significant meaning with a beginning and an end; and that, despite its accidental nature, its extraterritoriality with respect to the continuity of life, it nevertheless connects with the character and identity of the bearer of that life—that it does so in the widest sense, transcending, by a mysterious necessity, life's more narrowly rational aspects [1959, p. 246].

It is interesting that, while Simmel's conception of the adventure so well characterizes the experiencing of life and time of those who have legitimated themselves as dying, he himself sees the adventure as belonging to the life-style of youth rather than of the aged:

> Old age is "objective"; it shapes a new structure out of the substance left behind in a peculiar sort of timelessness by the life which has slipped by. The new structure is that of contemplativeness, impartial judgment, freedom from that unrest which marks life as being present. It is all this that makes adventure alien to old age [1959, p. 255].

Simmel argues this despite his also claiming that "life as a whole may be perceived as an adventure. . . . To have such a remarkable attitude toward

*From "The Adventure," by G. Simmel. In K. H. Wolff (Ed.), *Essays on Sociology, Philosophy and Aesthetics*. Copyright 1959 by Harper Torchbooks. This and all other quotations from this source are reprinted by permission.

life, one must sense above its totality a higher unity, a super-life, as it were" (1959, p. 247). This, I submit, is what is attained through the reconstruction of biography and the acceptance of impending death.

Perhaps Simmel's failure to see the possibility for adventure in old age stems from his view of the adventure as of necessity implying a disregard for the continuity of life: "The adventure lacks that reciprocal interpretation with adjacent parts of life which constitutes life-as-a-whole. It is like an island in life which determines its beginning and end according to its own formative powers" (1959, p. 244). But legitimation of biography and death erases the relevancy of death as an end point. As such, it allows for the freedom that Lyman and Scott note:

> Because of this fundamental disconnectedness, because of its existence in time and space *sui generis,* the adventure functions as a relief and respite to those on fatalistic time tracks. For its duration, the individual is freed from the dictated importunities of time, subjected to his own abilities, re-created as a potential master of the scene [1970, p. 193].

Major theoretical insights in this area will come from phenomenology, where the experience of time is seen to be intrinsically interwoven with the recognition of mortality. Luijpen, from this perspective, implies the same kind of freedom that I have suggested stems from acceptance of death:

> In his being-toward-death man must apprehend the possibility of death as a possibility without minimizing it; he must culture it as a possibility, "endure" it as a possibility. The authentic response to the consciousness of being-toward-death is "expectation" . . . in the realization that in the light of this extreme, yet present, possibility, it is futile to busy oneself with things and with the company of fellowmen [1969, pp. 393–394].

The person who is ready to die lives in a world of freedom—freedom from whims of others—for their whims become unimportant and time-bound.

It seems at first paradoxical that the aging person must be ready both to die and to live. However, this attitude follows from the certainty of death but the concomitant uncertainty of its timing. Planning for death and dying and making arrangements for the survivors become important with heightened awareness of finitude, and being able to make such plans undoubtedly enhances the sense of self-control of the aging and dying person and minimizes the degree to which he or she might become an emotional or financial burden to descendants.

Perhaps facilitating successful legitimation of the self-as-dying is the most feasible way to ensure that the aged can live out their days with some sense of tranquility. Near to his death, Pope John was reported to have said "My bags are packed, and I can go with a tranquil heart at any moment" (Saunders, 1969, pp. 77–78). Another wise man, Lao-tze, remarked "Who dies and dying, does not protest his death, he has known a true old age" (cited

in Feifel, 1965). Perhaps a "true old age"—that kind of life that we characterize with the few positive stereotypes we attribute to the aged, such as wisdom
and serenity—comes only when the developmental tasks of preparation for
death are completed. Ralph Harper, in his book *Nostalgia,* said "We cannot
know what is beyond the end of our days, but we can enter into an order
of things which can make us say, 'I'm not afraid'" (cited in Saunders, 1969,
p. 78).

The Future
of Aging and Dying

Death poses problems for individuals, as we have seen. But the response to death is never fully individual, for never is the individual completely
divorced from society. "Death gives rise to personal emotional responses,
which initiate culturally oriented responses and reactions" (Pine, 1972, p.
150). Culturally or societally oriented responses provide the framework within
which individuals must do their own dying. It is important to emphasize that
the cultural or societal responses are organized by humans for both personal
and social reasons.

Our ways of making sense of aging and dying are thus different from
those of our predecessors. Ritual maintenance of meanings of aging and dying
is no longer strong and no longer brings together all the generations. The
aging and the dying are seldom brought together as in days past. Making sense
of the self-as-dying has become a process initiated only later in life when
awareness of finitude is heightened, as described in Chapter Five, and the
ways in which people come to terms with their finitude have become lodged
not in the total community but in the informal social organization in which the
aging are embedded.

What, then, are the effects of organizational factors in the social-
psychological processes outlined in this book through which the dying can
make sense of their last days and impending death? They are factors that lead
to heightened awareness of finitude, factors that bear on the availability of
conversational others with whom one can interactively construct the meaning
of biography and death, and factors that bear on the wider pool of meanings
that can be utilized in the legitimation process.

The availability of conversational others depends to a large extent on
demographic factors that, we have seen, are changing and reducing the availability of close kinship relationships. And it is the intimate friend or relative,
rather than the acquaintance, who is important for reminiscence and legitimation of death.

Although it is difficult to predict the future, it seems certain that there
will be many more older people in the decades after the turn of the century and

especially when the baby-boom cohort reaches later life around 2010–2020. Of these, larger proportions than now will be very old people. This can be reasonably estimated for much of that period, because those who will be old in the foreseeable future are already alive.

We do not know how much, if at all, life expectancy itself will be extended. Deaths from cardiovascular disease and renal diseases might well be eliminated, giving a possible increased life expectancy at birth of almost 11 years and at age 65 of about 10 years (Shanas & Hauser, 1974). Conquering cancer would add an additional year or two, as would better nutrition, housing, and health care. A decline in the birth rate would lessen mortality risks that are associated with pregnancy and childbirth (Shanas & Hauser, 1974). A trend toward providing better housing conditions for the aged will probably continue and will probably lead to increased life expectancy (Carp, 1977).

Uhlenberg (1977) has persuasively argued that the demographic changes for the remainder of this century will not be as dramatic or consequential as those that have already occurred. He points out that the death of any cohort and its replacement by successors have great potential for change, since, in a decade, about 60% of those over age 65 will be replaced in this manner. However, the extent of change depends on the extent to which successive cohorts differ from one another, and Uhlenberg argues that many of the points of difference reached a maximum or limit around mid-century. Analyzing White cohorts for the United States, he concludes that inter-cohort differences on urbanization, educational attainment, immigration, fertility patterns, and mortality rates are now declining. Adjacent cohorts are no longer experiencing as great a difference in the proportion surviving to old age as was the case, for example, around the beginning of this century. Except for the disturbing effects of the baby-boom cohort, who will reach old age around 2010–2020, demographic factors will be less important as change agents than they have been (for a similar argument for Canada, see Denton & Spencer, 1975, 1979).

The cumulative effects of gradual demographic change, however, will add about five years to the life expectancy of cohorts entering old age around and after the turn of the century. These cohorts are also expected to be healthier in this extended old age (Carp, 1977; Neugarten, 1974, 1975; Tobin, 1975). However, as has been suggested by Neugarten and Tobin, the incapacities and dependencies of very late life will probably not be eradicated, and preterminal and terminal phases at the end of life will probably be no shorter than they are now (see especially Tobin, 1975).

Tobin (1975) does anticipate important changes in three areas, all of which have implications for the analytical dimensions discussed in this book. First, he sees a continuation of the trend toward community-based and locally controlled health and social-service delivery on a neighborhood basis. Second, and related to the first one, he sees a move toward smaller long-term-care institutions, despite current official guidelines suggesting an optimum size, on grounds of efficiency, of 180 beds for nursing homes and despite the increased per-patient costs of smaller institutions. Third, he anticipates that the growth of the hospice movement (see Stoddard, 1978) will continue, with terminal-care centers both incorporated in and independent of hospitals, and will serve the purpose of educating people toward the values and the techniques of giving good psychosocial care to the dying.

Changes in the ways in which people can control their own dying, as well as changes in the meaning of death and dying, are likely to emanate largely from within medical settings, although not always at the instigation of physicians (see Parsons, Fox, & Lidz, 1973; Veatch, 1976), for it is within those settings that much of the drama over control and the necessity for balancing the meaning of death with that of life occurs. However, the movement for reform is broad-based and embraces many nonmedical "consumers" of health and terminal care in what can be called a "social movement" (see Lofland, 1978). "However we may conceptualize the 'best death,' or even the 'successful death,'" Tobin (1975) argues, "the aged of the future will, in all likelihood, manifest a different set of attitudes and expectations regarding societal responsibilities for easing the dying process. The demand will grow for a wider range of options for the family in maintaining some degree of control over the management of death" (p. 36).

The perils of overinstitutionalization and early institutionalization, which so greatly reduce the individual's capacity for exercising control, seem to be widely recognized. A parallel recognition of the importance of providing the kind of home support services that will keep people out of institutions should also mean less institutionalization in the future (Tobin, 1975; for Canada, see Schwenger & Gross, 1979).

The place of death may, therefore, be returned to the community. These communities should be arrayed in rural-urban terms roughly the way they are at present, since the urbanization process that had characterized North America until 1970 has now apparently reached its end (Beale, 1976; De Jong & Sell, 1977; Tucker, 1976; Wardwell, 1977). Of course, what communities will be like in the future is a matter of some speculation, but the overall difference between rural and urban communities on variables such as educational levels and general life-style phenomena should decrease. Because of the pervasiveness of nationwide communications systems, cultural differences between rural and urban areas should lessen.

While technology is often evoked as the "enemy" (Lofland, 1978, pp. 88–92) and death with dignity is often seen as death without benefit of high-technology support systems, perhaps paradoxically technology can be of great value to older people, through much of their terminal status passage, in helping them gain greater control over their environment. Architectural design is increasingly premised on adapting the environment to the needs of older and infirm persons (Kahana, 1974; Tobin, 1975). New telemetry and computer communications and control systems can help older institutional residents, and even people living in their own homes, to have greater control over their lives and to engage in better self-monitoring of their health (see, for example, Carp, 1976; Hardiman, Holbrook, & Hedrick, 1979; Tobin, 1975). Communication and many other functions can be maintained through new technological advances in the design of prosthetic environments despite severe sensory or functional impairment. Technology is not, therefore, an enemy in itself; it can counter isolation and loss of control in many instances, and the trend for technology to do so should increase.

A cautionary note is in order. Peterson, Powell, and Robertson (1976) call our attention to difficulties in making forecasts about technological change. They observe that, in a 1937 report to President Roosevelt, the National Resources Committee "totally overlooked the discovery of nuclear power, jet propulsion, aviation as a primary transportation system, and the transistor; all of which were in use within 15 years" (p. 264). Our uncertainty about the technological future is exacerbated by an apparent need, within the foreseeable future, to find alternative energy sources to fuel that technology.

As Cohen (1976) has argued, if technological change is difficult to predict, social and political change is even more difficult. Peterson, Powell, and Robertson predict that the American society will move toward a more liberal philosophy, which will give a more equitable share of national resources to the aged, and that a clearly defined national policy toward the aged will be articulated. They also argue that a voting block of age-conscious elders will emerge to support its political interests. Neugarten (1975) envisions a society in which government will intrude more extensively into everyday life, even though there will be increasing concern among a well-educated elder population for pursuing values of self-fulfillment.

If, on the other hand, this "conservatively optimistic" imagery of a future society is not realized, we may see increasing conflict between the generations concerning allocation of scarce resources and a possible resentment of the middle-aged against the growing numbers of older people who are economically, and otherwise, dependent on them (Marshall & Tindale, 1978–1979; the work of Dowd & Brooks, 1978, is also relevant).

A situation of increased generational conflict might particularly affect the very old, who are closest to death. If maintaining life-support systems for the old is perceived as very costly, support for active euthanasia might increase. Lofland has argued that, in a society devoted to natural and nontechnological death, the individual who wishes to use mechanical life-support technology becomes the deviant (Lofland, 1978, p. 108).

Certainly the burden of the old has been linked to euthanasia policies in science fiction. A good example is Lawrence Sanders' novel *The Tomorrow File* (1975), in which he has a U.S. president in the year 1988 proclaim "We can no longer afford an obsolete society of obsolete people," and in which the "Department of Bliss"—formerly the Department of Happiness and, before that, the Department of Health, Education and Welfare—has a gerontology team that develops a plan to pay a large sum to indigent and obsolete people who agree to enjoy it for 30 days before being "stopped" (Sanders, 1975, p. 64).

The somewhat optimistic projections of the future that rely on the young-old/old-old distinction (Neugarten, 1974, 1975) have tended to focus on the younger of those two categories and have had what Beattie refers to as "an upper-to-middle-class orientation in regard to education and life-style" (1975, p. 39). If generational conflict does emerge in the future, one might safely predict that the lower- and working-class elderly will suffer more than their higher-class fellow-cohort members.

While all the above demographic, social, political, and technological factors will change in ways not entirely clear to us at this time, we should not lose sight of the fact that these are not totally alien features. Changes on these dimensions will not just happen; we will make them happen. More than ever before, we are consciously dealing with these factors. Although death remains inevitable, the way we age and die is clearly not inevitably fixed. That is one new realization that emerges from and gives impetus to scholarship in this area.

Similarly, the *meaning* of aging and dying is also changing and will continue to change in relation to the various factors discussed above and not through any impetus that is solely its own. Ideas do not change ideas; people change ideas.

It should not be surprising that religion is relatively unimportant for many people when they try to make sense of death, just as it should not be surprising that many other vocabularies seem to be successfully invoked by people in legitimating their terminal status passage and its end in death. After all, we are by nature sense-making creatures who abhor meaninglessness as nature abhors a vacuum, and the meanings on which we draw to make sense of death can be drawn quite naturally from our culturally available vocabulary (see Lofland, 1978, especially Chap. 3, for a development of this argument). By contrast with the vocabulary provided through the Judeo-Christian religious tradition, the language that people commonly use to legitimate their dying is more suited to our secular age, precisely because it is secular. There is nothing to suggest that secular language works any less well than religious language might have worked in earlier eras.

Research and scholarship in the general area of aging and dying, including efforts such as this book, are part of the sense-making and meaning-constructing endeavor. Through a better understanding of the last chapters of life, we may hope to better the aging and dying of others. Such knowledge might also facilitate an acceptance of a life that draws to a close and of death itself and enable those who are approaching death to continue to live lives that can be viewed as appropriate.

Pascal said:

> Man is only a reed, the feeblest reed in nature; but he is a thinking reed. There is no need for the entire universe to arm itself in order to annihilate him; a

vapour, a drop of water, suffices to kill him. But were the universe to crush him, man would yet be more noble than that which slays him, because man knows that he dies, and the advantage that the universe has over him; of this the universe knows nothing. Thus all our dignity lies in thought [cited by May, 1967, p. 57].

Knowledge of our mortality opens up the possibility suggested by Simmel that we can know of our mortality and interweave this knowledge into our lives in diverse and enriching ways.

Review Questions
for Chapter 7

1. *This chapter presents a number of legitimations for death, or verbal formulae that people sometimes use to make sense of the fact that they, as others, must die. A topic not discussed in the chapter is legitimations for continued living—belief systems that argue the inappropriateness of death. A prominent contemporary example is the cryonics movement, whose adherents believe that people should be suspended in a frozen state and reactivated in some later era, when death has been defeated. Examination of this movement, its ideology, and the social character of its adherents is beyond the scope of this book but would be an interesting exercise. Should the cryonogenic techniques be realized? What are the social and political forces that would affect the possible adoption of such techniques on a wide scale? Do we really want people to be able to live forever? What would society be like if people could live forever?*

2. *Many people claim that religion is not fading in importance but, rather, is changing its form. What, if any, is the role of the changing character of death in the development of new forms of religion?*

3. *With changing communications technology, how different will the social aspects of aging and dying be 50 years from now? Why? What technological changes other than those in communications will affect these aspects?*

4. *How do the meanings people attach to death, the degree of control they are able to assume, or wish to assume, over their aging and dying, and the "objective" features of aging, such as health and longevity, reflect class differences? How does social class affect the community contexts in which people age and die?*

References

Aberle, D. F., Cohen, A. K., Davis, A. K., Levy, M. J., Jr., & Sutton, F. X. "The Functional Prerequisites of a Society." *Ethics*, 1950, *60*(January): 100–111.

Acsádi, G., & Nemeskéri, J. *History of Human Life Span and Mortality*. Budapest: Akadémiai Kiadó, 1970.

Adams, B. N. "The Middle Class Adult and His Widowed and Still Married Mother." *Social Problems*, 1968, *16*(Summer): 50–59.

Aitken-Swan, J. "Nursing the Late Cancer Patient at Home." *Practitioner*, 1959, *183:*64.

Albrecht, G. L., & Gift, H. C. "Adult Socialization: Ambiguity and Adult Life Crises." Ch. 15, pp. 237–251, in N. Datan & L. H. Ginsberg (Eds.), *Life-Span Developmental Psychology: Normative Life Crises*. New York: Academic Press, 1975.

Aldridge, G. "The Role of Older People in a Florida Retirement Community." *Geriatrics*, 1956, *11:*223–226.

Alexander, I. E., & Adlerstein, A. "Death and Religion." Ch. 16, pp. 271–283, in H. Feifel (Ed.), *The Meaning of Death*. New York: McGraw-Hill, 1959.

Anthony, S. *The Discovery of Death in Childhood and After*. London: Lane, Penguin Books, 1971.

Arensberg, C. *The Irish Countryman*. New York: Macmillan, 1937.

Ariès, P. "La mort inversée. Le changement des attitudes devant la mort dans les sociétés occidentales." *Archives Européenes de Sociologie*, 1967, *8:*169–195. Translated as "The Reversal of Death: Changes in Attitudes toward Death in Western Societies." Pp. 134–158 in D. E. Stannard (Ed.), *Death in America*. Philadelphia: University of Pennsylvania Press, 1975.

Ariès, P. *Western Attitudes toward Death: From the Middle Ages to the Present*. Baltimore: Johns Hopkins University Press, 1974.

Ariès, P. *L'Homme devant la Mort*. Paris: Editions du Seuil, 1977.

Arling, G. "The Elderly Widow and Her Family, Neighbors and Friends." *Journal of Marriage and the Family*, 1976, *38*(November): 757–768.

Atchley, R. C. "Dimensions of Widowhood in Later Life." *The Gerontologist*, 1975, *15*(2): 176–178.

Back, K. W. "Social Behavior: Theory and Method." Ch. 16, pp. 403–431, in R. Binstock & E. Shanas (Eds.), *Handbook of Aging and the Social Sciences*. New York: Van Nostrand Reinhold, 1976.

Back, K. W., & Baade, H. W. "The Social Meaning of Death and the Law." Ch. 11, pp. 302–329, J. C. McKinney & F. T. de Vyver (Eds.), *Aging and Social Policy*. New York: Appleton-Century-Crofts, 1966.

Back, K. W., & Gergen, K. J. "Cognitive and Motivational Factors in Aging and Disengagement." Ch. 18, pp. 289–295, in I. H. Simpson & J. C. McKinney (Eds.), *Social Aspects of Aging*. Durham, N. C.: Duke University Press, 1966. (a)

Back, K. W., & Gergen, K. J. "Personal Orientation and Morale of the Aged." Ch. 19, pp. 296–305, in I. H. Simpson & J. C. McKinney (Eds.), *Social Aspects of Aging*. Durham, N. C.: Duke University Press, 1966. (b)

Baer, D. "An Age-Irrelevant Concept of Development." *Merrill-Palmer Quarterly*, 1970, *16:* 238–245.

Bakan, D. *Disease, Pain, and Sacrifice*. Chicago: University of Chicago Press, 1968.

Ball, J. F. "Widow's Grief: The Impact of Age and Mode of Death." *Omega*, 1976–1977, *7*(4):307–333.

Baltes, P. B. "Life-Span Developmental Psychology: Some Observations on History and Theory." Presidential Address, Division 20 (Adult Development and Aging) of the American Psychological Association, San Francisco, August 1977.

Barrett, C. J. "Sex Differences in the Experience of Widowhood." Paper presented at the annual meeting of the American Psychological Association, Toronto, September 1978.

Bartlett, F. C. *Remembering: A Study in Experimental and Social Psychology*. Cambridge: Cambridge University Press, 1967. (Originally published, 1932.)

Bascue, L. O., & Lawrence, R. E. "A Study of Subjective Time and Death Anxiety in the Elderly." *Omega*, 1977, *8*(1):81–90.

Beale, C. L. "A Further Look at Nonmetropolitan Population Growth Since 1970." *American Journal of Agricultural Economics*, 1976, *58*(5):953–958.

Beattie, W. M., Jr. "Discussion," *The Gerontologist*, 1975, *15*(1, Pt. 2):39–40

Becker, H. S. "Notes on the Concept of Commitment." *American Journal of Sociology*, 1960, *66*(July):32–40.

Becker, H. S., & Bruner, D. "Attitude toward Death and the Dead and Some Possible Causes of Ghost Fear." *Mental Hygiene*, 1931, *15:*828–837.

Becker, H. S., & Strauss, A. L. "Careers, Personality and Adult Socialization." *American Journal of Sociology*, 1956, *62*(November):253–263.

Bendiksen, R. "The Sociology of Death." Ch. 4, pp. 59–81, in R. Fulton & R. Bendiksen (Eds.), *Death and Identity* (rev. ed.). Bowie, Md.: Charles Press, 1976.

Bengtson, V. L. *The Social Psychology of Aging*. Indianapolis: Bobbs-Merrill, 1973.

Bengtson, V. L., Cuellar, J. B., & Ragan, P. K. "Stratum Contrasts and Similarities in Attitudes toward Death." *Journal of Gerontology*, 1977, *32*(1, January):76–88.

Bengtson, V. L., & Kuypers, J. "Generational Differences and the Developmental Stake." *Aging and Human Development*, 1971, *2*(4):249–260.

Bennett, R. "Living Conditions and Everyday Needs of the Elderly with Particular Reference to Social Isolation." *International Journal of Aging and Human Development*, 1973, *4*(3): 179–198.

Berardo, F. M. "Survivorship and Social Isolation: The Case of the Aged Widower." *The Family Coordinator*, 1970, *1*(January):11–25.

Berger, P. L. *Invitation to Sociology*. Garden City, N. Y.: Doubleday Anchor, 1963.

Berger, P. L. *The Sacred Canopy*. Garden City, N. Y.: Doubleday Anchor, 1969.

Berger, P. L., & Kellner, H. "Marriage and the Construction of Reality." *Diogene*, 1964, *46*:3–32.

Berger, P. L., & Luckmann, T. J. *The Social Construction of Reality* (2nd ed.). Garden City, N. Y.: Doubleday Anchor, 1967.

Berman, A. L. "Belief in Afterlife, Religion, Religiosity and Life-Threatening Experiences." *Omega*, 1974, *5*(2):127–135.

Berman, A. L., & Hays, J. E. "Relation between Death Anxiety, Belief in Afterlife, and Locus of Control." *Journal of Consulting and Clinical Psychology*, 1973, *41*:318.

Blau, Z. S. *Old Age in a Changing Society*. New York: Watts, 1973.

Blauner, R. "Death and Social Structure." *Psychiatry*, 1966, *29*(November):378–394.

Bottomore, T. B. *Karl Marx: Selected Writings in Sociology and Social Philosophy*. New York: McGraw-Hill, 1956.

Botwinick, J. *Aging and Behavior: A Comprehensive Integration of Research Findings* (2nd ed.). New York: Springer, 1978.

Boylin, W., Gordon, S. K., & Nehrke, M. F. "Reminiscing and Ego Integrity in Institutionalized Elderly Males." *The Gerontologist*, 1976, *16*(2, April):118–124.

Bradburn, N. N., & Caplovitz, C. *Reports on Happiness: A Pilot Study of Behavior Related to Mental Health*. Chicago: Aldine, 1965.

Bradshaw, J., Clifton, M., & Kennedy, J. *Found Dead: A Study of Old People Found Dead*. Mitcham Surrey, England: Age Concern England, 1978.

Breytspraak, L. M. "Achievement and the Self-Concept in Middle Age." Pp. 221–231 in E. Palmore (Ed.), *Normal Aging 2*. Durham, N. C.: Duke University Press, 1974.

Breytspraak, L. M. "Self-Concept in Adulthood: Emergent Issues and the Response of the Symbolic Interactionist Perspective." Paper presented at the 28th Annual Meeting of the Gerontological Society, Louisville, October 1975.

Breytspraak, L., & George, L. "Self-Concept and Self-Esteem." In D. J. Mangen & W. A. Peterson (Eds.), *Research Instruments in Social Gerontology*. Minneapolis: University of Minnesota Press, in press.

Brody, S. J. "Comprehensive Health Care for the Elderly: An Analysis." *The Gerontologist*, 1973, *13*(4):412–418.

Bromley, D. B. "An Approach to Theory Construction in the Psychology of Development and Aging." Ch. 4, pp. 71–114, in L. R. Goulet & P. B. Baltes (Eds.), *Life-Span Developmental Psychology: Research and Theory*. New York: Academic Press, 1970.

Brotman, H. B. "Life Expectancy: Comparison of National Levels in 1900 and 1974 and Variations in State Levels, 1969–1971." *The Gerontologist*, 1977, *17*(1, February):12–22.

Bugen, L. A. "Human Grief: A Model for Prediction and Intervention." *American Journal of Orthopsychiatry*, 1977, *47*:196–206.

Bunch, J. "Recent Bereavement in Relation to Suicide." *Journal of Psychosomatic Research*, 1972, *16*:361–366.

Burgess, E. W. "Aging in Western Culture." Ch. 1, pp. 3–28, in E. W. Burgess (Ed.), *Aging in Western Societies*. Chicago: University of Chicago Press, 1960.

Butler, R. "The Life Review: An Interpretation of Reminiscence in the Aged." *Psychiatry: Journal for the Study of Inter-Personal Processes*, 1963, *26*:65–76.

Bynum, J. "Social Status and Rites of Passage: The Social Context of Death." *Omega*, 1973, *4*(4):323–332.

Cain, L. D. "Aging and the Law." Pp. 342–368 in R. H. Binstock & E. Shanas (Eds.), *Handbook of Aging and the Social Sciences*. New York: Van Nostrand Reinhold, 1976.

Cain, L. D. "Counting Backward from Projected Death: An Alternative to Chronological Age in Assigning Status to the Elderly." Paper delivered at the Policy Center on Aging, Maxwell School, Syracuse University, March 22, 1978.

Calkins, K. "Shouldering a Burden." *Omega*, 1972, *3*(1):23–36.

Calvert, P., Northeast, J., & Dax, E. C. "Death in a Country Area and Its Effect on the Health of Relatives." *The Medical Journal of Australia*, 1977, *2*:635–638.

Cameron, P., Stewart, L., & Biber, H. "Consciousness of Death across the Life Span." *Journal of Gerontology*, 1973, *28*(1):92–95.

Cappon, D. "Attitudes of and toward the Dying." *Canadian Medical Association Journal*, 1962, *87*:693–700.

Carp, F. M. "Housing and Living Environments of Older People." Ch. 10, pp. 244–271, in R. H. Binstock & E. Shanas (Eds.), *Handbook of Aging and the Social Sciences*. New York: Van Nostrand Reinhold, 1976.

Carp, F. M. "Impact of Improved Living Environment on Health and Life Expectancy." *The Gerontologist*, 1977, *17*(3):242–249.

Carpenter, E. S. "Eternal Life and Self-Definition among the Aivilik Eskimos." *American Journal of Psychiatry*, 1954, *110*:840–843.

Carpenter, J. O., & Wylie, C. M. "On Aging, Dying, and Denying." *Public Health Reports*, 1974, *89*(5):403–407.

Carter, H., & Glick, P. C. *Marriage and Divorce: A Social and Economic Study*. Cambridge, Mass.: Harvard University Press, 1970.

Cartwright, A., Hockey, L., & Anderson, J. L. *Life before Death*. London and Boston: Routledge & Kegan Paul, 1973.

Cassell, E. J. "Dying in a Technological Society." *Hastings Center Studies*, 1974, *2*(2):31–36.

Cavan, R. S., Burgess, E. W., Havighurst, R. J., & Goldhamer, H. *Personal Adjustment in Old Age*. Chicago: Science Research Associates, 1949.

Chappell, N. L. "Awareness of Death in the Disengagement Theory: A Conceptualization and an Empirical Investigation." *Omega*, 1975, *6*(4):325–343.

References

Chasin, B. "Neglected Variables in the Study of Death Attitudes." *The Sociological Quarterly,* 1971, *12*(Winter):107–113.

Chellam, G. "The Disengagement Theory: Awareness of Death and Self-Engagement." D.S.W. Thesis, Western Reserve University, 1964. (University Microfilms No. 65-2318)

Chevan, A., & Korson, J. H. "The Widowed Who Live Alone: An Examination of Social and Demographic Factors." *Social Forces,* 1972, *51*(September):45–53.

Childe, V. G. "Directional Changes in Funerary Practices during 50,000 Years." *Man,* 1945, *45*:16–18.

Chiriboga, D. "Perceptions of Well-Being." Ch. 5, pp. 84–98, in M. F. Lowenthal, M. Thurnher, & D. Chiriboga, et al., *Four Stages of Life.* San Francisco: Jossey-Bass, 1975.

Chiriboga, D., & Gigy, L. "Perspectives on Life Course." Ch. 7, pp. 122–145, in M. F. Lowenthal, M. Thurnher, D. Chiriboga, et al., *Four Stages of Life.* San Francisco: Jossey-Bass, 1975.

Chiriboga, D., & Thurnher, M. "Concept of Self." Ch. 4, pp. 62–83, in M. F. Lowenthal, M. Thurnher, D. Chiriboga, et al., *Four Stages of Life.* San Francisco: Jossey-Bass, 1975.

Christ, A. "Attitudes toward Death among a Group of Acute Geriatric Psychiatric Patients." *Journal of Gerontology,* 1961, *16:*56–59.

Cicourel, A.B. *Method and Measurement in Sociology.* New York: Free Press, 1964.

Clausen, J. A. "Glimpses into the Social World of Middle Age." *International Journal of Aging and Human Development,* 1976, *7*(2):99–106.

Clayton, P., Desmarais, L., & Winokur, G. "A Study of Normal Bereavement." *American Journal of Psychiatry,* 1968, *121*(1):168–178.

Clayton, P., Halikes, J., & Maurice, W. "The Bereavement of the Widowed." *Diseases of the Nervous System,* 1971, *120*(1):597–604.

Coffin, M. M. *Death in Early America.* Nashville and New York: Nelson, 1976.

Cohen, E. S. "Editor's Note." *The Gerontologist,* 1976, *16*(3):270–275.

Coleman, P. G. "Measuring Reminiscence Characteristics from Conversation as Adaptive Features of Old Age." *International Journal of Aging and Human Development,* 1974, *5* (3):281–294.

Collette, C. L. "Death with Dignity: Unsolicited Responses to a Gubernatorial Statement." *The Gerontologist,* 1973, *13*(3, Pt. 1):327–331.

Coombs, R. H., & Goldman, L. J. "Maintenance and Discontinuity of Coping Mechanisms in an Intensive Care Unit." *Social Problems,* 1973, *20*(3):342–355.

Counts, D. "The Good Death in Kaliai: Preparation for Death in Western New Britain." *Omega,* 1976–1977, *7*(4):367–372.

Cox, P., & Ford, J. R. "The Mortality of Widows Shortly after Widowhood." *The Lancet,* 1964, (1):163–164.

Crane, D. *The Sanctity of Social Life: Physicians' Treatment of Critically Ill Patients.* New York: Russell Sage Foundation, 1975.

Cumming, E. "Further Thoughts on the Theory of Disengagement." *International Social Science Bulletin,* 1963, *15:*377–393.

Cumming, E. "Engagement with an Old Theory." *International Journal of Aging and Human Development,* 1975, *6*(3):187–191.

Cumming, E., Dean, L., Newell, D., & McCaffrey, I. "Disengagement: A Tentative Theory of Aging." *Sociometry,* 1960, *23:*23–35.

Cumming, E., & Henry, W. *Growing Old: The Process of Disengagement.* New York: Basic Books, 1961.

Curl, J. S. *The Victorian Celebration of Death.* Detroit: Partridge Press, 1972.

Damianopoulos, E. "A Formal Statement of Disengagement Theory." Ch. 12, pp. 210–218, in E. Cumming & W. Henry, *Growing Old: The Process of Disengagement.* New York: Basic Books, 1961.

Davidson, G. W. "Histories and Rituals of Destiny: Implications for Thanatology." *Soundings,* 1971, *54*(4, Winter):415–434.

Dawe, A. "The Two Sociologies." *British Journal of Sociology,* 1970, *21:*207–218.

Degner, L. "The Relationship between Some Beliefs Held by Physicians and Their Life-Prolonging Decisions." *Omega,* 1974, *5*(3):223–232.

DeJong, G. F., & Sell, R. R. "Population Redistribution, Migration, and Residential Preferences." *Annals of the American Academy of Political and Social Sciences,* 1977, *429:* 130–144.

Denton, F. T., & Spencer, B. G. "Health-Care Costs When the Population Changes." *Canadian Journal of Economics*, 1975, *8*(1):34–48.

Denton, F. T., & Spencer, B. G. "Canada's Population and Labour Force: Past, Present and Future." Ch. 2 in V. W. Marshall (Ed.), *Aging in Canada: Social Perspectives*. Toronto: Fitzhenry & Whiteside, 1979.

Denzin, N. K. *The Research Act*. Chicago: Aldine, 1970.

Diggory, J. *Self-Evaluation: Concepts and Studies*. New York: Wiley, 1966.

Diggory, J., & Rothman, D. "Values Destroyed by Death." *Journal of Abnormal and Social Psychology*, 1961, *63*:205–210.

Dilthey, W. *Pattern and Meaning in History* (edited by H. P. Rickman). New York: Harper Torchbooks, 1962.

Donaldson, P. "Denying Death: A Note Regarding Some Ambiguities in the Current Discussion." *Omega*, 1972, *3*:285–290.

Douglas, A. "Heaven Our Home: Consolation Literature in the Northern United States, 1830—1880." Pp. 49–68 in D. E. Stannard (Ed.), *Death in America*. Philadelphia: University of Pennsylvania Press, 1975.

Douglas, M. *Purity and Danger*. New York: Praeger, 1966.

Dowd, J. J., & Brooks III, F. P. "Anomia and Aging: Normlessness or Class Consciousness?" Unpublished paper, Department of Sociology, University of Georgia, 1978.

Drake, M. (Ed.). *Population in Industrialization*. London: Methuen, 1969.

Dudley, D. L., Verhey, J. W., Masuda, M., Martin, C. J., & Holmes, T. H. "Long-Term Adjustment, Prognosis, and Death in Irreversible Diffuse Obstructive Pulmonary Syndromes." *Psychosomatic Medicine*, 1969, *31*(4):310–325.

Duff, R. S., & Hollingshead, A. B. *Sickness and Society*. New York: Harper & Row, 1968.

Dumont, R. G., & Foss, D. C. *The American View of Death: Acceptance or Denial?* Cambridge, Mass.: Schenkman, 1972.

Eastman, M. (Ed.). *Capital, The Communist Manifesto, and Other Writings by Karl Marx*. New York: Modern Library, 1932.

Eaton, J. W. "The Art of Aging and Dying." *The Gerontologist*, 1964, *4*(2, Pt. 1):94–100.

Eisenstadt, S. N. *From Generation to Generation*. Glencoe, Ill.: Free Press, 1956.

Eissler, K. R. *The Psychiatrist and the Dying Patient*. New York: International Universities Press, 1955.

Elder, G. H., Jr. *Children of the Great Depression: Social Change in Life Experience*. Chicago: University of Chicago Press, 1974.

Enos, D. D., & Sultan, P. *The Sociology of Health Care: Social, Economic and Political Perspectives*. New York: Praeger, 1977.

Erikson, E. *Young Man Luther*. London: Faber & Faber, 1958.

Erikson, E. "Identity and the Life Cycle." *Psychological Issues*, 1959, *1*(1).

Erikson, E. *Childhood and Society* (2nd rev. ed.). New York: Norton, 1963.

Falk, J. M. "The Organization of Remembered Life Experience of Older People: Its Relation to Anticipated Stress, to Subsequent Adaptation, and to Age." Doctoral Dissertation, Committee on Human Development, University of Chicago, 1970.

Faunce, W. A., & Fulton, R. "The Sociology of Death: A Neglected Area of Research." *Social Forces*, 1958, *36*:205–209.

Feifel, H. "Attitudes toward Death in Some Normal and Mentally Ill Populations." Ch. 8, pp. 114–130, in H. Feifel (Ed.), *The Meaning of Death*. New York: McGraw-Hill, 1959.

Feifel, H. "The Function of Attitudes toward Death." Ch. 5, pp. 632–641, in *Death and Dying: Attitudes of Patient and Doctor*. Group for the Advancement of Psychiatry, Vol. 5, Symposium No. 11, 1965.

Feifel, H. "Religious Conviction and Fear of Death among the Healthy and the Terminally Ill." *Journal for the Scientific Study of Religion*, 1974, *13*(3):353–360.

Feldman, M. J., & Hersen, M. "Attitudes toward Death in Nightmare Subjects." *Journal of Abnormal Psychology*, 1967, *72*(5):421–425.

Felton, B., & Kahana, E. "Adjustment and Situationally Bound Locus of Control among Institutionalized Aged." *Journal of Gerontology*, 1974, *29*(3):295–301.

Festinger, L. "A Theory of Social Comparison Processes." *Human Relations*, 1954, *7*:117–140.

Foote, N. N. "The Movement from Jobs to Careers in American Industry." *Transactions of the Third World Congress of Sociology*, International Sociological Association, 1956 (2): 30–40.

Foote, N. N. "Concept and Method in the Study of Human Development." In M. Sherif & M. C. Wilson (Eds.), *Emerging Problems in Social Psychology*. Norman: University of Oklahoma Press, 1957.

Fourastié, J. "De La Vie Traditionnelle à la Vie 'Tertiaire,'" *Population*, 1959, *14*:417–423.

Fraisse, P. *The Psychology of Time*. New York: Harper & Row, 1963.

French, S. "The Cemetery as Cultural Institution: The Establishment of Mount Auburn and the 'Rural Cemetery' Movement." Pp. 69–91 in D. E. Stannard (Ed.), *Death in America*. Philadelphia: University of Pennsylvania Press, 1975.

Freud, S. *Beyond the Pleasure Principle*. London: Hogarth Press, 1948. (Originally published, 1920.)

Freud, S. "Thoughts for the Times on War and Death." In *The Standard Edition of the Complete Psychological Works of Sigmund Freud* (Vol. 14, pp. 275–300). London: Hogarth, 1957. (Originally published, 1915.)

Fulton, R. (Ed.). *Death and Identity* (Rev. ed.). Bowie, Md.: Charles Press, 1976.

Garrity, T. F., & Wyss, J. "Death, Funeral and Bereavement Practices in Appalachian and Non-Appalachian Kentucky." *Omega*, 1976, *7*(3):209–228.

Gatch, M. M. *Death: Meaning and Morality in Christian Thought and Contemporary Culture*. New York: Seabury Press, 1969.

Geertz, C. "Ritual and Social Change: A Javanese Example." *American Anthropologist*, 1957, *59*:32–54.

Geertz, C. "Religion as a Cultural System." Pp. 1–46 in M. Banton (Ed.), *Anthropological Approaches to the Study of Religion* (A.S.A. Monograph 3). New York: Praeger, 1966.

Gerber, I., Rusalem, R., Hannon, M., Battin, D., & Arkin, A. "Anticipatory Grief and Aged Widows and Widowers." *Journal of Gerontology*, 1975, *30*(2):225–229.

Giambra, L. M. "Daydreaming across the Life Span: Late Adolescent to Senior Citizen." *International Journal of Aging and Human Development*, 1974, *5*(2):115–140.

Giambra, L. M. "A Factor Analytic Study of Daydreaming, Imaginal Process, and Temperament: A Replication on an Adult Male Life-Span Sample." *Journal of Gerontology*, 1977, *32*(6):675–680. (a)

Giambra, L. M. "Daydreaming about the Past: The Time Setting of Spontaneous Thought Intrusions." *The Gerontologist*, 1977, *17*(1):35–38. (b)

Glaser, B. G. "The Social Loss of Aged Dying Patients." *The Gerontologist*, 1966, 6 (June): 77–80.

Glaser, B. G., & Strauss, A. L. "The Social Loss of Dying Patients." *The American Journal of Nursing*, 1964, *64*(June):119–121.

Glaser, B. G., & Strauss, A. L. *Awareness of Dying*. Chicago: Aldine, 1965.

Glaser, B. G., & Strauss, A. L. *Time for Dying*. Chicago: Aldine, 1968.

Glaser, B. G., & Strauss, A. L. *Status Passage*. Chicago and New York: Aldine-Atherton, 1971.

Glass, D. V., & Eversley, D. E. C. (Eds.). *Population in History*. Chicago: Aldine, 1965.

Glick, I. O., Weiss, R. S., & Parkes, C. M. *The First Year of Bereavement*. New York: Wiley-Interscience, 1974.

Glick, P. C. "The Family Cycle." *American Sociological Review*, 1947, *12*(April):164–174.

Glick, P. C., & Parke, R., Jr. "New Approaches in Studying the Life Cycle of the Family." *Demography II*, 1965:187–202.

Goffman, E. "On the Characteristics of Total Institutions." Pp. 1–24 in E. Goffman, *Asylums*. Garden City, N. Y.: Doubleday Anchor, 1961. (a)

Goffman, E. "Role Distance." Pp. 83–152 in E. Goffman, *Encounters*. Indianapolis: Bobbs-Merrill, 1961. (b)

Goffman, E. "The Medical Model and Mental Hospitalization: Some Notes on the Vicissitudes of the Tinkering Trades." Pp. 321–386 in E. Goffman, *Asylums*. Garden City, N. Y.: Doubleday Anchor, 1961. (c)

Goldscheider, C. *Population, Modernization and Social Structure*. Boston: Little, Brown, 1971.

Goldstein, A. M. "Denial and External Locus of Control as Mechanisms of Adjustment in Chronic Medical Illness." *Essence*, 1976, *1*(1):5–22.

Goody, J. *Death, Property and the Ancestors*. Palo Alto, Calif.: Stanford University Press, 1962.

Goody, J., Thirsk, J., & Thompson, E. P. (Eds.). *Family and Inheritance: Rural Society in Western Europe, 1200–1800* (First paperback edition). Cambridge: Cambridge University Press, 1978.

Gorer, G. *Death, Grief and Mourning*. Garden City, N. Y.: Doubleday Anchor, 1965. (a)

Gorer, G. "The Pornography of Death." Reprinted in G. Gorer, *Death, Grief and Mourning*. Garden City, N. Y.: Doubleday Anchor, 1965. (Originally published, 1955.) (b)

Gorney, J. E. "Experiencing and Age: Patterns of Reminiscence Among the Elderly." Doctoral Dissertation, Committee on Human Development, University of Chicago, 1968.

Gould, R. L. "The Phases of Adult Life: A Study in Developmental Psychology." *American Journal of Psychiatry*, 1972, *129*(5):33–43.

Gould, R. L. *Transformations*. New York: Simon & Schuster, 1978.

Greven, P., Jr. *Four Generations: Population, Land and Family in Colonial Andover, Massachusetts*. Ithaca, N. Y.: Cornell University Press, 1970.

Gubrium, J. F. *Living and Dying at Murray Manor*. New York: St. Martin's Press, 1975. (a)

Gubrium, J. F. "Death Worlds in a Nursing Home." *Urban Life*, 1975, *4*(3, October):317–338. (b)

Gubrium, J. F., & Buckholdt, D. R. *Toward Maturity*. San Francisco: Jossey-Bass, 1977.

Guemple, D. L. "Human Resource Management: The Dilemma of the Aging Eskimo." *Sociological Symposium*, 1969, 2(Spring): 59–74.

Guptill, C. S. "Aging and Attitude toward Dying." Paper presented at 29th Annual Meeting of the Gerontological Society, October 1976.

Gustafson, E. "Dying: The Career of the Nursing Home Patient." *Journal of Health and Social Behavior*, 1972, *13*(September): 226–235.

Haan, N. "Personality Organizations of Well-Functioning Younger People and Older Adults." *International Journal of Aging and Human Development*, 1976, 7(2):117–127.

Habakkuk, H. J. *Population Growth and Economic Development since 1750*. Leicester: Leicester University Press, 1972.

Hall, G. S. "Note on Early Memories." *Pediatric Seminar*, 1898, *6:*311–318.

Hardiman, C. J., Holbrook, A., & Hedrick, D. L. "Nonverbal Communication Systems for the Severely Handicapped Geriatric Patient." *The Gerontologist*, 1979, *19*(1):96–101.

Harvey, C. D., & Bahr, H. M. "Widowhood, Morale, and Affiliation." *Journal of Marriage and the Family*, 1974, *36*(February):97–106.

Hauser, P. M. "Aging and World-Wide Population Change." Ch. 3, pp. 59–86 in R. H. Binstock & E. Shanas (Eds.), *Handbook of Aging and the Social Sciences*. New York: Van Nostrand Reinhold, 1976.

Havighurst, R. J., & Glasser, R. "An Exploratory Study of Reminiscence." *Journal of Gerontology*, 1972, *27:*245–253.

Havighurst, R. J., Neugarten, B., & Tobin, S. "Disengagement and Patterns of Aging." Unpublished paper presented at the meeting of the International Association of Gerontology, Copenhagen, August 1963. Abridged as Ch. 16, pp. 161–172, in B. L. Neugarten (Ed.), *Middle Age and Aging*. Chicago: University of Chicago Press, 1968.

Hays, W. L. *Quantification in Psychology*. Monterey, Calif.: Brooks/Cole, 1967.

Heenan, E. "Sociology of Religion and the Aged: The Empirical Lacunae." *Journal for the Scientific Study of Religion*, 1972, 2:171–176.

Heidegger, M. *Being and Time* (translated by J. McQuarrie & E. Robinson). New York: Harper & Row, 1962.

Heidel, A. (Trans.). *The Gilgamesh Epic and Old Testament Parallels*. Chicago: University of Chicago Press, Phoenix Edition, 1963.

Hendrix, L. "Death Themes in Anglo-American Folk Balladry." Paper presented at the meeting of the American Sociological Association, Chicago, 1977.

Henripin, J. "From Acceptance of Nature to Control: The Demography of the French Canadians since the Seventeenth Century." *Canadian Journal of Economics and Political Science*, 1957, *25*(1):10–19.

Henry, W. "The Theory of Intrinsic Disengagement." Pp. 415–418 in P. F. Hansen (Ed.), *Age with a Future*. Proceedings of the 6th International Conference on Gerontology, Copenhagen, 1963. Philadelphia: Davis, 1964.

Herlihy, D. "Deaths, Marriages, Births, and the Tuscan Economy." Pp. 136–164 in R. D. Lee, R. A. Easterlin, P. H. Lindert, & E. Van de Walle (Eds.), *Population Patterns in the Past*. New York: Academic Press, 1977.

Hertz, R. *Death and the Right Hand* (translated by R. C. Needham). Aberdeen: Cohen & West, 1960.

Hewitt, J. *Self and Society*. Boston: Allyn & Bacon, 1976.

References　　　　　　　　　　　　　　　　　　　　　　　　　　　　　　　*203*

Hinton, J. M. "The Physical and Mental Distress of the Dying." *Quarterly Journal of Medicine,* 1963, *32:*1–21.

Hinton, J. M. *Dying.* Harmondsworth: Penguin, 1967.

Hochschild, A. R. *The Unexpected Community.* Englewood Cliffs, N. J.: Prentice-Hall, 1973.

Hochschild, A. R. "Disengagement Theory: A Critique and Proposal." *American Sociological Review,* 1975, *40*(5):553–569.

Hoggatt, L., & Spilka, B. "The Nurse and the Terminally Ill Patient: Some Perspectives and Projected Actions." *Omega,* 1978–1979, *9*(3): 255–266.

Homans, G. C. "Anxiety and Ritual: the Theories of Malinowski and Radcliffe-Brown." *American Anthropologist,* 1941, *43:*164–172. Reprinted, pp. 123–128, in W. Lessa & E. Z. Vogt (Eds.), *Reader in Comparative Religion* (2nd ed.). New York: Harper & Row, 1965.

Howard, A., & Scott, R. A. "Cultural Values and Attitudes toward Death." *The Journal of Existentialism,* 1965–1966, *6*(22):161–174.

Howard, E. "The Effect of Work Experience in a Nursing Home on Attitudes toward Death Held by Nurse Aides." *The Gerontologist,* 1974, *14:*54–56.

Hughes, E. C. "Institutional Office and the Person." *American Journal of Sociology,* 1937, *43*(November):404–413.

Hughes, E. C. "Good People and Dirty Work." Pp. 23–36 in H. Becker (Ed.), *The Other Side: Perspectives on Deviance.* New York: Free Press, 1964.

Hughes, E. C. "Cycles, Turning Points, and Careers." Reprinted in E. C. Hughes, *The Sociological Eye: Selected Papers on Institutions and Race.* Chicago: University of Chicago Press, 1971.

Illich, I. *Limits to Medicine. Medical Nemesis: The Expropriation of Health.* Toronto: McClelland & Stewart, and London: Marion Boyars, 1976.

Ingram, D. K., & Barry, J. R. "National Statistics on Deaths in Nursing Homes: Interpretations and Implications." *The Gerontologist,* 1977, *17*(4):303–308.

Inkeles, A. "Sociology and Psychology." Pp. 317–387 in S. Koch (Ed.), *Psychology: A Study of a Science* (Vol. 6). New York: McGraw-Hill, 1963.

Jackson, E. N. *Understanding Grief.* New York: Abingdon Press, 1957.

Jacobson, P. "Cohort Survival for Generations Since 1840." *Milbank Memorial Fund Quarterly,* 1964, *42*(July):36–53.

Jacques, E. *Work, Creativity and Social Justice.* New York: International Universities Press, 1970.

Jeffers, F., Nichols, C., & Eisdorfer, C. "Attitudes of Older Persons toward Death: A Preliminary Study." *Journal of Gerontology,* 1961, *16:*53–56.

Jeffers, F., & Verwoerdt, A. "Factors Associated with Frequency of Death Thoughts in Elderly Community Volunteers." Pp. 401–406 in E. Palmore (Ed.), *Normal Aging.* Durham, N. C.: Duke University Press, 1970.

Jones, R. L. "Religious Symbolism in Limbu Death-by-Violence." *Omega,* 1974, *5*(3):257–266.

Jordan, Z. A. (Ed.). *Karl Marx: Economy, Class and Social Revolution.* London: Michael Joseph, 1971.

Jung, C. G. *Modern Man in Search of a Soul.* New York: Harcourt, Brace & World, 1933.

Kahana, E. "Matching Environments to Needs of the Aged: A Conceptual Scheme." Ch. 9, pp. 201–214, in J. F. Gubrium (Ed.), *Late Life, Communities and Environmental Policy.* Springfield, Ill.: Charles C Thomas, 1974.

Kalbach, W. E., & McVey, W. W. *The Demographic Bases of Canadian Society.* Toronto: McGraw-Hill, 1971.

Kalish, R. A. "Some Variables in Death Attitudes." *Journal of Social Psychology,* 1963, *59:* 137–145.

Kalish, R. A. "A Continuum of Subjectively Perceived Death." *The Gerontologist,* 1966, *6*(2, June):73–76.

Kalish, R. A. "Of Children and Grandfathers: A Speculative Essay on Dependency." Pp. 73–83 in R. A. Kalish (Ed.), *The Dependencies of Old People. Occasional Papers in Gerontology* (Vol. 6). Ann Arbor and Detroit: Institute of Gerontology, University of Michigan and Wayne State University, 1969. (a)

Kalish, R. A. "Experiences of Persons Reprieved from Death." In A. H. Kutscher (Ed.), *Death and Bereavement.* Springfield, Ill.: Charles C Thomas, 1969. (b)

Kalish, R. A. "Of Social Values and the Dying: A Defense of Disengagement." *The Family Coordinator,* 1972, *21:*81–94.

Kalish, R. A. "Death and Dying in a Social Context." Ch. 19, pp. 483–507, in R. H. Binstock & E. Shanas (Eds.), *Handbook of Aging and the Social Sciences*. New York: Van Nostrand Reinhold, 1976.

Kalish, R. A., & Johnson, A. I. "Value Similarities and Differences in Three Generations of Women." *Journal of Marriage and the Family*, 1972, *34*(February):49–54.

Kalish, R. A., & Reynolds, D. K. "Widows View Death: A Brief Research Note." *Omega*, 1974, *5*(2):187–192.

Kalish, R. A., & Reynolds, D. K. *Death and Ethnicity: A Psychocultural Study*. Los Angeles: University of Southern California Press, 1976.

Kalson, L. "The Therapy of Independent Living for the Elderly." *Journal of the American Geriatrics Society*, 1972, *20:*394–397.

Kamen, H. *The Iron Century: Social Change in Europe, 1550–1660*. London: Sphere Books, 1976. (Revised from the original 1971 edition published by Wiedenfeld and Nicholson.)

Kapleau, P. (Ed.). *The Wheel of Death*. New York: Harper & Row, 1971.

Kastenbaum, R. "Engrossment and Perspective in Later Life: A Developmental Field Approach." Ch. 1, pp. 3–18, in R. Kastenbaum (Ed.), *Contributions to the Psychology of Aging*. New York: Springer, 1965.

Kastenbaum, R. "On the Meaning of Time in Later Life." *Journal of Genetic Psychology*, 1966, *109:*9–25.

Kastenbaum, R. "The Mental Life of Dying Geriatric Patients." *The Gerontologist*, 1967, *7*(2, Pt. 1):97–100. (a)

Kastenbaum, R. "Multiple Perspectives on a Geriatric 'Death Valley.'" *Community Mental Health Journal*, 1967, *3:*21–29. (b)

Kastenbaum, R. "The Foreshortened Life Perspective." *Geriatrics*, 1969, *24*(August):126–133.

Kastenbaum, R. *Death, Society, and Human Experience*. St. Louis: Mosby, 1977.

Kastenbaum, R., & Aisenberg, R. *The Psychology of Death*. New York: Springer, 1972.

Kastenbaum, R., & Candy, S. "The Four Percent Fallacy: A Methodological and Empirical Critique of Extended Care Facility Program Statistics." *Aging and Human Development*, 1973, *4*(1):15–21.

Katona, G. "Private Pensions and Individual Saving." (Monograph No. 40, Survey Research Center, Institute for Social Research.) Ann Arbor: University of Michigan, 1965.

Keith, P. M. "Life Changes and Perceptions of Life and Death among Older Men and Women." *Journal of Gerontology*, 1979, *34*(6): 870–878.

Kett, J. F. "Growing Up in Rural New England, 1800–1840." Pp. 1–16 in T. K. Hareven (Ed.), *Anonymous Americans: Explorations in Nineteenth Century Social History*. Englewood Cliffs, N. J.: Prentice-Hall, 1971.

Kiefer, C. W. *Changing Cultures, Changing Lives*. San Francisco: Jossey-Bass, 1974.

Kimsey, L. R., Roberts, J. L., & Logan, D. L. "Death, Dying, and Denial in the Aged." *American Journal of Psychiatry*, 1972, *129*(2):161–166.

Knodel, J. "Family Limitation and the Fertility Transition: Evidence from the Age Patterns of Fertility in Europe and Asia." *Population Studies*, 1977, *31*(2):219–249.

Koestenbaum, P. "The Vitality of Death." *Journal of Existentialism*, 1964, *18*(Fall):139–166. Reprinted in *Omega*, 1971, *2:*253–271.

Komarovsky, M. "Presidential Address: Some Problems in Role Analysis." *American Sociological Review*, 1973, *38:*(6):649–662.

Kroeber, A. L., & Kluckhohn, C. *Culture: A Critical Review of Concepts and Definitions*. New York: Vintage, 1952.

Kübler-Ross, E. "The Dying Patient as Teacher: An Experiment and an Experience." *The Chicago Theological Seminary Register*, 1966, *57:*1–10. (Author listed as Elizabeth Ross.)

Kübler-Ross, E. *On Death and Dying*. New York: Macmillan, 1969.

Kuhlen, R. G., & Monge, R. H. "Correlates of Estimated Rate of Time Passage in the Adult Years." *Journal of Gerontology*, 1968, *23*(4, October):427–433.

Kuhn, T. *The Structure of Scientific Revolutions* (2nd ed.). Chicago: University of Chicago Press, 1970.

Kuypers, J. A. "Internal-External Locus of Control, Ego Functioning, and Personality Characteristics in Old Age." *The Gerontologist*, 1972, *12*(2, Pt. 1):168–173.

Kuypers, J. A., & Bengtson, V. L. "Social Breakdown and Competence." *Human Development*, 1973, *16:*181–201.

Langer, W. L. "Europe's Initial Population Explosion." *American Historical Review*, 1963, *69*(1, October):1–17. Reprinted in D. M. Heer (Ed.), *Readings on Population*. Englewood Cliffs, N. J.: Prentice-Hall, 1975.

Laslett, P. "Size and Structure of the Household in England over Three Centuries: Part I." *Population Studies*, 1969, *23:*199–223.

Laslett, P. *The World We Have Lost* (2nd ed.). New York: Scribner's, 1971.

Laslett, P. "Societal Development and Aging." Ch. 4, pp. 87–116, in R. H. Binstock & E. Shanas (Eds.), *Handbook of Aging and the Social Sciences*. New York: Van Nostrand Reinhold, 1976.

Laslett, P. *Family Life and Illicit Love in Earlier Generations*. New York: Cambridge University Press, 1977.

Laurence, M. *The Stone Angel*. Toronto: McClelland & Stewart, 1968.

Lee, R. D. (Ed.). *Population Patterns in the Past*. New York: Academic Press, 1977.

Leming, M. R. "Religion and Death: A Test of Homan's Thesis." Paper presented at meeting of the American Sociological Association, Chicago, September 1977.

Lemon, B. W., Bengtson, V. L., & Peterson, J. A. "An Exploration of the Activity Theory of Aging: Activity Types and Life Satisfaction among In-Movers to a Retirement Community." *Journal of Gerontology*, 1972, *27*(4):511–523.

Lerner, M. "When, Why and Where People Die." Pp. 5–29 in O. G. Brim, Jr., H. E. Freeman, S. Levine, & N. A. Scotch (Eds.), *The Dying Patient*. New York: Russell Sage Foundation, 1970.

Lesnoff-Caravaglia, C. "The Five Per Cent Fallacy." *International Journal of Aging and Human Development*, 1978–1979, *9*(2):187–192.

Lester, D. "A Scale Measuring the Fear of Death: Its Construction and Consistency." Unpublished manuscript, ADA Auxiliary Publications Project Document No. 9449, Library of Congress, Washington, D. C., 1966.

Lester, D. "Inconsistency in the Fear of Death of Individuals." *Psychological Reports*, 1967, *20:*1084. (a)

Lester, D. "Experimental and Correlational Studies of the Fear of Death." *Psychological Bulletin*, 1967, *67:*27–36. (b)

Lester, D. "Psychology and Death." *Continuum*, 1967, *5:*50–59. (c)

Lester, D. "Religious Behavior and Fear of the Dead." *Omega*, 1970, *1*(3):181–188.

Leveton, A. "Time, Death and Ego-Chill." *Journal of Existentialism*, 1966, *6:*69–80.

Levin, S., & Kahana, R. J. (Eds.). *Psychodynamic Studies on Aging: Creativity, Reminiscing, and Dying*. New York: International Universities Press, 1967.

Levinson, D. J., Darrow, C. M., Klein, E. B., Levinson, M. H., & McKee, B. *The Seasons of a Man's Life*. New York: Knopf, 1978.

Levy, M. J., Jr. *The Structure of Society*. Princeton, N. J.: Princeton University Press, 1952.

Levy, M. J., Jr. *Modernization and the Structure of Societies* (2 vols.). Princeton, N. J.: Princeton University Press, 1966.

Lewis, C. N. "Reminiscing and Self-Concept in Old Age." *Journal of Gerontology*, 1971, *26*(2):240–243.

Lieberman, M. A. "Observations on Death and Dying." *The Gerontologist*, 1966, *6*(2):70–72, 125.

Lifton, R. J. *Death in Life: Survivors of Hiroshima*. New York: Random House, 1967.

Lifton, R. J. *Boundaries*. New York: Random House, 1969.

Lifton, R. J. (Ed.). *History and Human Survival*. New York: Vintage, 1971.

Linn, M. W. "Perceptions of Childhood: Present Functioning and Past Events." *Journal of Gerontology*, 1973, *28*(2):202–206.

Liton, J., & Olstein, S. C. "Therapeutic Aspects of Reminiscence." *Social Casework*, 1969, *50:*263–268.

Livson, F. B. "Patterns of Personality Development in Middle-Aged Women: A Longitudinal Study." *International Journal of Aging and Human Development*, 1976, *7*(2):107–115.

Loeb, M. B., Pincus, A., & Mueller, B. J. "A Framework for Viewing Adjustment in Aging." *The Gerontologist*, 1966, *6*(4, December): 185–187, 236.

Lofland, L. H. *The Craft of Dying: The Modern Face of Death*. Beverly Hills and London: Sage Publications, 1978.

Lopata, H. Z. *Widowhood in an American City*. Cambridge, Mass.: Schenkman, 1973. (a)

Lopata, H. Z. "Loneliness: Forms and Components." Pp. 102–115 in R. S. Weiss (Ed.), *Loneliness: The Experience of Social Isolation.* Cambridge, Mass.: MIT Press, 1973. (b)

Lopata, H. Z. "Contributions of Extended Families to the Support Systems of Metropolitan Area Widows: Limitations of the Modified Kin Network." *Journal of Marriage and the Family,* 1978, *40*(May):355–364.

Lopata, H. Z. *Women as Widows: Support Systems.* New York: Elsevier North-Holland, 1979.

Lowenthal, M. F. "Intentionality: Toward a Framework for the Study of Adaptation in Adulthood." *Aging and Human Development,* 1971, *2*(May):79–95.

Lowenthal, M. F. "Toward a Sociopsychological Theory of Change in Adulthood and Old Age." Ch. 6, pp. 116–127, in J. E. Birren, K. W. Schaie, et al. (Eds.), *Handbook of the Psychology of Aging.* New York: Van Nostrand Reinhold, 1977.

Lowenthal, M. F., & Chiriboga, D. "Transition to the Empty Nest: Crisis, Challenge or Relief?" *Archives of General Psychiatry,* 1972, *26*(January):8–14.

Lowenthal, M. F., & Chiriboga, D. "Social Stress and Adaptation: Toward a Life-Course Perspective." Pp. 281–310 in C. Eisdorfer & M. P. Lawton (Eds.), *The Psychology of Adult Development and Aging.* Washington: American Psychological Association, 1973.

Lowenthal, M. F., & Haven, C. "Interaction and Adaptation: Intimacy as a Critical Variable." *American Sociological Review,* 1968, *33:*20–30.

Lowenthal, M. F., Thurnher, M., & Chiriboga, D. *Four Stages of Life.* San Francisco: Jossey-Bass, 1975.

Lozier, J., & Althouse, R. "Retirement to the Porch in Rural Appalachia." *International Journal of Aging and Human Development,* 1975, *6*(1):7–15.

Lucas, R. "Social Implications of the Immediacy of Death." *The Canadian Review of Sociology and Anthropology,* 1968, *5*(1):1–16.

Lucas, R. *Men in Crisis.* New York: Basic Books, 1969.

Luijpen, W. A. *Existential Phenomenology* (Rev. ed.). Pittsburgh: Duquesne University Press, 1969.

Lyman, S., & Scott, M. "On the Time Track." Pp. 189–212 in S. Lyman and M. Scott, *A Sociology of the Absurd.* New York: Appleton-Century-Crofts, 1970.

Maddison, D., & Walker, W. "Factors Affecting the Outcome of Conjugal Bereavement." *British Journal of Psychiatry,* 1967, *113:*2(503):1057–1067.

Maddox, G. "Persistence of Life Style among the Elderly." Pp. 309–311 in *Proceedings of the 7th International Congress of Gerontology.* Reprinted in E. Palmore (Ed.), *Normal Aging.* Durham, N. C.: Duke University Press, 1970.

Malinowski, B. *Magic, Science and Religion, and Other Essays.* Glencoe, Ill.: Free Press, 1948.

Malinowski, B. "The Role of Magic and Religion." Pp. 102–112 in W. A. Lessa & E. Z. Vogt (Eds.), *Reader in Comparative Religion* (2nd ed.). New York: Harper & Row, 1965.

Manard, B. B., Kart, C. S., & van Gils, D. W. L. *Old-Age Institutions.* Lexington, Mass.: Heath, 1975.

Mannheim, K. "The Problem of Generations." Ch. 7, pp. 276–322, in *K. Mannheim, Essays on the Sociology of Knowledge* (P. Kecskemeti, Ed.). London: Routledge & Kegan Paul, 1952.

Marcuse, H. "The Ideology of Death." Ch. 5, pp. 64–76, in H. Feifel (Ed.), *The Meaning of Death.* New York: McGraw-Hill, 1959.

Markson, E. W. "Disengagement Theory Revisited." *International Journal of Aging and Human Development,* 1975, *6*(3):183–186.

Marris, P. *Widows and Their Families.* London: Routledge & Kegan Paul, 1958.

Marshall, V. W. "Continued Living and Dying as Problematical Aspects of Old Age." Unpublished doctoral dissertation, Department of Sociology, Princeton University, 1973. (a)

Marshall, V. W. "Game-Analyzable Dilemmas in a Retirement Village: A Case Study." *International Journal of Aging and Human Development,* 1973, *4*(4):285–291. (b)

Marshall, V. W. "The Last Strand: Remnants of Engagement in the Later Years." *Omega,* 1974, *5*(1):25–35. (a)

Marshall, V. W. "The Life Review as a Social Process." Paper presented at the 27th Annual Meeting of the Gerontological Society, Portland, 1974. (b)

Marshall, V. W. "Socialization for Impending Death in a Retirement Village." *American Journal of Sociology,* 1975, *80*(5, March):1124–1144. (a)

Marshall, V. W. "Age and Awareness of Finitude in Developmental Gerontology." *Omega,* 1975, *6*(2):113–129. (b)

Marshall, V. W. "Organizational Features of Terminal Status Passage in Residential Facilities for the Aged." *Urban Life*, 1975, *4*(3, October):349–368. (c)

Marshall, V. W. "The Denial Concept in Canadian and American Death and Dying Research." Paper presented at the Symposium *Death and Dying in Different Cultures*, 11th International Congress of Gerontology, Tokyo, 1978. Abstracted in the *Proceedings*, p. 156.

Marshall, V. W. "No Exit: A Symbolic Interactionist Perspective on Aging." *International Journal of Aging and Human Development*, 1978–1979, *9*(4):345–358.

Marshall, V. W. "No Exit: A Symolic Interactionist Perspective on Aging." *International Journal of Aging and Human Development*, 1978–1979, *9*(4):345–358.

Marshall, V. W. "Death, Dying, and Adjustment to Death and Dying." In D. Mangen & W. A. Peterson (Eds.), *Research Instruments in Social Gerontology*. Minneapolis: University of Minnesota Press, in press.

Marshall, V. W., & Tindale, J. A. "Notes for a Radical Gerontology." *International Journal of Aging and Human Development*, 1978–1979, *9*(2):163–175.

Matthews, A. M. "Women and Widowhood." Ch. 15 in V. W. Marshall (Ed.), *Aging in Canada: Social Perspectives*. Toronto: Fitzhenry & Whiteside, 1979.

Matthews, S. H. "Old Women and Identity Maintenance: Outwitting the Grim Reaper." *Urban Life*, 1975, *4*(3, October):339–348.

Matthews, S. H. *The Social World of Old Women*. Beverly Hills and London: Sage Publications, 1979.

May, R. *Existential Psychotherapy*. Toronto: CBC Publications, 1967.

McCrae, R. R., Bartone, P. T., & Costa, P. T. "Age, Anxiety, and Self-Reported Health." *International Journal of Aging and Human Development*, 1976, *7*(1):49–58.

McHugh, P. *Defining the Situation*. Indianapolis: Bobbs-Merrill, 1968.

McInnis, R. M. "Childbearing and Land Availability: Some Evidence from Individual Household Data." Pp. 201–227 in R. D. Lee (Ed.), *Population Patterns in the Past*. New York: Academic Press, 1977.

McIntosh, J. *Communication and Awareness in a Cancer Ward*. London and New York: Croom Helm and Prodist, 1977.

McKeown, T. *The Role of Medicine: Dream, Mirage or Nemesis?* London: Nuffield Provincial Hospitals Trust, 1976.

McKeown, T., & Brown, R. G. "Medical Evidence Related to English Population Changes in the Eighteenth Century." *Population Studies*, 1955, *9*(2).

McKeown, T., Record, R. G., & Turner, R. D. "An Interpretation of the Decline of Mortality in England and Wales during the Twentieth Century." *Population Studies*, 1975, *29*:391–422.

McKinlay, J. B., & McKinlay, S. M. "The Questionable Contribution of Medical Measures to the Decline of Mortality in the United States in the Twentieth Century." *MMFQ/Health and Society*, 1977, *55*(3, Summer):405–428.

McMahon, W. W., & Rhudick, P. J. "Reminiscing: Adaptational Significance in the Aged." *Archives of General Psychiatry*, 1964, *10*:292–298.

McNeil, B., Weichselbaum, R., & Pauker, S. G. "Fallacy of the Five-Year Survival in Lung Cancer." *The New England Journal of Medicine*, 1978, *299*(25):1397–1401.

Mead, G. H. *Mind, Self, and Society: From the Standpoint of a Social Behaviorist* (C. W. Morris, Ed.). Chicago: University of Chicago Press, 1934. (a)

Mead, G. H. "The Self and the Process of Reflection." Supplementary Essay III in G. H. Mead, *Mind, Self and Society: From the Standpoint of a Social Behaviorist* (C. W. Morris, Ed.). Chicago: University of Chicago Press, 1934. (b)

Mead, G. H. "The Social Self." Ch. 12, pp. 142–149, in A. J. Reck (Ed.), *Mead: Selected Writings*. Indianapolis: Bobbs-Merrill, 1964.

Messer, M. "Possibility of an Age-Concentrated Environment Becoming a Normative System." *The Gerontologist*, 1967, *17*(Winter):247–251.

Michalowski, R. J., Jr. "The Social Meanings of Violent Death." *Omega*, 1976, *7*(1):83–93.

Millman, M. *The Unkindest Cut: Life in the Backrooms of Medicine*. New York: Morrow, 1977.

Mindel, C. H., & Vaughan, C. E. "A Multidimensional Approach to Religiosity and Disengagement." *Journal of Gerontology*, 1978, *33*(1):103–108.

Mischel, W. "Continuity and Change in Personality." *American Psychologist*, 1969, *24*:1012–1018.

Mitchell, D. L., & Goldfarb, A. I. "Psychological Needs of the Aged Patients at Home." *American Journal of Public Health*, 1966, *56*(10):1716–1720.

Moore, R. J., & Newton, J. H. "Attitudes of the Life Threatened Hospitalized Elderly." *Essence*, 1977, *1*(3):129–138.

Moore, W. E. *Man, Time, and Society*. New York: Wiley, 1963.

Moore, W. E. "Aging and the Social System." Pp. 23–41 in J. C. McKinney & F. T. de Vyver (Eds.), *Aging and Social Policy*. New York: Appleton-Century-Crofts, 1966.

Morgan, J. N. "Planning for the Future and Living with Risk." *The American Behavioral Scientist*, May 1963.

Morgenthau, H. J. "Death in the Nuclear Age." Pp. 69–77 in N. A. Scott, Jr. (Ed.), *The Modern Vision of Death*. Richmond, Va.: John Knox, 1967.

Moriwaki, S. Y. "Self-Disclosure, Significant Others and Psychological Well-Being in Old Age." *Journal of Health and Social Behavior*, 1973. *14*(3):226–232.

Morley, J. *Death, Heaven and the Victorians*. Pittsburgh: University of Pittsburgh Press, 1971.

Munnichs, J. M. A. *Old Age and Finitude*. Basel and New York: Karger, 1966.

Munnichs, J. M. A. "Taboo on Death and Dying: Some Explanatory Notes." Paper presented at a conference on Aging and Social Policy, sponsored by l'Institut de la Vie, Vichy, France, 1977.

Myerhoff, B. G. "A Symbol Perfected in Death: Continuity and Ritual in the Life and Death of an Elderly Jew." Ch. 5, pp. 163–202, in B. G. Myerhoff & A. Simić (Eds.), *Life's Career: Aging*. Beverly Hills and London: Sage Publications, 1978.

Nehrke, M., Bellucci, G., & Gabriel, S. J. "Death Anxiety, Locus of Control and Life Satisfaction in the Elderly: Toward a Definition of Ego-Integrity." *Omega*, 1977–1978, *8*(4): 359–368.

Nelson, L. D. "Religious Conditioning of Death Avoidance." Paper presented at the annual meeting of the American Sociological Association, Chicago, September 5–9, 1977.

Nelson, L. D., & Nelson, C. C. "A Factor Analytic Inquiry into the Multidimensionality of Death Anxiety." *Omega*, 1975, *6*(2):171–178.

Neugarten, B. L. (Ed.). *Personality in Middle and Late Life: Empirical Studies*. New York: Atherton, 1964.

Neugarten, B. L. "Adult Personality: A Developmental View." *Human Development*, 1966, *9*:61–73.

Neugarten, B. L. "Dynamics of Transition of Middle Age to Old Age." *Journal of Geriatric Psychiatry*, 1970, *4*(1, Fall):71–87. (a)

Neugarten, B. L. "The Old and the Young in Modern Societies." *American Behavioral Scientist*, 1970, *14*(1):13–24. (b)

Neugarten, B. L. "Personality and the Aging Process." *The Gerontologist*, 1972, *12*(I, Pt. 1): 9–15.

Neugarten, B. L. "Patterns of Aging, Past, Present, and Future." *Social Service Review*, 1973, *47*(4):571–580.

Neugarten, B. L. "Age Groups in American Society and the Rise of the Young-Old." *Annals of the American Academy of Political and Social Science*, 1974, *415*(September):187–198.

Neugarten, B. L. "The Future and the Young-Old." *The Gerontologist*, 1975, *15*(1, Pt. 2):4–9.

Neugarten, B. L. "Aging in the Future." Pp. 2–26 in B. T. Wigdor (Ed.), *Canadian Gerontological Collection I, Selected Papers*. Calgary: Canadian Association on Gerontology, 1977.

Neugarten, B. L., Crotty, W., & Tobin, S. "Personality Types in an Aged Population." Ch. 8, pp. 159–187, in B. L. Neugarten (Ed.), *Personality in Middle and Late Life: Empirical Studies*. New York: Atherton, 1964.

Neugarten, B. L., & Datan, N. "Sociological Perspectives on the Life Cycle." Ch. 3, pp. 53–69, in P. B. Baltes & K. W. Schaie (Eds.), *Life-Span Developmental Psychology: Personality and Socialization*. New York and London: Academic Press, 1973.

Neugarten, B. L., & Hagestadt, G. O. "Age and the Life Course." Ch. 2, pp. 35–55, in R. H. Binstock & E. Shanas (Eds.), *Handbook of Aging and the Social Sciences*. New York: Van Nostrand Reinhold, 1976.

Noyes, R. "The Experience of Dying." *Psychiatry*, 1972, *35*(May):174–184.

Nydegger, C. N. "Middle Age: Some Early Returns—A Commentary." *International Journal of Aging and Human Development*, 1976, *7*(2):137–141.

Osarchuk, M., & Tatz, S. J. "Effects of Induced Fear of Death on Belief in Afterlife." *Journal of Personality and Social Psychology*, 1973, *27*:256–260.

Palmore, E. "The Effects of Aging on Activities and Attitudes." *The Gerontologist,* 1968, *8:*259–263.

Palmore, E. "Sociological Aspects of Aging." Ch. 3, pp. 33–69, in E. W. Busse & E. Pfeiffer (Eds.), *Behavior and Adaptation in Late Life.* Boston: Little, Brown, 1969.

Palmore, E. "Total Chance of Institutionalization among the Aged." *The Gerontologist,* 1976, *16*(6):504–507.

Palmore, E., & Luikart, C. "Health and Social Factors Related to Life Satisfaction." *Journal of Health and Social Behavior,* 1972, *13:*68–80.

Pandey, R. E., & Templer, D. I. "Use of the Death Anxiety Scale in an Inter-Racial Setting." *Omega,* 1972, *3*(2):127–130.

Parkes, C. M. "Recent Bereavement as a Cause of Mental Illness." *British Journal of Psychiatry,* 1964, *110:*198–204. (a)

Parkes, C. M. "Effects of Bereavement on Physical and Mental Health: A Study of the Medical Records of Widows." *British Medical Journal,* 1964, *2:*274–279. (b)

Parkes, C. M. "The First Year of Bereavement." *Psychiatry,* 1970, *33:*444–467.

Parkes, C. M. *Bereavement: Studies of Grief in Adult Life.* New York: International Universities Press, 1972.

Parkes, C. M., Benjamin, B., & Fitzgerald, R. G. "Broken Heart: A Statistical Study of Increased Mortality among Widowers." *British Medical Journal,* 1969, *1:*740.

Parsons, T. *The Social System.* Glencoe, Ill.: Free Press, 1951.

Parsons, T. "Death in American Society: A Brief Working Paper." *The American Behavioral Scientist,* 1963, *6*(May):61–65.

Parsons, T., Fox, R. C., & Lidz, V. M. "The 'Gift of Life' and Its Reciprocation." Pp. 1–49 in A. Mack (Ed.), *Death in American Experience.* New York: Schocken, 1973.

Parsons, T., & Lidz, V. M. "Death in American Society." Pp. 133–140 in E. S. Shneidman (Ed.), *Essays in Self-Destruction.* New York: Science House, 1967.

Parsons, T., Shils, E., Naegele, K. D., & Pitts, J. R. (Eds.). *Theories of Society* (2 vols.). New York: Free Press, 1961.

Payne, E. C., Jr. "The Physician and His Patient Who Is Dying." Pp. 111–163 in S. Levin and R. J. Kahana (Eds.), *Psychodynamic Studies on Aging: Creativity, Reminiscing, and Dying.* New York: International Universities Press, 1967.

Pearlman, J., Stotsky, R. A., & Dominick, J. R. "Attitudes toward Death among Nursing Home Personnel." *Journal of Genetic Psychology,* 1969, *144:*63–75.

Peck, R. C. "Psychological Developments in the Second Half of Life." Ch. 9, pp. 88–92, in B. Neugarten (Ed.), *Middle Age and Aging.* Chicago: University of Chicago Press, 1968.

Peterson, D. A., Powell, C., & Robertson, L. "Aging in America: Toward the Year 2000." *The Gerontologist,* 1976, *16*(3):264–270.

Phillips, B. "A Role Theory Approach to Adjustment in Old Age." *American Sociological Review,* 1957, *22:*212–217.

Pine, V. R. "Comparative Funeral Practices." *Practical Anthropology,* 1969, *16:*49–62.

Pine, V. R. "Social Organization and Death." *Omega,* 1972, *3*(2):149–153.

Pine, V. R. *Caretaker of the Dead: The American Funeral Director.* New York: Irvington Publishers, 1975.

Pine, V. R., & Phillips, D. L. "The Cost of Dying: A Sociological Analysis of Funeral Expenditures." *Social Problems,* 1970, *17*(3):405–417.

Postan, M. M. *The Medieval Economy and Society.* London: Weidenfeld & Nicolson, 1972.

Pressat, R. *Demographic Analysis: Methods, Results, Applications.* Chicago and New York: Aldine, Atherton, 1972. (Originally published, 1969.)

Preston, C. E., & Williams, R. H. "Views of the Aged on the Timing of Death." *The Gerontologist,* 1971, *11*(4, Winter, Pt. 1):300–304.

Preston, S. H. "The Changing Relation between Mortality and Level of Economic Development." *Population Studies,* 1975, *29:*231–248.

Preston, S. H. "Mortality Trends." *Annual Review of Sociology,* 1977, *3:*163–178.

Radcliffe-Brown, A. R. "Taboo." Pp. 112–123 in W. A. Lessa & E. Z. Vogt (Eds.), *Reader in Comparative Religion* (2nd ed.). New York: Harper & Row, 1965. (Originally published, 1939.)

Raether, H. C., & Slater, R. C. "Immediate Postdeath Activities in the United States." Ch. 13, pp. 233–248, in H. Feifel (Ed.), *New Meanings of Death.* New York: McGraw-Hill, 1977.

Rea, M. P., Greenspoon, S., & Spilka, B. "Physicians and the Terminal Patient: Some Selected Attitudes and Behavior." *Omega*, 1975, *6*(4):291–302.

Rees, W. D., & Lutkins, S. G. "Mortality of Bereavement." *British Medical Journal*, 1967, *4*:13.

Reid, W. S., Gilmore, A. J. J., Andrews, G. R., & Caird, F. I. "A Study of Religious Attitudes of the Elderly." *Age and Aging*, 1978, *7*:40–45.

Reynolds, D. K., & Kalish, R. A. "Anticipation of Futurity as a Function of Ethnicity and Age." *Journal of Gerontology*, 1974, *29*(2):224–231.

Rheinstein, M. "Motivation of Intergenerational Behavior by Norms of Law." Ch. 11, pp. 241–266, in E. Shanas & G. F. Streib (Eds.), *Social Structure and the Family: Generational Relations*. Englewood Cliffs, N. J.: Prentice-Hall, 1965.

Riley, J. W., Jr. "Old Age in American Society: Notes on Health, Retirement, and the Anticipation of Death." *American Society of Chartered Life Underwriters Journal*, 1968, *22*:27–32.

Riley, J. W., Jr. "What People Think about Death." Ch. 2, pp. 30–41, in O. G. Brim, Jr., H. E. Freeman, S. Levine, & N. A. Scotch (Eds.), *The Dying Patient*. New York: Russell Sage Foundation, 1970.

Riley, M., & Foner, A. *Aging and Society: An Inventory of Research Findings* (Vol. 1). New York: Russell Sage Foundation, 1968.

Riley, M., Foner, A., Hess, B., & Toby, M. L. "Socialization for the Middle and Later Years." Pp. 951–982 in D. Goslin (Ed.), *Handbook of Socialization Theory and Research*. Chicago: Rand McNally, 1969.

Roberts, J. L., Kimsey, L. R., Logan, D. L., & Shaw, G. "How Aged in Nursing Homes View Dying and Death." *Geriatrics*, 1970, *25*(April):115–119.

Rose, A. "A Current Theoretical Issue in Social Gerontology." *The Gerontologist*, 1964, *4*: 46–50.

Rosen, J., & Neugarten, B. "Ego Functions in the Middle and Later Years: A Thematic Apperception Study." Ch. 4, pp. 90–101, in B. L. Neugarten (Ed.), *Personality in Middle and Late Life, Empirical Studies*. New York: Atherton, 1964.

Rosenfeld, J. P. *The Legacy of Aging: Inheritance and Disinheritance in Social Perspective*. Norwood, N. J.: Ablex, 1979.

Rosenthal, C. J., Marshall, V. W., Macpherson, A. S., & French, S. P. *Nurses, Patients and Families: Care and Control in the Hospital*. London: Croom Helm, 1980.

Rosow, I. *Social Integration of the Aged*. New York: Free Press, 1967.

Rosow, I. *Socialization to Old Age*. Berkeley: University of California Press, 1973.

Rosow, I. *Socialization to Old Age*. Berkeley: University of California Press, 1974.

Rosow, I. "Status and Role Change through the Life Span." Ch. 18, pp. 457–482, in R. H. Binstock & E. Shanas (Eds.), *Handbook of Aging and the Social Sciences*. New York: Van Nostrand Reinhold, 1976.

Ross, J. K. *Old People, New Lives*. Chicago: University of Chicago Press, 1977.

Rossman, I., & Kissick, W. L. "Home Care and the Cancer Patient." In *The Physician and the Total Care of the Cancer Patient*. New York: American Cancer Society, 1961.

Roth, J. *Timetables*. Cleveland: Bobbs-Merrill, 1963.

Rotter, J. B. "Generalized Expectancies for Internal versus External Control of Reinforcement." *Psychological Monographs*, 1966, *80*(1, Whole No. 609).

Russell, J. C. *British Medieval Population*. Albuquerque: University of New Mexico Press, 1948.

Ryder, N. B. "The Cohort as a Concept in the Study of Social Change." *American Sociological Review*, 1965, *30*(6):834–861.

Sackett, D. L., & Torrance, G. W. "The Utility of Different Health States as Perceived by the General Public." *Journal of Chronic Disease*, 1978, *31*:697–704.

Sanders, L. *The Tomorrow File*. New York: Berkeley Publishing, 1975.

Saunders, C. "The Moment of Truth: Care of the Dying Person." In L. Pearson (Ed.), *Death and Dying: Current Issues in the Treatment of the Dying Person*. Cleveland: Case Western Reserve University Press, 1969.

Schactel, E. "On Memory and Childhood Amnesia." *Psychiatry*, 1947, *10*:1–26.

Schaie, K. W. "Developmental Processes and Aging." Pp. 151–156 in C. Eisdorfer & M. P. Lawton (Eds.), *The Psychology of Adult Development and Aging*. Washington, D. C.: American Psychological Association, 1973.

Schulz, R., & Aderman, D. "Clinical Research and the Stages of Dying." *Omega,* 1974, *5* (2):137–143.

Schulz, R., & Aderman, D. "How the Medical Staff Copes with Dying Patients: A Critical Review." *Omega,* 1976, *7*(1):11–21.

Schutz, A. "Common Sense and Scientific Interpretation of Human Action." Pp. 7–47 in M. Natanson (Ed.), *Alfred Schutz: Collected Papers I* (2nd ed.). The Hague: Nijhoff, 1967. (Originally published, 1953.) (a)

Schutz, A. "On Multiple Realities." Pp. 207–259 in M. Natanson (Ed.), *Alfred Schutz: Collected Papers I* (2nd ed.). The Hague: Nijhoff, 1967. (Originally published, 1945.) (b)

Schwenger, C. W., & Gross, M. J. "Institutional Care and Institutionalization of the Elderly in Canada." Ch. 23 in V. W. Marshall (Ed.), *Aging in Canada: Social Perspectives.* Toronto: Fitzhenry & Whiteside, 1979.

Seguin, M. "Opportunity for Peer Socialization in a Retirement Community." *The Gerontologist,* 1973, *13*(Summer):208–214.

Shanas, E. "The Family as a Social Support System in Old Age." *The Gerontologist,* 1979, *19*(2):169–174.

Shanas, E., & Hauser, P. M. "Zero Population Growth and the Family Life of Old People." *Journal of Social Issues,* 1974, *30*(4):79–92.

Shanas, E., Townsend, P., Wedderburn, D., Friis, H., Milhøj, P., & Stehouwer, J. *Old People in Three Industrial Societies.* New York: Atherton, 1968.

Sharma, K. L., & Jain, U. C. "Religiosity and Fear of Death in Young and Retired Persons." *Indian Journal of Gerontology,* 1969, *1*(4):110–114.

Sheehy, G. *Passages: Predictable Crises of Adult Life.* New York: Dutton, 1977.

Sherman, S. A. "Mutual Assistance and Support in Retirement Housing." *Journal of Gerontology,* 1975, *30*(4):479–483.

Shibutani, T. *Improvised News.* Indianapolis and New York: Bobbs-Merrill, 1966.

Shneidman, E. S. *Deaths of Man.* Baltimore: Penguin Books, 1974. (Originally published, 1973.)

Shneidman, E. S. *Death: Current Perspectives.* Palo Alto, Calif.: Mayfield, 1976.

Shorter, E. *The Making of the Modern Family.* New York: Basic Books, 1977.

Silverman, D. *The Theory of Organisations.* London: Heinemann Educational Books, 1970.

Simić, A., & Myerhoff, B. "Conclusion." Pp. 231–246 in B. Myerhoff & A. Simić (Eds.), *Life's Career: Aging.* Beverly Hills and London: Sage Publications, 1978.

Simko, A. "Death and the Hereafter: The Structuring of Immaterial Reality." *Omega,* 1970, *1*(2):121–135.

Simmel, G. "The Adventure." Pp. 243–258 in K. H. Wolff (Ed.), *Essays on Sociology, Philosophy and Aesthetics.* New York: Harper Torchbooks, 1959.

Simmons, S., & Given, B. "Nursing Care of the Terminal Patient." *Omega,* 1972, *3*(3):217–225.

Spence, D. L. "The Role of Futurity in Aging Adaptation." *The Gerontologist,* 1968, *8*:180–183.

Spencer, D. L. "The Meaning of Engagement." *International Journal of Aging and Human Development,* 1975, *6*(3):193–198.

Spence, D. L., & Lonner, T. D. "Career Set: A Resource through Transitions and Crises." *International Journal of Aging and Human Development,* 1978–1979, *9*(1):51–65.

Spiro, M. E. "Culture and Personality." *Psychiatry,* 1951, *14*(February):19–46.

Spiro, M. E. "Social Systems, Personality, and Functional Analysis." Ch. 2, pp. 93–127, in B. Kaplan (Ed.), *Studying Personality Cross-Culturally.* Evanston: Harper & Row, Peterson, 1961.

Stannard, C. I. "Old Folks and Dirty Work: The Social Conditions for Patient Abuse in a Nursing Home." *Social Problems,* 1973, *20*(3):329–343.

Stannard, D. E. "Death and the Puritan Child." Pp. 9–29 in D. E. Stannard (Ed.), *Death in America.* Philadelphia: University of Pennsylvania Press, 1975.

Stannard, D. E. *The Puritan Way of Death.* New York: Oxford University Press, 1977.

Statistical Bulletin. "Gains in Longevity Continue." 1978, *59*(3):7–9.

Stoddard, S. *The Hospice Movement: A Better Way of Caring for the Dying.* New York: Vintage Books, 1978.

Strauss, A. *Mirrors and Masks.* Mill Valley, Calif.: Sociology Press, 1969.

Streib, G. F. "Social Stratification and Aging." Ch. 7, pp. 160–185, in R. H. Binstock & E. Shanas (Eds.), *Handbook of Aging and the Social Sciences.* New York: Van Nostrand Reinhold, 1976.

Sudnow, D. *Passing On: The Social Organization of Dying* (paperback ed.). Englewood Cliffs, N.J.: Prentice-Hall, 1967.

Sussman, M. B., Cates, J. N., & Smith, D. T. *The Family and Inheritance.* New York: Russell Sage Foundation, 1970.

Swenson, W. M. "Attitudes toward Death among the Aged." *Minnesota Medicine,* 1959, *42:* 399–402.

Swenson, W. M. "Attitudes toward Death in an Aged Population." *Journal of Gerontology,* 1961, *16:*49–52.

Tallmer, M., & Kutner, B. "Disengagement and the Stresses of Aging." *Journal of Gerontology,* 1969, *24:*70–75.

Tashjian, D., & Tashjian, A. *Memorials for Children of Change: The Art of Early New England Stone Carving.* Middleton, Conn.: Wesleyan University Press, 1974.

Teahan, J., & Kastenbaum, R. "Subjective Life Expectancy and Future Time Perspective as Predictors of Job Success in the Hard-Core Unemployed." *Omega,* 1970, *1*(3):189–200.

Templer, D. I. "The Construction and Validation of a Death Anxiety Scale." *Journal of Genetic Psychology,* 1970, *82:*165–177.

Templer, D. I. "The Relationship between Verbalized and Non-Verbalized Death Anxiety." *Journal of Genetic Psychology,* 1971, *119:*211–214. (a)

Templer, D. I. "Death Anxiety as Related to Depression and Health of Retired Persons." *Journal of Gerontology,* 1971, *26*(4):521–523. (b)

Templer, D. I. "Death Anxiety in Religiously Very Involved Persons." *Psychological Reports,* 1972, *31:*361–362.

Templer, D. I., & Dotson, E. "Religious Correlates of Death Anxiety." *Psychological Reports,* 1970, *26:*895–897.

Templer, D. I., & Ruff, C. "Death Anxiety Scale Means, Standard Deviations, and Embedding." *Psychological Reports,* 1971, *29:*173–174.

Templer, D. I., Ruff, C., & Franks, C. M. "Death Anxiety: Age, Sex and Parental Resemblances in Diverse Populations." *Developmental Psychology,* 1971, *4:*108.

Thomas, J. M., & Weiner, E. A. "Psychological Differences among Groups of Critically Ill Hospitalized Patients, Noncritically Ill Hospitalized Patients, and Well Controls." *Journal of Consulting and Clinical Psychology,* 1974, *42*(2):274–279.

Thorson, J. A. "Variations in Death Anxiety Related to College Students' Sex, Major Field of Study, and Certain Personality Traits." *Psychological Reports,* 1977, *40:*857–858.

Thorson, J. A., & Perkins, M. "A Factor Analytic Study of a Scale Designed to Measure Death Anxiety." Paper presented at the 30th Annual Scientific Meeting of the Gerontological Society, San Francisco, 1978.

Thurnher, M. "Goals, Values, and Life Evaluations at the Preretirement Stage." *Journal of Gerontology,* 1974, *29*(1, January):85–96.

Thurnher, M. "Midlife Marriage: Sex Differences in Evaluation and Perspectives." *International Journal of Aging and Human Development,*1976, *7*(2):129–135.

Thurnher, M., & Chiriboga, D. "Self-Concept: An Adult Life Perspective." Paper presented at the 25th Annual Meeting of the Gerontological Society, San Juan, P. R., December 1972.

Thurow, L. C. "The Optimum Lifetime Distribution of Consumption Expenditures." *American Economic Review,* 1969, *59:*324–330.

Tobin, S. S. "Social and Health Services for the Future Age." *The Gerontologist,* 1975, *15*(1, February, Pt. 2):32–37.

Tobin, S. S. "Social and Health Services for the Future Age." *The Gerontologist,* 1975, *15*(1, Psychiatry, 1968, *19:*434–444.

Tobin, S. S., & Lieberman, M. A. *Last Home for the Aged.* San Francisco: Jossey-Bass, 1976.

Tolor, A., & Murphy, V. "Some Psychological Correlates of Subjective Life Expectancy." *Journal of Clinical Psychology,* 1967, *23:*21–24.

Toronto Globe & Mail. "Canadians Edged by Americans as Top Buyers of Life Insurance." October 31, 1978.

Townsend, P. *The Last Refuge.* London: Routledge & Kegan Paul, 1962.

Townsend, P. *The Family Life of Old People* (Abr. ed.). Harmondsworth: Penguin Books, 1963. (Originally published, 1957.)

Toynbee, A. *Man's Concern with Death.* New York: McGraw-Hill, 1968.

Travis, T. A., Noyes, R., Jr., & Brightwell, D. R. "The Attitudes of Physicians toward Prolonging Life." *International Journal of Psychiatry in Medicine,* 1974, *5*(1):17–26.

References   *213*

Troll, L. E. *Early and Middle Adulthood*. Monterey, Calif.: Brooks/Cole, 1975.

Tucker, C. J. "Changing Patterns of Migration between Metropolitan and Nonmetropolitan Areas in the United States: Recent Evidence." *Demography*, 1976, *13*(4):435–443.

Tunstall, J. *Old and Alone*. London: Routledge & Kegan Paul, 1966.

Turner, R. "Role-Taking: Process versus Conformity." In A. Rose (Ed.), *Human Nature and Social Processes*. Boston: Houghton-Mifflin, 1962.

Turner, R. "Is There a Quest for Identity?" *The Sociological Quarterly*, 1975, 16(2, Spring): 148–161.

Turner, R. "The Real Self: From Institution to Impulse." *American Journal of Sociology*, 1976, *81*(5, March):989–1016.

Turner, V. *The Forest of Symbols*. Ithaca, N. Y.: Cornell University Press, 1967.

Uhlenberg, P. R. "A Study of Cohort Life Cycles: Cohorts of Native Born Massachusetts Women, 1830–1920." *Population Studies*, 1969, *23*:407–420.

Uhlenberg, P. R. "Cohort Variations in Family Life Cycle Experiences of U. S. Females." *Journal of Marriage and the Family*, 1974, *36*(May):284–292.

Uhlenberg, P. R. "Changing Structure of the Older Population of the USA During the Twentieth Century." *The Gerontologist*, 1977, *17*(3):197–202.

Uris, L. *Trinity*. Garden City, N. Y.: Doubleday, 1976.

Vachon, M. L. S. "The Final Illness in Cancer: The Widow's Perspective." *Canadian Medical Association Journal*, 1977, *117*(November):1151–1154.

Vachon, M. L. S. "Identity Change over the First Two Years of Bereavement: Social Relationships and Social Support." Unpublished doctoral dissertation, Department of Sociology, York University, Toronto, Ontario, 1979.

Vachon, M. L. S., Formo, A., Freedman, K., Lyall, W. A. L., Rogers, J., & Freeman, S. J. J. "Stress Reactions to Bereavement." *Essence*, 1976, *1*(1): 23–33.

Vallee, F. G. "Burial and Mourning Customs in a Hebridean Community." *Journal of the Royal Anthropological Institute*, 1955, *85*(Pts. 1 and 2):119–130.

Vallin, J. "La Mortalité dans les Pays du Tiers Monde: Evolution et Perspectives." *Population*, 1968 (September–October):845–868.

van Gennep, A. *The Rites of Passage* (translated by M. B. Vizedom & G. L. Caffee). Chicago: University of Chicago Press, 1960.

Veatch, R. M. *Death, Dying, and the Biological Revolution*. New Haven and London: Yale University Press, 1976.

Vernon, G. *Sociology of Death: An Analysis of Death-Related Behavior*. New York: Ronald Press, 1970.

Vernon, G. "Death Control." *Omega*, 1972, *3*(2):131–138.

Vischer, A. L. *On Growing Old* (translated by G. Onn). Boston: Houghton-Mifflin, 1967. (Revised edition originally published, 1961.)

Vovelle, M. *Piété baroque et déchristianisation*. Paris: Plon, 1973. Cited in P. Ariès, *Western Attitudes toward Death*. Baltimore and London: Johns Hopkins University Press, 1974:64.

Waitzkin, H., & Stoeckle, J. D. "The Communication of Information about Illness." *Advances in Psychosomatic Medicine*, 1972, *8*:180–215.

Walker, W. J. "Changing United States Life-Style and Declining Vascular Mortality: Cause or Coincidence?" *New England Journal of Medicine*, 1977, *297*(3, July 21): 163–165.

Wallach, M. A., & Green, L. R. "On Age and the Subjective Speed of Time." *Journal of Gerontology*, 1961, *16*:71–74.

Walton, D. "On the Rationality of Fear of Death." *Omega*, 1976, 7(1):1–10.

Wardwell, J. M. "Equilibrium and Change in Non-Metropolitan Growth." *Rural Sociology*, 1977, *42*(2):156–179.

Warner, W. L. *The Family of God*. New Haven, Conn.: Yale University Press, 1961.

Warner, W. *American Life, Dream and Reality* (Rev. ed.). Chicago and London: University of Chicago Press, 1962.

Warren, R. I. *The Community in America* (2nd ed.). Chicago: Rand McNally, 1972.

Weber, M. *The Protestant Ethic and the Spirit of Capitalism* (translated by T. Parsons). New York: Scribner's, 1958. (Originally published, 1904–1905.)

Weber, M. *Max Weber: The Theory of Social and Economic Organization* (translated and edited by A. M. Henderson & T. Parsons). New York: Free Press, 1964.

Weisman, A. *On Dying and Denying*. New York: Behavioral Publications, 1972.

Weisman, A., & Kastenbaum, R. *The Psychological Autopsy*. New York: Community Mental Health Journal Monograph No. 4, 1968.

Wells, R. V. "Demographic Change and the Life Cycle of American Families." Pp. 85–94 in T. K. Rabb & R. I. Rotberg (Eds.), *The Family in History*. New York: Harper & Row, 1973.

Wershow, H. J. "Days beyond Recall: Subsistence Homesteading in the Rural South, Circa 1920." *International Journal of Aging and Human Development*, 1975, *6*(1):1–5.

Wershow, H. J. "The Four Percent Fallacy: Some Further Evidence and Policy Implications." *The Gerontologist*, 1976, *16*(1, Pt. 1, February):52–55.

Williams, M. "Changing Attitudes to Death: Survey of Contributions in Psychological Abstracts over a Thirty Year Period." *Human Relations*, 1966, *19:*405–423.

Williams, R. H. "Our Role in the Generation, Modification and Termination of Life." *Archives of Internal Medicine*, 1969, *124:*215–237.

Williams, R. H., & Wirths, C. G. *Lives through the Years*. New York: Atherton, 1965.

Winch, P. *The Idea of a Social Science and Its Relation to Philosophy*. London: Routledge & Kegan Paul, 1958.

Wirth, L. "The Scope and Problems of the Community." Ch. 11, pp. 165–177, in A. J. Reiss, Jr. (Ed.), *Louis Wirth on Cities and Social Life*. Chicago: University of Chicago Press, 1964. (Originally published, 1933.)

Wittgenstein, L. *Philosophical Investigations* (translated by G. M. Anscombe). New York: Macmillan, 1953.

Wolff, K. H. (Ed. and trans.) *The Sociology of Georg Simmel*. New York: Free Press of Glencoe, 1950.

Wuthnow, R. "Recent Patterns of Secularization: A Problem of Generations?" *American Sociological Review*, 1976, *41*(October):850–867.

Young, M., Benjamin, B., & Wallis, C. "Mortality of Widowers." *Lancet*, 1963, *2:*454.

Zelizer, V. A. "Human Values and the Market: The Case of Life Insurance and Death in 19th Century America." *American Journal of Sociology*, 1978, *84*(3, November):591–610.

Ziegler, P. *The Black Death*. London: Collins, 1969.

Zinsser, H. "Two Sonnets, II." In H. Husted (Ed.), *Love Poems of Six Centuries*. New York: Coward-McCann, 1950.

Name Index

Cameron, P., 98–102
Candy, S., 141
Caplovitz, C., 113
Cappon, D., 66–67
Carp, F. M., 191–193
Carpenter, E. S., 35
Carpenter, J. O., 155
Carter, H., 147
Cartwright, A., 137, 144, 146, 147
Cassell, E. J., 54
Cates, J. N., 33, 135
Cavan, R. S., 82
Chappell, N. L., 106, 139, 155, 165, 178
Charmaz, K. C., 145
Chasin, B., 153
Chevan, A., 149
Childe, V. G., 30–31
Chiriboga, D., 101–102, 111–112, 113, 128, 182, 187
Christ, A., 66
Cicourel, A. B., 66
Clausen, J. A., 111–112
Clayton, P., 148
Clifton, M., 144
Coffin, M. M., 31, 46
Cohen, A. K., 28–29
Cohen, E. S., 193
Coleman, P. G., 109, 115, 116, 120
Collette, C. L., 139
Cooley, C. H., 119
Coombs, R. H., 156
Costa, P. T., 172–173
Counts, D., 33–34, 151
Cox, P., 148
Crane, D., 139, 143
Crotty, W., 86, 113
Cuellar, J. B., 73, 75–76, 100–101, 103, 104, 106, 152, 154, 165, 169
Cumming, E., 80–81, 111
Curl, J. S., 46

Damianopoulos, E., 81
Darrow, C. M., 85–89, 110, 120
Datan, N., 84
Davidson, G. W., 32, 48–50, 59, 183
Davis, A. K., 28–29
Dawe, A., 3
Dax, E. C., 148
Dean, L., 80
Degner, L., 139
DeJong, G. F., 192
Denton, F. T., 191
Denzin, N. K., 66
Desmarais, L., 148
Diggory, J., 70–71, 77, 78, 166, 171, 178
Dilthey, W., 108
Dominick, J. R., 155
Donaldson, P., 65
Dotson, E., 72, 178

Douglas, A., 46
Douglas, M., 43
Dowd, J. J., 193
Drake, M., 12
Dudley, D. L., 158–159
Duff, R. S., 137, 143
Dumont, R. G., 58, 65, 67, 68
Durkheim, E., 31

Eastman, M., 29
Eaton, J. W., 153
Eisdorfer, C., 66, 76, 165, 179
Eisenstadt, S. N., 29
Eissler, K. R., 67
Elder, G. H., Jr., 112
Enos, D. D., 141
Erikson, E., 85, 86, 87–90, 92, 107, 111, 118, 166
Etigson, E., 109
Eversley, D. E. C., 12

Falk, J. M., 115–116
Faunce, W. A., 179
Feifel, H., 137, 176, 178–180, 190
Feldman, M. J., 73
Felton, B., 157
Festinger, L., 105
Fitzgerald, R. G., 148
Foner, A., 72, 75, 83, 100, 134, 136
Foote, N. N., 125
Ford, J. R., 148
Formo, A., 148, 150
Foss, D. C., 58, 65, 67, 68
Fourastié, J., 12, 21
Fox, R. C., 54, 136, 192
Fraisse, P., 128
Francks, C. M., 72, 73
Freedman, K., 148, 150
Freeman, S. J. J., 148, 150
French, S., 46
French, S. P., 137, 143, 147, 155, 156
Freud, S., 59, 67, 68, 86
Friis, H., 91
Fulton, R., 65, 179

Gabriel, S. J., 72, 157–158
Garrity, T. F., 48
Gatch, M. M., 35, 90
Geertz, C., 2–3, 43, 181
George, L., 113
Gerber, I., 148
Gergen, K., 168
Giambra, L. M., 103, 114–115
Gift, H. C., 113
Gigy, L., 112, 182
Gilgamesh, 1–2
Given, B., 140
Glaser, B. G., 103, 124, 126, 137, 141, 143–144, 146, 155, 156, 172, 183

Glass, D. V., 12
Glasser, R., 108, 116
Glick, I. O., 148–150
Glick, P. C., 19–21, 147
Goffman, E., 137–138
Goldfarb, A. I., 142
Goldhamer, H., 82
Goldman, L. J., 156
Goldscheider, C., 10–11, 13
Goldstein, A. M., 157
Goody, J., 32–33, 34, 36, 37, 135
Gordon, S. K., 116–117
Gorer, G., 47, 58, 102
Gorney, J. E., 115–117
Gould, R. L., 110, 120
Green, L. R., 128
Greenspoon, S., 139
Greven, P., Jr., 12–13, 41
Gross, M. J., 141, 192
Gubrium, J. F., 84, 152, 155
Guemple, D. L., 35, 173
Guptill, C. S., 102
Gustafson, E., 155

Haan, N., 111–112
Habakkuk, H. J., 40–41
Hagestadt, G. O., 84, 151
Halikes, J., 148
Hall, G. S., 108
Hannon, M., 145
Hardiman, C. J., 193
Harper, R., 190
Harvey, C. D., 149
Hauser, P. M., 11, 191
Haven, C., 119
Havighurst, R. J., 80–82, 108, 111, 116
Hays, J. E., 178, 182
Hays, W. L., 66
Hedrick, D. L., 193
Heenan, E., 177
Heidegger, M., 98
Heidel, A., 1–2
Hendrix, L., 51–54
Henripin, J., 12
Henry, W., 80–81, 111
Herlihy, D., 11
Herson, H., 73
Hertz, R., 31–32, 34–35, 37, 43
Hess, B., 83, 165
Hewitt, J., 125
Hinton, J. M., 137, 141, 143, 181
Hochschild, A. R., 76, 81, 119, 138, 152
Hockey, L., 137, 144, 146, 147
Hoggatt, L., 139
Holbrook, A., 193
Hollingshead, A. B., 137, 143
Holmes, T. H., 158–159
Homans, G., 36
Howard, A., 54

Howard, E., 155–156
Hughes, E. C., 124–125, 156

Illich, I., 143
Ingram, D. K., 142
Inkeles, A., 2

Jackson, E. N., 55
Jacques, E., 110
Jain, U. C., 76, 165
James, W., 128
Jeffers, F., 66, 76, 165, 179
Johnson, A. I., 76–77, 165
Jones, R. L., 34
Jung, C. G., 86, 110

Kahana, E., 157, 192
Kahana, R. J., 67
Kalish, R. A., 49, 57, 58, 66, 69, 72–78,
    83, 101–106, 128, 132, 146, 149, 151,
    155, 165, 168–169, 173, 178, 180
Kalson, L., 155
Kamen, H., 18, 37
Kapleau, P., 120
Kart, C. S., 142
Kastenbaum, R., 24, 106, 128, 132, 141,
    143, 155, 156
Katona, G., 129
Keith, P., 166–168, 178
Kellner, H., 4
Kennedy, J., 144
Kett, J. F., 20–22
Kiefer, C. W., 84
Kimsey, L. R., 157
Kissick, W. L., 143
Klein, E. B., 85–89, 110, 120
Kluckhohn, C., 2
Knodel, J., 11
Koestenbaum, P., 127–128
Komarovsky, M., 84
Korson, J. H., 149
Kroeber, A. L., 2
Kübler-Ross, E., 67–69, 150
Kuhlen, R. G., 128
Kuhn, T., 68
Kutner, B., 116
Kuypers, J. A., 80, 119, 135, 157, 182

Langer, W. L., 10
Lao-tse, 189
Laslett, P., 10, 11, 12, 13, 18, 20, 23, 24,
    37–42
Laurence, M., 146
Lawrence, R. E., 138
Lee, R. D., 12
Leming, M. R., 36, 180
Lemon, B. W., 79, 82
Lerner, M., 141
Lesnoff-Caravaglia, C., 141

Pincus, A., 132
Pine, V., 49, 55–56, 63, 190
Pitts, J. R., 2–3
Postan, M. M., 10
Powell, C., 193
Pressat, R., 37
Preston, C. E., 139
Preston, S. H., 11, 16, 18, 20, 40

Rabb, T. K., 22
Radcliffe-Brown, A. R., 35–36
Raether, H. C., 55
Ragan, P., 73, 75–76, 100–101, 103, 104, 106, 152, 154, 165, 169
Rea, M. P., 139
Record, R. G., 16
Rees, W. D., 148
Reid, W. S., 178
Reynolds, D. K., 49, 72–76, 101–106, 132–138, 149, 151, 165, 168–169, 178
Rheinstein, M., 135
Rhudick, P. J., 108–109
Riley, J. W., Jr., 72, 73, 75–78, 100–102, 106, 134–136, 165
Riley, M. W., 72, 75, 83, 100, 134, 136, 165
Roberts, J. L., 157
Robertson, L., 193
Rogers, J., 148, 150
Rose, A., 81
Rosen, J., 108, 111
Rosenfeld, J. P., 33, 135
Rosenthal, C., 137, 143, 147, 155, 156
Rosow, I., 78, 82–83, 84, 126, 144, 154
Ross, J. K., 152–153
Rossman, I., 143
Roth, J., 138, 155
Rothman, D., 70–71, 77, 78, 166, 171, 178
Rotter, J. B., 117, 157
Ruff, C., 72, 73, 76, 165
Rusalem, R., 148
Russell, J. C., 10

Sackett, D. L., 140
Sanders, L., 193–194
Saunders, C., 189, 190
Schactel, E., 108
Schaie, K. W., 85, 113
Schulz, R., 156
Schutz, A., 4, 98
Schwenger, C. W., 141, 192
Scott, M., 187–189
Scott, R. A., 54
Seguin, M., 155
Sell, R. R., 192
Shanas, E., 91, 147, 149–150, 191
Sharma, K. L,. 76, 165
Shaw, G., 157

Sheehy, G., 86
Sherman, S. A., 154
Shibutani, T., 51
Shils, E., 2–3
Shneidman, E. S., 35, 101, 178
Shorter, E., 34, 39–40
Silverman, D., 3
Simić, A., 125
Simko, A., 165
Simmel, G., 1, 188–189
Simmons, S., 140
Slater, R. C., 55
Smith, D. T., 33, 35
Spence, D. L., 81, 124–125, 127, 128
Spencer, B., 191
Spilka, B., 139
Spiro, M. E., 3
Stannard, C. I., 155
Stannard, D. E., 12, 30–31, 46, 50–51
Stehouwer, J., 91
Stewart, L., 98–102
Stoddard, S., 192
Stoeckle, J. D., 137, 155
Stotsky, R. A., 155
Strauss, A., 103, 124, 126, 130, 137, 141, 143–144, 146, 155, 156, 172, 183, 187
Streib, G. F., 40, 57
Sudnow, D., 103, 143, 156
Sultan, P., 141
Sussman, M. B., 33, 135
Sutton, F. X., 28–29
Swenson, W. M., 70–71, 77, 158, 165, 175, 179, 180

Tallmer, M., 116
Talz, S. J., 178
Tashjian, A., 31, 42, 46, 51
Tashjian, D., 31, 42, 46, 51
Teahan, J., 106
Templer, D. I., 72, 73, 76, 138, 147, 157, 165, 172, 178–179
Thirsk, J., 135
Thomas, J. M., 158
Thompson, E. P., 135
Thorson, J. A., 73, 158
Thurnher, M., 101–102, 111–112, 114, 187
Thurow, L. C., 129
Tindale, J. A., 80, 193
Tobin, S. S., 80–81, 86, 106, 108, 109, 111, 113, 116, 191–193
Toby, M. L., 83, 165
Tolor, A., 107
Tolstoy, L., 91
Torrance, G. W., 140
Townsend, P., 91, 146, 147, 152, 155, 156
Toynbee, A., 11
Travis, T. A., 139
Troll, L. E., 109, 113

Tucker, C. J., 192
Turnstall, J., 149
Turner, R., 84, 109–110
Turner, R. D., 16
Turner, V., 43

Uhlenberg, P. R., 19–22, 191
Uris, L., 39

Vachon, M. L. S., 148, 150
Vallee, F. G., 31, 34
Vallin, J., 16
van Gennep, A., 32
van Gils, D. W. L., 142
Vaughan, C. E., 177–178
Veatch, R. M., 192
Verhey, J. W., 158–159
Vernon, G., 65, 172
Vischer, A. L., 65, 79
Vovelle, M., 46, 48

Waitzkin, H., 137, 155
Walker, W., 148
Walker, W. J., 16–17
Wallach, M. A., 128
Wallis, C., 148
Walton, D., 168

Wardwell, J. M., 192
Warner, W. L., 49
Warren, R. I., 151
Waugh, E., 46
Weber, M., 3, 50, 181
Wedderburn, D., 91
Weichselbaum, R., 139–140
Weiner, E. A., 158
Weisman, A., 69–70, 156
Weiss, R. S., 148–150
Wells, R. V., 19, 21–22
Wershow, H. J., 141–142
Williams, M., 65
Williams, R. H., 139
Winch, P., 4
Winokur, G., 148
Wirth, L., 151
Wittgenstein, L., 164
Wolff, K. H., 188
Wuthnow, R., 182–183
Wylie, C. M., 155
Wyss, J., 48

Young, M., 148

Zelizer, V. A., 133–134
Ziegler, P., 29
Zinsser, H., 176

Subject Index